Self-Injury

Self-Injury

PSYCHOTHERAPY WITH PEOPLE
WHO ENGAGE IN SELF-INFLICTED VIOLENCE

ROBIN E. CONNORS, PH.D.

JASON ARONSON INC.
Northvale, New Jersey
London

Production Editor: Elaine Lindenblatt

This book was set in 11½ New Baskerville, and printed and bound by Book-mart Press, Inc. of North Bergen, NJ.

Library of Congress Cataloging-in-Publication Data

Connors, Robin.
    Self-injury : psychotherapy with people who engage in self-inflicted violence /
    Robin Connors.
       p. cm.
    Includes bibliographical references and index.
    ISBN 0-7657-0264-9
    1. Self-injurious behavior.   2. Self-injurious behavior—Treatment.
    3. Psychotherapy.   I. Title.
  RC569.5.S48 C66 2000
  616.85'820651—dc21   00-022517

Printed in the United States of America on acid-free paper. For information and catalog write to Jason Aronson Inc., 230 Livingston Street, Northvale, NJ 07647-1726, or visit our website: www.aronson.com

This book is dedicated to the spirit of possibility

Contents

2

Understanding Self-Injury   33

Distinguishing Self-Injury from Suicidality • Traumatic
Antecedents of Self-Injury: What the Research Shows • "Felt
Experience": The Ground beneath Self-Injury • How Self-Injury
Helps: Function and Meaning • Reenactment of the Original
Trauma • Expression of Feelings and Needs • Way to Organize
Self and Regain Homeostasis • Management and Maintenance of
the Dissociative Process • Overlapping Functions and Needs
• The Addiction Model: Does It Help Make Sense of Self-Injury?
• Anchoring Our Perception of Self-Injury in a Continuum of
Self-Harm • The Basic Point: Self-Injury Helps

3

Trauma, Wounding, and Healing   67

The Power of Love • The Power of Fear • Emotions as
Players in the Mind–Body Experience • Movement out of
Stuckness, from Fear to Love • The Role of Balance • The Impact
of Trauma • The Presence of Fear and the Absence of Love: How
Trauma Gets Stuck • Context as a Regulator of Impact • Brain
Functioning during and after Traumatic Events • Self-Injury and
the Psychobiology of Trauma • Freeing Up Energy by Removing
the Blocks in Our Energy Fields • Self-Injury as a Beacon

4

The Incomplete Self-Boundary   91

Basic Theory about Attachment and the Sense of Self
• The Development of the Self-Boundary • Disruptions in the
Developmental Process • Holes and Weak Links: The Inadequate
Self-Boundary • Operating with an Inadequate Self-Boundary:
How It Feels • The Impact of Incomplete Individuation: Self-Injury
and Other Clues • Ego States or Alter Personalities: A Concrete
and Sometimes Confounding Element • Implications for the
Therapeutic Relationship • Borderline Personality Disorder or
Inadequate Self-Boundary: What's in a Name? • Summary

II

RESPONDING TO PEOPLE WHO SELF-INJURE

• Finding Alternatives • Highly Dissociative Clients and Self-Intervention: A Complex Task • Assessing and Managing the Level of Harm • Tolerating "Failure" • Making Lists: A Way to Manage the Limitations of State-Dependent Memory • Helping Clients Talk to Others • The Use of Contracts • Using a Twelve-Step/Addiction Recovery Model with Self-Injury • Keeping Perspective: Helping the Client Intervene

8

Repairing and Completing the Self-Boundary 231

The Broad Framework: How to Approach This Work • Communicating Basic Concepts About the Individuation Process • Teaching Key Strategies that Facilitate Healing • Developing New and Enhancing Existing Skills in Self-Management • Solidifying the Self-Boundary: Common Steps • Individual Differences, Many Pathways • The Role of Current Attachment Figures: Therapists, Partners, Friends, and Co-Workers • Reenactment within the Therapeutic Relationship: A Relational Working-Through • Working with the Original Attachment Figure in the Present • Healing the Self: Is It Reparenting or Not?

9

Working with Core Issues and Other Interventions 269

Resolution of Old Traumas • Two Metaphors that Frame the Process of Healing • Managing Intrusive Imagery and Affect • Working with Dissociative Process • Processing and Integrating Traumatic Events • Adjuncts and Alternatives to Talk Therapy: Body–Mind Approaches • Newer Methods of Uncertain Mechanisms • Energy-Based Approaches • Medication and Self-Injury • The Presence of a Substance Addiction • Clients' Concerns about Scars • Addressing the Needs of Family Members and Support People • What About Spirituality? • Conclusion

III

MANAGING OUR OWN RESPONSES
TO SELF-INJURY

Preface

People who directly injure their bodies are increasingly requesting help from psychotherapists and other health care providers. For many self-injurers, the disclosure of such generally private behavior is fraught with intensity and meaning. As clinicians, we may not initially realize all of what people bring to us when they ask for assistance. For the most part, people who self-injure harbor a deep desire for clinicians to perceive the pain and need beneath their behavior. They long to be understood, respected, and helped in ways that can be difficult to articulate. They seek a listener skilled at hearing the layers of meaning and truth they endeavor to tell through word and action. And they fear, often with good reason, that others will react in a controlling, shaming, or dismissive fashion.

The mental health professions have struggled to understand self-injury for decades, with varying degrees of success and compassion. Because of the potent nature of self-injury and the variety of issues touched in us as helpers, clinical responses to self-injury have often been only moderately beneficial and, in too many cases, distinctly harmful. My hope is that this book can offer some helpful guidelines to clinicians who wish to improve their capacity to respond usefully to people who seek their services.

The book is organized into three parts: Understanding Self-Injury as the Tip of the Iceberg, Responding to People Who Self-Injure, and Managing Our Own Responses to Self-Injury. The first part delineates various forms of self-injuring behavior, its place in the psychiatric literature, and some demographic information about people who self-injure. The functions that self-injury serves and its relationship to prior traumas and losses are described. The impact of trauma, particularly as a disruption in the formation of the self-boundary, is discussed as a contributor to the use of self-injury as a coping mechanism.

The second part focuses on therapeutic interventions with self-injuring clients or patients. It discusses fundamental therapy tasks with people who self-injure, why a compassionate presence is so important, and the nature of a viable therapeutic relationship. Attention to the power dynamics in the therapy relationship, along with concrete recommendations for interacting with clients about their self-injury, are described in detail. A range of related issues are addressed as well, including some basic approaches to resolving prior traumatic events, tasks related to repairing the inadequate self-boundary, the use of adjunct therapies, coexisting addictions, the role of spirituality in healing, and the needs of family members and support people.

The final part highlights the complexity and range of issues that arise for clinicians working with people who self-injure. The task of determining the right action in light of strong countertransferential responses is explored, including situations where self-injury occurs in our presence. Some thoughts about self-care are also posed.

At the core of working therapeutically with people who self-injure is the necessity of bringing our selves into the room. By meeting our clients or patients with the fullness of our presence, we offer a relational context—a vibrant, enlivened container— within which self-injuring people can heal core issues. This essential value weaves through the book. It is my hope that this book augments the readers' capacity to embody compassion in their clinical work.

Robin E. Connors
Pittsburgh, Pennsylvania

Acknowledgments

I extend great appreciation to the clients and other people who have talked to me about their self-injury. Their willingness to risk and speak honestly has allowed this book to take form. A special thanks to everyone who gave me permission to quote them or share their experiences. I also feel a deep gratitude to my clients for all they have taught me about the process of therapy, my own vulnerabilities, and the potency of kindness and truth.

Three dear friends provided unwavering support and read every word, chapter by chapter, as I wrote it. I offer heartfelt thanks to Anita Mallinger, my clinical colleague of nearly twenty years, who read the manuscript like the editor she used to be, and who always, fiercely, stands with me in "the work"; Kristy Trautmann, my comrade as trainer/educator, whose initial encouragement allowed me to conceive this book and who helped me think through knotty issues time after time; and Reed Williams, librarian extraordinaire, whose humor, perspective, and unfailing belief in my ability sustained and nourished me throughout the process of writing, and who helped me find needed sources.

I also thank another old and dear friend, Carol Mullen, who read the completed manuscript and brought her writer's eye to the overall structure and content. Several colleague-friends also read every word and offered insightful feedback. I thank Ruta Mazelis, whose prompting and practical help first got me writing on the topic of self-injury, and whose vision to change how self-injury is viewed has inspired important shifts in our collective awareness, and Maureen Burke, who traveled across the Atlantic bringing confirmation about how to compassionately respond to people who self-injure.

A delighted thank you to Kathy Heart, another cherished friend and former colleague, for generously allowing her artwork to be used on the cover. Thank you to Joyce Aronson for appreciating my work and encouraging me to write this book, editors Anne Marie Dooley for her support and guidance and Elaine Lindenblatt for her careful shepherding of the production process, and copy editor David Kaplan for making this a better book.

A special thank you to Ann Begler, Kathy Reed, and Judith Vollmer. While not directly involved with the creation of this manuscript, their contributions to my work and the wide-ranging ideas we explored together through the years inspire this text. The influence of my early mentors at Arsenal Family and Children's Center, especially Sara Arnaud and Nancy Curry, shines through as well. I also want to acknowledge the memory of my colleague Ruth Gumerman, who embodied integrity better than anyone I have ever known. More than fifteen years ago, Ruth and I presented a paper on the importance of attending to power dynamics in the therapeutic relationship; this was my first attempt at articulating the core of what has become this book. Thank you, too, to other former colleagues at Pittsburgh Action Against Rape alongside whom I learned the value and ethics of respectful listening and simple presence.

Thanks so much to my brother Chris for creating the diagrams in Chapter 4, my parents for always endorsing my curiosity and independent thinking (even when it made life more complicated!), and my siblings and their families for their love and their faith in me.

And, finally, Jan: I really couldn't have done this without your love, constancy, and patience. Thank you, my beloved.

I

Understanding Self-Injury as the Tip of the Iceberg

1

What Is Self-Injury?

When hidden pain starts to speak, it will speak silently. Its voice may appear as a cut on the leg, a burn on the arm, skin ripped and scratched repeatedly. There will be no sound, not any, only unfelt and silent pain which makes its appearance in another pain, self-inflicted, and when that second, collateral pain emerges, it will articulate in blood or blisters the open definition you desire, although it may not be in a language you care to see. This, it says, is pain, and this is real in any language you care to speak. [McLane 1996, p. 111]

Self-injurious behavior challenges our sensibilities. We find it baffling, frustrating, confusing, and disturbing. We tend to startle when we see the scars of self-inflicted injuries on someone's arms. We wonder involuntarily, Why would some one *do* that? Self-injury seems to defy our fundamental instincts about survival and self-protection. We respond instinctively to physical attacks, fighting back and asserting our right to survive. We even embody this belief in our legal code, allowing for a "self-defense" argument. Some describe the body as the temple of the soul, a place of honor. We spend thousands of dollars to care for and maintain our physical selves. It would appear that as human beings we demonstrate a fierce determination to protect and care for ourselves.

Why, then, do some people directly injure themselves? What motivates people to carve marks into their arms or stomachs? Why do people take lit cigarettes and slowly press them into their thighs? What prompts people to punch or slap themselves in the face? Why do people douche with toxic or harsh substances? Or bang their heads on floors and walls?

To ground the answers to these questions, we need first to explore the ambivalent relationship we have with our bodies. Although we expend much effort and money caring for our bodies, at the same time we routinely and consistently disregard what is best for our physical (and mental/emotional/spiritual) selves. Taking a glance at the larger continuum of self-harming or self-destructive behaviors evident in Western culture fleshes out this ambivalence and provides a context within which to place self-injuring behavior. First, though, we need to start with language, since it is the modality utilized in this book.

The Language We Use to Describe Self-Injury

Our words reflect our beliefs. Whether conscious or unaware, the language we use for our observations and perceptions communicates what we believe, value, and feel. The particular words we use often tell more about our theoretical orientation and philosophical worldview than the actual ideas we describe with our words. Therefore, to frame the concepts central to working with clients who self-injure, I begin by describing the terms I find most useful in discussing self-harming behavior.

Self-injury has been called a range of other names: parasuicidal behavior (Gardner and Cowdry 1985), self-mutilation (Conn and Lion 1983, Favazza 1996, Walsh and

Rosen 1988), self-destructive behavior (Figueroa 1988), self-damaging behavior (Courtois 1988), deliberate self-harm (Morgan et al. 1975, Pattison and Kahan 1983), self-inflicted violence (Alderman 1997, Blessing 1990, Mazelis 1990) and self-abuse (Davies and Frawley 1994). The term *self-injury* has grown increasingly common in the last decade, and is the primary term used in this book. It is the most descriptive and least pejorative of the common phrases. The term *self-inflicted violence* is also used in this book because it too is an accurate descriptor.

Self-injury and *self-inflicted violence* both convey a fundamental sense of the behavior without attributing (often inaccurate) intent as do the terms *self-mutilation* and *self-destructive behavior*. Various forms of self-injury do not involve mutilation per se (e.g., head-banging, punching, ingesting objects), and many do not result from an intent of destruction. *Self-inflicted violence* is an apt term also in that it links violence to self-injury.

Another difficulty with some of the terminology associated with self-injury is the lack of clarity or generality of a phrase. *Self-harm* is a broad term used in this book to describe a wide range of behaviors that may or may not be seen as problematic; it includes but is not limited to self-injury. *Self-damaging behavior* and *self-abuse* are equally unclear as descriptors for self-injury because of their broad meaning. My concerns about the phrase *parasuicidal behavior* is that it links self-injury so clearly to suicidality, which is precisely in contradiction to the intent behind self-injury. (This concept is discussed in further detail in Chapter 2.) Even though parasuicidal behaviors *can* be unintentionally lethal (thus the linguistic link to suicide), generally self-injury is not, and to use the term *parasuicidal* often confounds the issues. Further, both *parasuicidal* and *self-mutilation* have also gathered a charged negativity through the years, creating a pejorative and less-than-respectful tone. Given the already complicated nature of addressing self-injury with clients, I believe it is useful to avoid such language, particularly when other options exist.

Defining Self-Injury

Self-injury consists of direct actions, outside of the realm of social acceptability, that hurt or harm one's body. Alderman (1997) defines self injury as "the intentional harm of one's own body without conscious suicidal intent . . . [or simply] the act of physically hurting yourself on purpose" (p. 7). She summarizes the key characteristics of self-inflicted violence as acts that are "done to oneself, performed by oneself, physically violent, not suicidal, and intentional and purposeful" (p. 9). In other words, self-injury is deliberate violence toward one's body that has a purpose other than suicide.

Part of what allows us to usefully define self-injury is the context of the behavior. Favazza (1996) has devoted considerable effort to exploring the anthropological and cross-species contexts within which we might approach a definition and understanding of self-injury. Walsh and Rosen (1988) also state that behavior in and of itself does not constitute self-injury.

Understanding the Significance of Context

The broad continuum of self-harming behavior incorporates many different kinds of actions (or inaction). Whether a certain act is perceived as self-harming is partly determined by social norms, the actor's intent, the psychological state accompanying the behavior, and how the act impacts the body/self. Any particular form of behavior can be viewed in different lights, depending on the social and personal context within which it occurs. For example, cutting or piercing one's skin may constitute self-injury, or it may be an act done to allow one to wear earrings within certain cultural contexts, or it may be part of an initiation rite in a particular culture. Any exploration of the meaning of a particular behavior needs to be grounded in the surrounding details.

The following story from a woman who has used self-injury in the past illustrates the significance of context.

Jessie's mother smoked cigarettes for thirty years. She attempted to stop several times, with no luck. Several years ago she was taken to the hospital with chest pains. An angioplasty found that several major arteries were blocked; surgery followed. Fortunately, there was no lasting damage and her recovery was promising. However, her doctors instructed her to stop smoking immediately. They said that if she smoked she would cause permanent damage to her heart and she would most likely die. They also said that they realized there was a good chance she would not be able to quit successfully, given her history. She was discharged and wished well in her recovery.

Reflecting on her mother's addiction to nicotine and Jessie's desire for her mother to stop smoking, Jessie realized what the hospital staff had *not* said to her mother. No doctor or nurse had said anything to her mother about involuntarily hospitalizing her if she thought about smoking, prescribing psychoactive medication to manage her feelings and impulses, and using restraints if she lit a cigarette. No one asked her what was wrong with her that she wanted to smoke. Even though they believed

that smoking would be life-threatening at this point, the
health care professionals acted as if Jessie's mother had
the right to decide what she did with her body. Jessie
knew that their responses would have been different had
her mother engaged in cutting her arms or burning her
chest, neither of which would be likely to endanger her
life.

Smoking is only one of the many socially acceptable
ways to harm or physically change one's body; most common are drinking alcohol, overeating, playing hard-contact
football, having unnecessary cosmetic surgery, getting tattoos, and piercing one's ears. In many social circles, these
are not unusual or harmful acts, but rather ones that are
sometimes encouraged and even given a certain status. In
this case, the self-harm—which may not even be perceived
as self-harm—results from what is seen as a necessary or
likely by-product of an activity done for pleasure or other
socially acceptable needs. In this context the harm or damage is judged to be temporary or insignificant in the face
of larger needs or wishes. Concomitantly, the intent is not
to cause self-harm, for the most part.

Other types of socially acceptable self-harm result from
various forms of oppression operating within our cultural
norms. For example, expectations about how women
should look leads to dieting, excessive exercise, eyebrow
plucking, and other forms of behavior that may result in
self-harm. The economic and/or political structure of many
cultures severely limits accessibility to healthy nutrition and
medical care for some classes of people, thereby leading to
poor nutrition and inadequate health care—often resulting
in significant self-harm.

On an even broader level, all of us are subjected to
certain environmental hazards or other harmful agents

such as airborne carcinogens and antibiotics in food. Although these problems are perpetrated by industry and are not patently self-harming, knowingly exposing ourselves might be construed as self-harm. In other words, if we know that certain foods are laden with pesticides and antibiotics (substances which are demonstrated to have negative health effects) are we engaging in self-harm if we choose to eat these foods? Clearly, the degree of choice we have regarding our exposure to such potential dangers depends on various factors, including our level of awareness about such concerns, our beliefs about health and illness, and economic privilege.

Several other forms of behavior might fit more accurately within the specific category of self-injury, but they tend to remain within the realm of social acceptability due to the relatively high frequency of the behaviors and the relatively low level of harm. They are commonly described as "nervous" behaviors and may serve similar functions to other forms of self-injury. Examples include nail-biting, pulling off scabs, unconscious scratching, and picking at acne or pimples. While such behavior may or may not be perceived by the person doing it as self-injury, this behavior is generally not identified as such by others due to social acceptability. Nail biting usually does not stand out to the average person the way cutting one's arms does. On the other hand, one might categorize pulling off scabs as self-injury, and yet the person doing it may not experience it as self-injury. (It should be acknowledged that all of these behaviors can become more extreme regarding level of harm, thereby impacting how one might perceive or experience the behavior; see Wells et al. [1999] for a discussion and study of the distinction between mild and severe nail-biting.)

In short, we need to exercise caution as we attempt to define self-injury, given the impact of context and individual perceptions in categorizing behavior. Particular care needs to be taken regarding attributions of meaning and function. A certain behavior may constitute self-injury for one person but not another; the same behavior may constitute self-injury for the same person at one point in time but not another. Rather than trying to narrowly articulate self-injury as a discrete class of behavior, I would posit that we are better served by clarifying and articulating the larger continuum of self-harm. This helps to demystify what might be called the more extreme forms of self-harm identified here as self-injury, and provides a grounded framework within which to understand self-injury as a psychological mechanism.

The Broad Continuum of Self-Harm

In an effort to more carefully define the larger continuum of body-altering, -injuring, or otherwise harmful-to-the-self behavior, four categories are delineated below. Examples illustrate each category. Some reflections on the complexity of self-harm and the artificiality of such categorization follow these definitions.

1. *Body alterations:* direct, self-chosen changes to the body, often to conform to cultural or group norms. Body alterations may or may not involve pain, and sometimes entail the use of anesthesia. The intent behind these common, socially sanctioned (at least by a subgroup if not by the dominant culture) actions is generally beautification or symbolic marking to indicate belonging. Examples are cosmetic surgery, tattoos, ear/body piercing, eyebrow plucking, and ceremonial or initiation scarring or marking.

2. *Indirect self-harm:* behaviors that can indirectly cause harm to the person's body and psychological well-being even though the apparent or conscious intent is not to harm the self. Examples are substance abuse, overeating, dieting, purging, smoking, staying in a damaging relationship, unnecessary surgeries, and excessive exercise.

3. *Failure to care for self:* an inadequate ability to provide self-care or protect self. Significant mental health problems, inadequate economic resources, and lack of information may contribute to or exaggerate these forms of self-harm. Examples include excessive risk-taking, accident proneness, not getting necessary medical care, and poor nutrition.

4. *Self-injury:* direct actions that injure the body that do not appear to fit in the category of body alterations noted above. A few examples are cutting, burning, and head-banging (more examples are given later).

"Apparent or conscious intent" (noted in category 2) can be a confusing concept, the meaning of which is dependent on how deeply we look for intent. Clearly, these are forms of harm to the self. However, these actions are not as direct as slicing one's arm with a razor blade. While the underlying dynamics and functions may operate in ways that are similar to direct and overt self-injury, the nature of the indirectness can complicate the sorting process for clients. I therefore find it useful to separate them out. Like all classification systems, these are arbitrary categories developed for the purpose of clarity in discussion, to facilitate conversation. They are not intended to be factual or rigid. In real life, the overlapping nature of these forms of self-harm becomes clearer as clients sort out what their behavior means to them. Most people who self-injure also

engage or have engaged in these first three categories of
general self-harm. Indeed, perhaps all of us have engaged
in some form of self-harm at some point in time.

Further, some people may discover that they engage
in socially acceptable forms of self-harm or body alteration
that operate psychologically like self-injury for them, such
as nail-biting, tattooing, piercing, and eyebrow plucking.
They may or may not determine these behaviors to be
problematic or cause for change. As noted, various forms
of indirect self-harm frequently operate psychologically in
ways very similar to direct self-injury. Troubled eating (a
phrase borrowed from Burstow [1992]) and substance
abuse are commonly related to the same issues underlying self-injury, and function in ways quite similar to self-
inflicted violence. Again, what is important is that the
person engaging in the behavior needs to determine what
is self-injury and what is not, as well as what to do (or not
do) about it.

Self-Injury as Violence

Perhaps what distinguishes self-injury from these other forms
of self-harm is the directness of the use of violence as a solution to a difficult problem or situation. Many people from
a range of cultures have learned to use violence to solve
what seem like intractable problems. These can be intrapersonal, interpersonal, or societal problems that we feel
we lack the skills to finesse in other ways. As nations we go
to war over boundary disputes, or to convince others to
believe as we do. Interpersonally, we use our physical
strength or intellectual prowess to control or intimidate
others. We act violently to resolve conflicts, or keep others
"in line." Unless taught otherwise, children often get the

toy they want by taking it forcibly from another child, or slap their friend when they don't like what their friend is saying. If children observe such behavior in their adult caregivers, they are even more likely to employ such solutions (de Zulueta 1993, Dutton 1995, Garbarino 1999a).

Self-injury is a violence-oriented solution to intrapersonal dilemmas. Too many feelings? Hit yourself. Overwhelming arousal? Bang your head until your body calms down. Feeling disconnected or dead? Cut until there is enough blood to prove you are alive. As many people who utilize self-injury have a history of childhood abuse, it is not surprising that the lessons of violence are well learned and used in the present as a coping style. This element of violent action distinguishes self-injury (for purposes of discussion) from other forms of self-harm. I should note that violence per se is not primarily a motivator or purpose for self-injury, but rather violence is the shape it takes. It is the form of the solution to the underlying need, although, as McLane (1996) notes, it takes this form because self-injury can "express the violence and contradictions [one] knows while controlling the expression and effect on others" (p. 115). The need to express previously unexpressed violence in some relatively safe form often exists for self-injuring clients. (The purpose and meaning of self-injury is explored in detail in the next chapter.)

Clearly, there is a continuum of violence and control. Seemingly passive behavior can be inherently violent and abusive. An interpersonal example is an abusive husband not allowing his wife to have access to money in order to control her, or never getting around to sitting down with her to review their financial situation. A societal example is an industry's ignoring citizens' complaints about downstream pollution from a factory. Alcohol addiction is similarly self-violent, albeit in a more passive fashion than hit-

ting oneself. Just as indirect self-harm can function dynami-
cally like self-injury, indirect self-harm can be inherently,
insidiously violent.

Self-Injury in the Psychiatric Literature

Self-injury has been discussed in the psychiatric literature
beginning with Menninger in 1935. While enjoying a long
history with sporadic contributions, the literature is largely
based on clinical data from a range of theoretical perspectives, augmented by more recent descriptive or epidemiological research, personal commentary, and informal interview. In a psychiatric context, self-injury has been
generally considered a hallmark symptom of borderline
personality disorder (Hamilton 1992, Kernberg 1985,
Leibenluft et al. 1987); it has also been evidenced by
people struggling with apparent psychosis and those with
organic impairments or under the influence of mind-
altering drugs (Favazza 1996, Favazza and Rosenthal 1993,
Walsh and Rosen 1988).

The last decade or so has seen a significant increase
in the number of journal articles and books addressing self-
injury. This seems to parallel the increase in the number
of clients who describe self-injuring behavior as they seek
the help of mental health professionals. Recently, journalists, clinicians, and other writers have endeavored to augment this literature with books for the general public as
well as academia (Alderman 1997, Conterio and Lader
1998, Hyman 1999, Levenkron 1997, Miller 1994, Strong
1998). (It should be noted that the majority of the current
books in the popular press are written by mental health
professionals experienced in therapeutic work with self-injuring clients, though a few are by journalists.)

The greater availability of information about self-injury also coincides with the increasing volume of knowledge about trauma, both in the professional and the popular press. In recent years, researchers and clinicians have begun to link self-injuring behavior to the experience of trauma in childhood (Arnold 1995, Briere and Gil 1998, Briere and Zaidi 1989, Bryer et al. 1987, Davies and Frawley 1994, deYoung 1982, DiClemente et al. 1991, Miller 1994, Nicholls et al. 1999, Romans et al. 1995, van der Kolk et al. 1991, Zlotnick et al. 1997) and to some extent in adulthood (Arnold 1995, Briere and Gil 1998, Greenspan and Samuel 1989, Pitman 1990, Zlotnick et al. 1997). Many authors writing about childhood trauma list self-injury among the long-term effects of trauma for adult and adolescent survivors (Briere 1992, Courtois 1988, Dolan 1991, Finney 1992, Herman 1992, Waites 1993). Some have addressed the functions self-injury serves for survivors (Blessing 1990, Briere 1992, Briere and Gil 1998, Burstow 1992, Calof 1995, Connors, 1996a, Davies and Frawley 1994, Farber 1998, Favazza 1996, Herman 1992, van der Kolk 1996a, Waites 1993, Walsh and Rosen 1988, Wise 1989).

Some writers have made an effort to classify self-injury (Burstow 1992, Favazza 1996, Figueroa 1988, Hawton 1990). Most attempt to incorporate several criteria in determining categorization schemes: the level of harm, associated features (such as rhythmicity or symbolic meaning), and the mental status of the person engaging in the behavior. Writing about the management of cutting among psychiatric inpatients, Hawton (1990) identifies superficial self-cutting, deep cutting, and self-mutilation. He writes that superficial self-cutting is generally not associated with suicidal intent, while deep cutting is usually associated with suicidality and involves endangering blood vessels, nerves, and tendons. He states that self-mutilation (using his definition) often involves disfigurement and is generally limited to people with psychosis.

Taking a slightly different approach, Figueroa (1988) chose the phrase *self-destructive behavior* to denote the broad category of self-harm, with five subtypes. Self-injurious behavior (as engaged in by people with mental retardation), suicidal behavior, and failures in self-care constitute three of his categories. The other two are self-mutilation/characterological and self-mutilation/psychotic, with the mental state determining the class of self-destructive behavior.

Favazza (1996) and his colleagues (Favazza and Rosenthal 1993, Favazza and Simeon 1995) list three types of self-mutilation (their broad naming): major, stereotypic, and superficial or moderate. Major self-mutilation involves significant tissue damage, often a removal of a body part, and is infrequent. It tends to be done while acutely intoxicated or during a psychotic episode, though it can occur rarely in other situations. Stereotypic self-mutilation is rhythmic and without symbolism, as with repetitive head-banging. These behaviors are often engaged in by people with metal retardation or other organic syndromes, particularly those who are institutionalized. They may also occur in people under the influence of drugs. The third category is superficial or moderate self-mutilation, involving little tissue damage or rhythmicity. This form tends to have symbolic meaning, and is evidenced by a range of people with mixed histories and diagnoses, including various types of trauma histories, eating problems, and personality disorders. Favazza goes on to further delineate this third type of self-injury by identifying three subcategories: compulsive (such as trichotillomania, which is compulsive hair-pulling), episodic, and repetitive.

In her descriptive approach, Burstow (1992) describes three levels of self-mutilation in women: women who self-mutilate lightly, women who mutilate lightly but occasionally hurt themselves badly, and women who injure themselves seriously. Burstow emphasizes the point that the majority of women who injure themselves do not engage in serious self-injury, such as cutting to the bone, using dirty instruments, or causing second-degree burns.

It is clear that some forms of direct self-injury are engaged in by people with organic retardation, people suffering from psychosis or autism, or people with acute obsessive-compulsive disorder (Favazza 1996, Walsh and Rosen 1988). The role of trauma in the etiology of self-injury as a coping mechanism in these populations is unclear, though there is some thought that obsessive-compulsive disorder can be trauma-based (de Silva and Marks 1999). It is also hard to readily classify trichotillomania, currently listed as an impulse disorder in the *Diagnostic and Statistical Manual of Mental Disorders* (*DSM-IV*; American Psychiatric Association 1994). Some would argue that it is a form of self-injury (Primeau and Fontaine 1987), while others (Stanley and Cohen 1999) describe it as an obsessive-compulsive disorder. Stein and Christenson (1999) tend to dismiss the classification of trichotillomania as self-injury, as they argue that only a minority of the people who engage in trichotillomania also cut or burn themselves. Interestingly, trichotillomania and a range of other habits noted by Stein and Christenson clearly cause self-harm, have been associated with loss and other traumatic life changes, and may or may not cause pain (as is true with self-injury). They also state that the clinical presentations of trichotillomania and the people affected by it are somewhat heterogeneous in nature. All of this suggests at least some similarity to what is defined as self-injury in this book. Perhaps it is simply a matter of language and perspective.

Self-injurious behavior in psychotic, organically impaired, drugged, or autistic people appears to operate with somewhat different or at least additional elements as trauma-based self-inflicted violence. While this book does not address self-injury in these populations particularly, some of the operative dynamics may be similar for trauma-based self-injury, such as serving the functions of tension reduction, self-soothing, or expression of feelings (Favazza 1996, Figueroa 1988), particularly frustration. Certainly, the role of stress contributes to the use of self-injury by mentally impaired individuals.

Many self-injurers who come into contact with health and mental health professionals, however, would fit into Hawton's (1990) class of superifical self-cutters, Figueroa's (1988) self-mutilation/characterological group, Favazza's (1992) two latter subcategories of episodic and repetitive superficial/moderate self-mutilators, and Burstow's (1992) first two categories (women who mutilate lightly and women who occasionally hurt themselves badly). This book addresses psychotherapy with people who are not suffering from a major organic impairment but rather people who would fit loosely into the various categories just noted, and who are, in varying degrees, responsive to psychotherapy.

Forms and Variations of Self-Injury

Self-injury takes many forms. Most commonly identified is self-injury that involves the skin: cutting, burning, picking, scratching or scraping, tearing at cuticles or biting nails to the quick, using an eraser or steel wool to "burn" or tear the skin, taking scalding showers and baths, and interfering with the healing of wounds. Other forms include the use of force against the body such as slapping oneself, punching oneself or punching walls, head-banging, breaking bones, choking, and hitting oneself with objects. Sometimes the focus is on poking or inserting: stabbing or gouging skin and tissue, biting the inside of the mouth, biting other parts of the body, using harmful or painful enemas and douches (either with very hot or cold water, or with toxic substances), inserting large or sharp objects into the vagina or rectum, ingesting sharp objects (such as razor blades, staples, needles, and pins), and swallowing toxic substances. Deliberate overdoses not intended to kill may be included in this category. Other forms involve removal of parts of the body such as pulling out eyelashes or teeth, digging into the gums, cutting off a body part, and hair-pulling or -plucking (usually head or pubic hair).

In addition to constituting a wide variety of behaviors, variations may also exist in the way self-injury occurs. One is the degree of dissociation. Some self-injurers describe being dissociated from the pain; they sometimes perceive a dissociated part of the self to be the one engaging in self-injury. Others feel they self-injure in a trance, knowing they are doing it but feeling like they have no control over what they are doing. Some people describe watching themselves self-injure, or feeling that the self-injury "just happens." They may or may not feel pain. Others do experience pain and are acutely aware that they—rather than a dissociated part of self—are the one inflicting the violence.

Lisa describes watching herself cut her arm, knowing what she is doing but experiencing no pain or sensation. On occasion, she feels she is floating above her body, but for the most part she is simply detached from the pain.

Linda feels she only cuts when she hears someone inside (a dissociated part) telling her she must hurt herself. The voice is compelling, and offers detailed arguments about why Linda must cut herself as a punishment for doing something wrong or being inadequate.

West (1999) offers this powerful description of self-injury occurring while he was in a dissociated state:

> Looking out my upstairs bedroom window through a curtain of fog, I see a vague image under a street lamp. I squint my eyes, and as the image slowly becomes clearer, I can distinguish a human outline. I take a step closer and lean forward, placing my hands on the windowsill, pressing my forehead against the cool pane. *Who is that?*
>
> It's a slim, dark-haired man in a T-shirt and blue jeans. He's doing something, but I can't quite make it out. I rub my eyes and again press my face to the glass, straining to see. The dark-haired man is leaning over a white, free-standing sink with a mirror attached to the back of it. There appears to be something in his left hand—something sharp. *What's he doing?*
>
> Then I see that his right arm is covered with blood. Blood is dripping off the tips of his fingers and into the sink. He looks up into the mirror and back down at his arm. I follow his gaze and see blood dripping from a five-inch incision on his forearm. Large drops of blood fall from the end of the short steel blade of a knife. He makes another pass with the knife, and fresh blood fills the wound, training down his arm, splattering in the sink.
>
> Suddenly, a familiar force seizes me; a silent vacuum pulls my viscous self through the window and across the street. I'm now behind the man with the bloody arm, watching him lean over the sink. He spots me in the mirror, and like a balloon filling with molasses, I

slowly expand and fill his body. Now I am inside. I look down at the left hand holding the bloody knife, then at the open flesh oozing red. The eyes peer into the mirror, and from an island in my mind, I realize that it's my face looking back at me, it's my hand holding the knife, my arm bleeding into the sink. [p. 1]

A second variation is the presence or absence of sexualization. Some self-injury is highly sexualized and arousing. Other experiences of self-injury may produce feelings of peace or positive sensations, such as a sense of relief, but the sensations are not specifically sexual. The act of self-injury itself can be associated with sexual fantasy, or provide a release of sexual tension. Sexualized self-injury may be focused on the genitals, breasts, or buttocks, but harming other parts of the body can also be experienced as sexual if connected to sexual arousal or fantasy. Some self-injurers engage in both nonsexualized and sexualized self-injury, reporting that different kinds of self-injury serve different functions.

One of the forms of self-injury Marcy utilized for many years was to insert needles into her clitoris. It was both arousing and painful. What was most salient for her was the experience of pain in connection with sexual arousal. "When I hurt enough, I would have an orgasm." Marcy linked the insertion of needles to traumatic medical procedures in childhood. Recently, she has found she has stopped this form of self-injury, even though she still occasionally scratches herself when overwhelmed by feelings of frustration or self-blame. Marcy attributes the fact that the sexualized self-injury "just kind of stopped" to her resolution of many long-standing issues, including the early trauma.

A third variation occurs in the approach to the behavior. Some people who self-injure describe the behavior as habitualized, almost ritualized, self-inflicted violence. They may become aware of the need to self-injure some hours prior to engaging in self-injury; some describe actually planning it in detail or looking forward to it all day. For them, part of the process is the preparation, such as buying razor blades or canceling appointments so enough time is allocated after work. Sometimes just the preparation itself serves the purpose, without having to actually self-injure. As one woman said, "Just knowing I can hurt myself when I go home relieved the pressure so I could do my work. Sometimes I don't even have to do it when I do get home."

For others it is an impulsive act, often in response to intense affect triggered by an external event. "I just hit myself in a fury when I become helpless and frustrated. It's as if I can't bear to feel so out of control, so I do something to focus the rage, to feel in control momentarily. It happens in an instant." Again, some people experience elements of both methods, or find they utilize different styles in response to different feelings or needs. Understanding the need the behavior is meeting (the function it serves) often explains these variations.

How Common Is Self-Injury and Who Does It?

An accurate estimate of how many people self-injure, in either the population at large or in specific clinical populations, is difficult to ascertain. Little solid epidemiological research has been done. Briere and Gil (1998) surveyed several populations and found a rate of 4 percent in the general population and 21 percent in clinical populations. Conterio and Lader (1998) believe that approximately 1,400 out of every 100,000 people in the general population engage in self-injury. Unpublished research on clinical samples by Nicholls and colleagues (1999) reports a rate of 58 percent for direct self-injury (with even greater numbers reporting indirect self-harm). DiClemente and colleagues (1991) found that 61 percent of psychiatrically hospitalized adolescents engaged in self-cutting.

The role of specific variables such as gender or age in identifying self-harm is unclear. Some data and clinical reports suggest a higher incidence of self-injury among women and girls (Carmen et al. 1984, Miller 1994, Walsh and Rosen 1988), although this is not supported by several research studies. Briere and Gil (1998), Nicholls and colleagues (1999), and DiClemente and colleagues (1991) all report no significant differences in the rates of self-injury between genders in their samples. Historically, the clinical literature and most research studies have focused on women as self-injurers, as do many of the current trade books (Conterio and Lader 1998, Levenkron 1997). Several books on self-injury even limit their scope to women (Hyman 1999, Miller 1994). However, men also report self-injury (Briere and Gil 1998, Nicholls et al. 1999, Olson 1990, West 1999, Zweig-Frank et al. 1994b), as do children and adolescents of both genders (deYoung 1982, DiClemente et al. 1991, Green 1978, Ross and McKay 1979, Simpson and Porter 1981, Walsh and Rosen 1988).

The role of trauma in the etiology of self-injury along with the subsequent gender-mediated responses to the aftereffects of trauma would support the sense of imbalance regarding gender representation in mental health settings. Alderman (1997) offers a perspective on this, stating that while men and women self-injure with similar frequency, women are more likely to show up in mental health settings. This is consistent with clinical literature on trauma survivors in general, and those diagnosed with dissociative identity disorder in particular. The working hypothesis is that men may be less likely than women to readily identify or disclose abuse histories (Lew 1990), and that men with trauma histories are more likely to end up in prison than in clinicians' offices or hospitals (Conterio and Lader 1998, Putnam 1989, Urquiza and Crowley 1986, Urquiza and Keating 1990). This does not, however, suggest that men don't self-injure at the same rate. In fact, as noted, the limited research suggests little difference in frequency between genders (Briere and Gil 1998, DiClemente et al. 1991, Nicholls et al. 1999), and the reported incidence of self-injury in prison populations is somewhat high, regardless of gender (Potier 1993, Winchel and Stanley 1991). However, no firm conclusions can be drawn about self-injury with regard to gender, class, race, and other demographic variables until systematic, well-constructed research data are available.

Based on clinical experience and informal interview, I believe the dynamics of self-injury for men are similar to those for women considered within the context of differential gender socialization. The underlying issues and effects are similar, although the language and experiences will be slanted differently. For example, men have described what they identified as self-injury occurring within the context of male gender-role "games"—"I'm tougher than you are because I can take more self-inflicted cigarette burns"—or in conjunction with externally directed aggression, such as street fights and high-contact team sports. Women are less likely to self-injure in the context of a group or in a competitive manner. It is interesting to note that externally directed aggression such as fighting and high-contact sports involves a mix of both self-injury and other-injury. I suspect this is more common for men than women. This is consistent with gender socialization, wherein girls are encouraged to direct anger and frustration inward, and boys are supported to focus it outward.

Diagnostically, self-injury has been particularly associated with people diagnosed with borderline personality disorder, dissociative identity disorder, posttraumatic stress disorder, and various personality disorders (Chu 1998, Conterio and Lader 1998, Davies and Frawley 1994, Favazza and Conterio 1988, Linehan 1993, Strong 1998, Waites 1993, Winchel and Stanley 1991). Self-injury commonly coexists with alcohol or drug addictions, eating disorders, compulsive sexuality or sexual dysfunction, and body image distortions. People who self-injure tend to have difficulties with anxiety, mood regulation, and depression. In short, the clinical patterns following trauma appear consistently in the lives and histories of people who self-injure.

A clinical picture sometimes described with regard to age is that self-injury often starts during adolescence, increases during one's 20s, and begins to decline in one's 30s (Alderman 1997, Strong 1998). Perhaps it is simply that this pattern echoes what had been called the natural course of borderline personality disorder (American Psychiatric Association 1994). Some women have noted that their self-injury began soon after they reached menarche, and have questioned the role of hormones as a precipitant to self-harm. Certainly, stress contributes to self-injury, and hormonal changes can be stressful; they may be one of a group of contributing factors. So many relevant factors emerge at adolescence (such as issues about body image, sexuality, gender conflicts, separation issues, and current or prior abuse) that it is hard to know how they tie together. I am uncertain how accurate this pattern or these theories are, and I believe we need more data before we can conclude there is a pattern or course. The variations in individuals' lives are great, and factors such as external stressors, social supports, and the presence of addiction or other self-harming behavior separate from actual self-injury probably mediate the course of someone's experience with self-injury.

Regarding the democratic nature of self-injury: sometimes, depending on the client population we happen to encounter or the limitations of our personal knowledge, we conclude that people who self-injure fit a particular profile. We may think self-injurers as a group are somewhat low functioning if we work in a state hospital, or we may believe that only women self-injure because of the current rash of books and articles on cutting, or we may tend to classify self-injurers as people suffering from some form of severe psychiatric illness. I have found that a wide range of people self-injure, just as a wide range of people experience trauma and a wide range of people seek mental health services.

A number of the people identified as self-injurers who are quoted throughout this book are reasonably well-functioning individuals. They include professionals in various fields who have had the resources to avoid psychiatric hospitalization and the scrutiny that comes with that experience. Many of them struggle with the fear of being discovered as less functional than they appear to be from the outside; they have generally worked hard to keep their self-injury a secret. On the other hand, some of the people I quote *have* spent significant time in hospitals and the mental health/social services system, and have become more conversant and less secretive about their self-injury by necessity. They may appear to be somewhat blasé about their self-harm (or alternately quite focused on it). The important thing to remember is that appearances can be deceptive and that in spite of one's history as a 'patient,' the experience of self-injury, globally, is remarkably similar and, in detail, diverse.

The Essential Purpose of Self-Injury

Regardless of clinical diagnosis, gender, trauma history, or style of injuring, central to therapeutic work with people who self-injure is the necessity of understanding the purpose of self-inflicted violence. Self-injury is a fundamentally adaptive and life-preserving coping mechanism. It enables people struggling with overwhelming and often undifferentiated affect, intense psychological arousal, intrusive memories, poor or fluctuating self-esteem, and dissociative states to regulate their current experience of both past and present in order to stay alive (Davies and Frawley 1994, Hyman 1999, Mazelis 1993). Although self-injury may appear to be similar to suicidal gesturing, it is essentially different in that the self-injurer is attempting to avoid suicidality and death (see Chapter 2). Self-injury makes life bearable for some people by helping them manage intense internal and external experiences. In her richly written book on cutting, *A Bright Red Scream*, Marilee Strong (1998) offers this comment by a young woman. It eloquently describes how self-injury offers temporary but clear relief:

"I remember what it felt like to see the blood," recalls Lindsay of her first cutting experience at age fourteen. "It's weird to say this, but it was beautiful. It was as if the entire outside world had closed and everything was calm and quiet and peaceful. I cut very shallowly that first time—there was barely any bleeding—but it was enough then. For a few moments it seemed as if the poison in my blood was leaving—calmly, submissively. I was in control of it. It felt like rain.

"After the tranquility wore out, I was terrified at what I had just done. It scared me and I thought I was crazy. But I knew that those few moments had released

me from the chaos in my head. And I knew I could
do it again." [p. 55]

The Importance of the Person, Not the Behavior

In defining and focusing on self-injury, we give it center
stage. This has value, because in so doing we name it. If
we don't name it, it doesn't exist. Naming allows us to
clarify what we mean, acknowledge that self-injury not only
exists but has relevance and meaning, conduct research in
order to better understand it, and attempt to communicate
with clients about it, with the goal of helping in some way.
But, fundamentally, the statistics and categories and diagnostic labels don't really matter; they are mere constructions that organize our thoughts and observations. What
matters about self-injury is the person doing it. Self-injury is
just a behavior. Only when we look at the person behind the
behavior, the person controlling the behavior, the person
utilizing the behavior, the person needing the behavior, can
we begin to value the role of self-injury in a person's life.
Then, we may be able to be useful as clinicians or helpers.

    This book focuses on the *person* who self-injures rather
than on the self-injury. Many would say, "Well, of course
it's about the person." And yet, so often our interventions
are focused on the behavior, not the person in all of who
she is. Too frequently, our treatment plans address the
behavior, rather than conceptualizing what is happening
internally for the client, or finding ways to better support
the client. Extinguishing behavior becomes more important
than healing core issues. The policies we develop to guide
our actions highlight behavior, not the underlying needs
of the patient. In the end, focusing on the behavior fails
the person and what she asks of us.

Self-injury is a message, a metaphor, a form of communication, an attempt to cope with the unmanageable or unspeakable, a doorway into the client's internal world. It always serves a purpose—often more than one purpose. As Strong (1998) has noted, it is "a bright, red scream" in the language of the body. Hearing the pain behind the scream, being willing to peek through the doorway into the client's private experience of past and present, makes a difference. As we begin to grasp what self-injury means to the person engaging in the behavior, we then begin to be useful to clients seeking our help. And that, simply put, is our job.

2

Understanding Self-Injury

The key to effective response to self-injury, either by professionals or by the person injuring, is understanding what gives rise to the behavior. Identifying the antecedents and constructing a framework within which to view self-injury helps make sense of self-inflicted violence. Like most coping mechanisms, it does make sense once we are able to peer through the lens of the worldview of the people utilizing the behavior. This allows us to better perceive their experience, and be more useful in offering support or suggesting paths for change. For people who self-injure, understanding the links between their self-injury and various elements of their past gives a fuller picture of their internal experience and personal history, thus promoting healing of the self.

Distinguishing Self-Injury from Suicidality

Before we can make sense of self-injury, we need to separate it from suicidal gestures and failed suicide attempts. Historically, as indicated by one of the terms used to refer to self-injury, *parasuicidal behavior*, self-injury has been both misperceived and miscategorized. Cutting in particular is often confused with suicidal intent. Emergency room personnel and other health care providers may see self-inflicted violence as a suicidal gesture or attempt, because the obvious evidence of self-injury, such as scars and wounds,

35

appears to be so similar to some suicide attempts. Even the language used in reference to suicidal ideation ("Do you mean you want to hurt yourself?") is unclear and can be readily confused with self-injury.

As with many inquiries, our assumptions bias what we see and know. If clinicians' knowledge base includes information about suicidality but little or no information about self-injury, they will be inclined to limit their questions to observable wounds or scars, or make assumptions about what the injuries mean. This confusion is further compounded by the fact that people who self-injure often feel ashamed of their behavior, and find it easier to simply agree with professionals who assume they have attempted or are contemplating suicide. Even when some people who self-injure make an effort to clarify that their injuries are not related to wanting to die, it may be difficult for a professional to conceptualize any other explanation, thereby discounting what the patient is saying quite directly.

Although self-injury and suicidality both arise as an answer to overwhelming pain or anguish, they differ in how clients use them as solutions. Suicide presents a final escape from emotional distress. Self-injury offers a way to stay alive and keep going after achieving the temporary relief of distress. One woman with a dissociative identity structure said, "Our self-abuse was not meant as a bid for attention or a cry for help or an attempt at suicide. It was a little death to prevent a bigger death" (Cohen et al. 1991, p. 80).

As Walsh and Rosen (1988) suggest, the similarities between suicidal behavior and self-injury reside in global characteristics; both are self-directed behavior that "result in concrete physical harm" and stem from "frustrated psychological needs" (p. 51). However, as they explore in some depth, "the differences . . . are more striking" (p. 52), and more apparent as one looks more carefully and specifically at self-injury and suicide. They employ Shneidman's (1985) framework for defining and understanding suicide in order to compare suicide and self-injury, considering such elements as stimulus, stressor, purpose, goal, cognitive state, and action. This definitional approach is informative.

Clinically, what matters most is that we not make assumptions about scars, recent wounds, or clients' references to hurting themselves. We need to remain open and curious, and ask questions with sensitivity to encourage clients to tell us what is going on. Any concern or uncertainty about actual suicidality needs to be addressed directly, drawing on a good risk assessment and developing a plan for safety as indicated. Self-injury and suicidality often co-exist for trauma survivors, and the importance of distinguishing between suicidality and self-injury does not imply that the risk of suicide is not a clinical concern.

A recent study by Hawton and colleagues (1999) highlights common questions about the interconnection of suicidality and self-injury. In their study of young people who completed suicide, they found that 45 percent had previously engaged in deliberate self-harm. It is not clear from their data whether these acts were prior suicide attempts or forms of self-injury. While one might conclude from this study (as well as others addressing suicide) that there is a link between self-injury and suicide, it isn't clear what that link is. It might be confirmation that accidental deaths occur more frequently as a result of self-injury than we have previously thought. I suspect, however, that it probably reflects a basic overlap in the populations of people who self-injure and people who commit suicide; these populations are often the same people, struggling to manage unresolved pain. The frequency with which self-injurers actually attempt or commit suicide is not known.

Traumatic Antecedents of Self-Injury:
What the Research Shows

Clinicians have made connections between clients' self-injuring behavior and aspects of the same clients' histories. Earlier work (primarily) focused on women who cut themselves. Leibenluft and colleagues (1987), Malon and Berardi (1987), and Grunebaum and Klerman (1967) noted connections between women's cutting and their past histories. In this context, links were sometimes made with past trauma histories. As Malon and Berardi noted in their report on using hypnotic techniques with self-cutters to manage arousal, "This new-found sense of security and self-control led some patients to spontaneously reveal early traumatic incidents" (p. 538).

Since the advent of our heightened awareness of the role trauma plays in psychological distress over the last twenty years, more writers have posited that self-injury is related to prior traumatic events. Miller (1994) states unequivocally that regardless of the form of women's self-harm, "they are all women who hurt their bodies as a result of interpersonal or family trauma" (p. 8). Various clinical texts devoted to working with trauma survivors note self-injury as a common residual effect of childhood trauma (Briere 1992, Burstow 1992, Chu 1998, Courtois 1988, Herman 1992, Waites 1993), as do numerous journal articles (Connors 1996a, Farber 1998, Green 1978, Potier 1993, Saunders and Arnold 1991, van der Kolk 1989, Wise 1989).

Research studies over the past twenty years have also correlated a number of childhood experiences with self-inflicted violence. DeYoung (1982) noted that 58 percent of the paternal incest survivors in her sample engaged in self-injury. In all cases, the self-harm began after the abuse started. Walsh and Rosen (1988) identified a range of childhood experiences present in the histories of adolescents who self-injured. These included separation and loss experiences, and out-of-home placements as well as abuse. Van der Kolk and colleagues (1991) found histories of childhood abuse to be significant predictors of adult self-injury. Favazza and Conterio (1988) report that 62 percent of the self-injuring women in their study experienced childhood abuse, while DiClemente and colleagues (1991) state that 83 percent of the adolescents in their sample reported a history of sexual abuse.

In more recent work, Briere and Gil (1998), who studied both general population and clinical samples with regard to self-injuring behavior, found a significant relationship between self-injury in adulthood and a history of childhood sexual abuse, in particular. Other traumatic childhood experiences (such as physical abuse, domestic violence, and parental alcoholism) were statistically related to self-injury only when sexual abuse was also present. In studying several clinical populations, Nicholls and colleagues (1999) confirm this fundamental fact. They found that 58 percent of their total sample of partial hospital patients and psychotherapy outpatients engaged in some form of direct self-injury, and those with childhood abuse histories were even more likely to self-injure.

Drawing on these and other works, including recent texts in the popular press (Alderman 1997, Conterio and Lader 1998, Favazza 1996, Hyman 1999, Levenkron 1997, Strong 1998) as well as a range of informal reports from people who self-injure, there appears to be a working consensus that one or more childhood trauma and loss experiences generally exist in the histories of people who self-injure. These may include physical, sexual, or emotional abuse; neglect; invasive caregiving; loss, abandonment, and placement outside the home; surgery or significant illness; witnessing family violence or alcoholism; and ritual abuse (Arnold 1995, Briere and Gil 1998, de Zulueta 1993, diClemente et al. 1991, Favazza and Conterio 1988, McClory 1986, Miller 1994, Nicholls et al. 1999, Pattison and Kahan 1983, Putnam 1989, van der Kolk et al. 1991, Walsh and Rosen 1988, Zlotnick et al. 1996).

Several authors whose work is based on self-report studies by self-injurers note that the antecedents to self-inflicted violence also include traumatic events in adulthood. Greenspan and Samuel (1989) reported self-cutting after rape in adulthood, and Pitman (1990) described self-injury among combat veterans. The Bristol Crisis Service for Women (Arnold 1995) found that 14 percent of the 76 women responding to their survey of self-injurers reported that adult experiences (with no reported history of childhood trauma) were related to their self-injury. These events generally included either loss or interpersonal violence similar to the childhood events most likely to be correlated with self-injury: rape, sexual assault, and abuse by partners. Poor communication and serious illness were also cited as contributing factors. Briere and Gil (1998) did not find this relationship between self-injury and trauma in adulthood.

A few studies have not shown a correlation between self-injury and prior trauma (Brodsky et al. 1995, Zweig-Frank et al. 1994a,b). These authors assessed the histories of women and men diagnosed with borderline personality disorder and found no statistically significant relationship between self-injury and childhood abuse, once they controlled for dissociation. Teasing out this complex relationship with dissociation needs more work, especially in light of the fact that many self-injurers dissociate, some describing high levels of dissociation (Hyman 1999, Mazelis 1991, Waites 1993).

The framework suggested by Linehan (1993) offers insight into a broader range of childhood experience that can result in a similar residue of experience for the adult, thereby accounting for the lack of relationship in some studies between traumatic events and self-injury. She describes the "invalidating environment" as a significant contributor to the development of borderline personality disorder, a diagnosis commonly ascribed to people who self-injure. "An invalidating environment is one in which communication of private experiences is met by erratic, inappropriate, and extreme responses" (p. 49).

The similarities in the "felt experiences" of both the invalidating environment and direct abuse or neglect are articulated neatly by transactional analysis clinical trainer Cornell (personal communication, 1995) who compares "strain" trauma and "shock" trauma. As can be deduced, strain trauma results from chronically inadequate or harmful situations that are part of the fabric of one's life, in contrast with shock trauma, which tends to be organized around specific events. Miller (1990) broadens this concept even further by suggesting that not only abuse but "normative" child-rearing practices are fundamentally inadequate and traumatic to many children. It seems a reasonable assumption that all of these less-than-ideal environments for children's growth (consistent invalidation, abuse, loss, neglect, and general inappropriateness) could create residual "felt experiences" with similar implications for the child's developing sense of self.

"Felt Experience": The Ground beneath Self-Injury

Traumatic experiences, whether based on specific events of abuse, abandonment, and neglect, or on a more chronic invalidating environment, often leave a residue of "felt experience" that characterize the worldview of the trauma-tized child—even when the child is an adult. This worldview, like all worldviews, includes beliefs, perceptions, affects, and sensations that are derived in this case from the traumatic experience and its immediate aftermath. While not comprehensive (an adult survivor's worldview is more com-plex and developed than simply consisting of the after-effects of childhood trauma), this residue often continues to operate both consciously and unconsciously in the present for the adolescent or adult survivor. Current life events as well as efforts to heal the original trauma may tap into this residue, causing what appears to be a strong overreaction. It is from this reactive place that people often self-injure.

Understanding this "felt experience," this operative worldview of the survivor, provides a ground from which we can better see the functions and meanings of self-injury. Some of the elements of this "felt experience" may be described as body alienation and disconnection from self, social isolation and a sense of disconnection from others, overwhelming feelings and an inadequate capacity to man-age or modulate them, intense physiological arousal and/ or disorganization, and a profound sense of inadequate (and therefore, chronically violated) boundaries. (The impact of trauma is explored in more detail in Chapters 3 and 4, but some key elements as they relate to self-injury are described here.)

Disconnection

One of the primary effects of trauma is disconnection (Herman 1992, Putnam 1985, Terr 1990). This is evidenced in a number of ways: disconnection from a cohesive or continuous sense of self; disconnection from one's body;

disconnection from ordinary, everyday life (even if the abuse occurs every day); disconnection from one's own history; and disconnection from others. The results of these disconnections are often described, variably, as isolation, numbing, internal emptiness, a sense of differentness, a lack of identity or sense of selfhood, discontinuous memory, out-of-body experiences, and self-alienation (Briere 1992, Chu 1998, Cornell and Olio 1991, Courtois 1988, Davies and Frawley 1994, Herman 1992, van der Kolk 1996a, Wisechild 1988).

Overstimulation and Inadequate Comfort

Another aspect of trauma is the overstimulation that occurs during the traumatic experience (Briere 1992, Davies and Frawley 1994, Matsakis 1994, van der Kolk 1987). Trauma overwhelms the capacity of the body and mind to make sense of and process the experience. There is too much information to manage. During the trauma, survivors often experience an overload of physiological and emotional arousal; this arousal is stored and then reexperienced in times of stress or in response to specific triggering events (van der Kolk 1987). The overwhelming nature of this arousal is particularly enhanced by the child's immature capacity to effectively sort and manage the often conflicting and highly charged information contained in a traumatic experience.

What happens, for example, when a child is sexually abused by a trusted adult? From the child's perceptive, the internal dialogue goes something like this: "How come Uncle John—who is supposed to take care of me—is doing these weird things that sometimes feel kind of good but it all feels kind of yucky, and I don't really know why he's doing it but he told me not to tell anyone so it must be bad, but I feel tickly down there, so how come it's bad if it tickles? I guess I'm bad but he told me I'm special, so maybe I'm not bad, but I hate the sticky stuff that comes out of his peepee, and sometimes I'm scared when he gets that look in his eyes and his hands are rough, and why am I special, I think I must be bad, I don't understand why he's doing this." In lived experience, this dialogue doesn't quite get formed as words but swims around internally with attendant anxiety and confusion. The unsorted, rambling nature of the experience, replete with contradiction and inconsistency, remains a part of the stored experience.

When the traumatic event occurs within a context of isolation, as is often the case with sexual abuse, the sense of being overwhelmed is heightened. In this case, only the victim and perpetrator are present. No one is available to stop the abuse or to aid the victim in processing the experience afterward. No one can provide words for the experience, or physical soothing. No one else shares the same (albeit, traumatic) experience, as is the case with natural disasters, or even with physical abuse or parental alcoholism occurring in the presence of siblings. Similarly, many loss and abandonment experiences, as well as chronically inadequate environments, are lived by the child in relative isolation. Being alone with an overwhelming and confusing situation adds to the overstimulation and stress.

This overstimulation and the inadequate ability to modulate affect results in "felt experiences" that remain fixed in the child-become-adult's internal worldview until there is resolution of the traumatic event. Survivors may be flooded by feelings, or experience generalized anxiety and panic. They often have an inability to name or even identify specific sensations and affects, or may carry chronic psychic and physical tension. Some vacillate between an inability and an impulsivity to express strong feelings. This overstimulation can also result in particular fears about expressing feelings or the inaccurate labeling of sensations and affects.

Boundary Violation

Further complicating this experience of overstimulation and an inadequate system within which to process the experiences is the role of boundary invasion. Trauma, by its nature, violates boundaries. It crosses the psychological and physical boundaries that help to define self. The intrusive nature of trauma serves to damage existing boundaries and interfere with the development of new boundaries and a cohesive, bounded sense of self (this dilemma is explored in detail in Chapter 4). This is particularly true when the traumatic event is a personal one (i.e., the perpetrator's conduct is focused on the victim), as opposed to an impersonal act (such as a car accident). The resulting difficulties with boundaries may be evidenced in a number of ways.

Some survivors have a recurrent sense of being impinged upon by the world, or operate with a low threshold for perceiving safety in the face of a high volume of external information. They may have an impaired capacity to delineate self from others, especially in terms of affects. They may "soak in" others' feelings, especially in high affect situations, or be unable to differentiate their own feelings from others. Survivors often, understandably, have low degrees of trust in others, even when help-seeking and needy. At the same time, some survivors develop elaborate self-protective, self-reliant skills and are very resourceful.

Resulting Self-Injury

In short, traumatized people, children in particular, struggle with a fundamental sense of disconnection from self and others, overstimulation, and disrupted boundaries. For children who have been victimized or abandoned or experience significant loss, these "felt experiences" are carried into adulthood along with the constructions of mis-meaning—the child's efforts to make sense out of an incomprehensible situation (Hartman and Burgess 1993, McCann and Pearlman 1992, Pearlman and Saakvitne 1995). These misperceptions and misunderstandings, which make good sense within the limited worldview of the child under stress, are often an integral part of the dynamics operating when self-injury occurs.

Self-injury is a coping mechanism employed to maintain self-integrity (in other words, not disintegrate) in the face of what is felt to be an overwhelming, unmanageable experience without any help from the outside world. In this way, self-injury itself mirrors the original traumatic situation, with the notable exception that this time the person trying to manage the experience (i.e., the one who is self-injuring) is also the person in charge of the pain or confusion. This exception is an important piece of the puzzle for many self-injurers, as the element of control is central to the dynamics of the process of self-inflicted violence.

How Self-Injury Helps: Function and Meaning

Seeing self-injury as a way to maintain self-integrity and avoid disintegration provides a larger backdrop for understanding self-injury. In finer detail are the varied meanings and functions of self-inflicted violence. They often overlap, with a number of functions served by one act. Or several different acts are utilized to meet the same need. The range of functions have been discussed variably as tension reducing (Briere 1992, Chu 1998, deYoung 1982); expressions of values or communication (Calof 1995, Mazelis 1993, Miller 1994); means of managing internal and external worlds, and affective regulation (Davies and Frawley 1994, Calof 1995, Figueroa 1988, Miller 1994, van der Kolk 1996a, Wise 1989); self-soothing (Chu 1998, Davies and Frawley 1994, Herman 1992); the avoidance of disintegration (Davies and Frawley 1994, deYoung, 1982, Mazelis 1993); and reenactment of trauma (Calof 1995, Miller 1994).

In Briere and Gil's (1998) recent studies, self-injurers report that self-inflicted violence serves a range of functions, often more than one at a time. At the top of the list were self-punishment, distraction from painful feelings, release of pent-up feelings, stress management, and tension reduction. Close behind were getting rid of anger and feeling self-control. However, twenty-three other reasons were given as well by a large percentage of the sample. Arnold (1995) discovered a similar picture, with relief of feelings, self-punishment, and control cited most frequently. Nicholls and colleagues (1999) state that distraction from feelings, punishment, and expression of feelings were cited most frequently as reasons for self-injury. Clearly, self-injury meets diverse needs, and is not readily categorized by function.

These various purposes, or the needs met by the self-injury, are organized here into four primary functions. This is not a definitive list. Rather, it offers a conceptualization for groups of related needs. The four primary purposes of self-injury are the reenactment of the original trauma, the expression of feelings and needs, a way to organize self and regain homeostasis, and the management and maintenance of dissociative process.

Reenactment of the Original Trauma

Trauma survivors, both adults and children, often reenact the original trauma in both literal and symbolic ways (Burstow 1992, Calof 1995, Chu 1998, Courtois 1988, Davies and Frawley 1994, de Zulueta 1993, Holiman 1997, Miller 1994, Terr 1990, van der Kolk 1989). Interpersonal relationship patterns (particularly strong attractions and addictions), posttraumatic play, and abusing others are some of the ways trauma is reenacted. For many survivors, reenactments are attempts to master a previously unmanageable situation. It is as if the survivor's operative belief states, "This time I'll be able to control what happens" or "This time I'll be in charge of the pain and decide when it's too much." Such a belief may be fundamentally connected to the survivor's efforts to regain a sense of power and control following a traumatic experience, or in the ongoing struggle to stop the internal experience of the abuse going on in the present. One woman described this, speaking from a "child-place" inside: "I hurt myself before she [mother] can hurt me. That way *I* get to do it."

Reenactments that involve self-injury can be connected to the infliction of physical pain during the trauma or reflect the site of trauma-related psychological distress. One survivor of multiple abuses in childhood and adolescence said it succinctly: "My sense is that certain body parts call to be hurt." Around the time she made this statement, she went to the gynecologist for a checkup. Much to her relief, he was sensitive and kind about the scars on her arms, legs, and torso. He pointed to the most recent scars on her abdomen and asked her if she knew that the marks were directly over her ovaries. (She did not.) What was most interesting to this client was that the issues she had been addressing in therapy around the time of the self-injury to her abdomen concerned a painful memory about being pregnant and her intensely difficult reactions to her pregnant friends.

Such reenactments demonstrate an effort to communicate about the trauma, to find a way to "tell" what happened. The need for telling may be to literally retrieve the memory of what occurred. For example, a survivor may bang her head in an effort to communicate about having her head repeatedly smashed against the wall. Because trauma is generally stored in nonverbal modes such as sensations and visual images (van der Kolk 1996b), survivors may unconsciously act out the event in their bodies. The need to tell or communicate may be directed outward to other people, or it may be the need to tell oneself, or another part of self. It may also stem from what appears to be an almost innate drive to release the stored information, or may feel like the only way to access nonverbal memories. For survivors who were distinctly told to not disclose their abuse, acting it out feels safer and less like a violation of that injunction. McLane (1996) "characterizes self-mutilation as the creation of a voice on the skin . . . a 'mouth' [that] can speak what the actual physical mouth has been forbidden to utter" (p. 115).

A fourth aspect of reenactment may be in response to programming or mind control techniques used during or after the original trauma. Particularly for survivors of sadistic or ritual abuse, the perpetrators may have employed posthypnotic suggestions and operant conditioning, giving the survivor direct messages about hurting herself if she ever discloses her abuse (Blessing 1990, Neswald 1991). Again, these messages may be acted upon without conscious awareness, where the survivor finds herself self-injuring without really knowing why other than feeling compelled to harm herself. Neswald (1991) suggests that self-injury was "taught" to child victims using sophisticated conditioned stimulus–response sequences in order to ensure nondisclosure and compliance. The logic of such methods is that if the survivor approaches disclosure (actual or anticipated), she will be internally prompted to self-injure. This in and of itself may be enough to discourage disclosure, or to punish her for not complying with the nondisclosure injunction. A further effect is that she herself as well as others will perceive her as crazy, thus discrediting any disclosure claims she may make (Mazelis 1997). The reenactment in this case, then, embodies the trauma of the mind-control techniques themselves; it may also incorporate other traumatic events linked to the same perpetrators.

Self-injury as reenactment may also serve to let the survivor "make real" the remembered traumas. When the trauma is reenacted, whether literally or symbolically, some survivors experience a sense of reality about what they have experienced that is more vivid than their normal perceptions. Since the struggle to sort out what is real and what is not real is a difficult one for many survivors, self-injury can serve as one vehicle in the sorting process. Given the heavily sensate nature of trauma storage combined with individual preferences of different modalities of knowing, some survivors find reenactment a powerful tool.

Expression of Feelings and Needs

Self-injury can also serve as a vehicle for the expression of feelings. Many self-injurers say they hurt themselves as a way to communicate feelings for which they don't have words. Lisa, who has cut since age 13, states "I need to talk and cry. The blood represents the tears." Common feelings expressed or released through self-injury are rage, frustration, shame, hurt, emotional pain, guilt, and a sense of badness. Childhood trauma survivors often describe their reluctance to express feelings of rage or frustration toward anyone, not wanting to hurt the other person. However, they may perceive themselves as a legitimate target and direct these feelings toward the self, both psychologically and physically (deYoung 1982, Hyman 1999).

This inwardly directed focus may be particularly true for female survivors. In contrast, one male survivor found playing football, a socially acceptable form of self-harm though not technically self-injury, to be an outlet for feelings of rage and hurt following abuse by his father. "Of course it was connected to the abuse. Why else do you think I was so good [at playing football]? It was a perfect way to get beat up and hurt others without getting in trouble." In this situation, he engaged in behavior that combined hurting himself with hurting others, an approach perhaps more common with men as noted earlier. (The use of another person's body to inflict hurt or pain is beyond the scope of the definition of self-injury used by Alderman [1997] and throughout this book; see Hyman [1999] for an exploration of these dynamics for women.)

Directing these feelings toward the self may also combine with a need for self-punishment. The internal rationale for self-punishment may include having feelings of any variety, simply being alive, or believing one is generically and globally "bad." Or, the felt need to punish may be connected to discomfort with having feelings of pleasure, longing, sadness, or arousal related to abusive events. Self-punishment as a function of self-injury may be particularly salient for some survivors regarding the sexual arousal accompanying sexual abuse. Self-injury directed toward the genitals can serve to express, release, and punish feelings of arousal and shame (Waites 1993). Sexualized self-injury (such as hitting, pinching, or cutting one's genitals) tends to incorporate self-punishment as well as offer a release of sexual tension. This type of self-injury is likely to serve a range of functions whose complexity is generally only understood over a significant period of time spent unraveling the connecting threads of pleasure, shame, desire, power, guilt, violence, and arousal.

Self-injury can also serve to express feelings of guilt and shame about having been needy and thus consciously or unconsciously tolerating the abuse in order to get attachment and other needs met. Some survivors of trauma feel a sense of complicity with the abuser—a response abusers may deliberately elicit through verbal framing of the experience. Such efforts to evoke guilt and responsibility (and thus silence) in the victim are often focused on sexual arousal and responsiveness (e.g., "If you didn't like this, you wouldn't be wet, now would you?"). Occasionally the victim's sense of complicity and responsibility centers on desiring sexual arousal or satisfaction, or reaching orgasm without even seeking such release. More often, it is related to the need for affection, recognition, or physical contact. Self-injury can be one mechanism to discharge the complex feelings and resulting confusion, as well as reflecting a reenactment of the complicated and confused power dynamics inherent in the situation.

Another purpose or meaning of self-injury in this domain is to express or communicate needs regarding the presence of psychic or emotional pain and the longing for comfort and containment. The next section addresses some of the dynamics involving comfort and containment, but the aspect raised here is the effort to express the depth of the pain to self and others, or to deny and avoid emotional pain. One survivor described it this way: "I hit myself because then I could know I was really hurt. Having the bruises and sore places helped me believe I had been hurt [by the abuse]—that the pain was real. Having such concrete proof of having been injured also helped me believe that I could heal, as if the physical healing [of the injuries] gave me hope about the possibility of psychic healing." Alternately, others describe the use of self-injury to distract from feelings. When an internal feeling state or sensation becomes intolerable, some people find that self-injuring can pull their attention away from their emotional pain.

Sometimes the need to externalize and concretize the pain is focused on helping the survivor give meaning and voice to an internal experience for himself. There also may be times when one of the functions is to let others know about the pain and to receive validation or get help. On occasion, survivors, consciously or unconsciously realizing the unresponsiveness of the mental health system, have self-injured in order to get needed care that would not be possible without a self-endangering act. This is in contrast with the fact that self-injury is often kept private and not communicated to others, and is not enacted primarily to communicate with others.

Way to Organize Self and Regain Homeostasis

From infancy on, human beings make an effort to organize a sense of themselves and their external environment, and to regain physiological and emotional homeostasis (Bowlby 1973, Kaplan 1978, Mahler 1975, Stern 1985). When nourishment is provided, diapers are changed, and restful sleep is achieved, homeostasis returns and the child experiences comfort. With adequate care and reasonably responsive caregivers, infants and young children move from being very dependent on others for soothing and for getting needs met to being able to use internalized soothing techniques. Their growing cognitive capacities allow them to create internal psychic structures or schemas, including ones related to self-nurturing, to help them manage increasingly demanding situations.

When such care is inadequate, or when trauma is experienced without any posttrauma intervention, children are left to fend for themselves in their efforts to regain a sense of being safe and okay—returning to homeostasis. The disequilibrium of trauma and the isolation experienced posttrauma make it extremely difficult, especially for young children, to calm themselves. To this end, they utilize a range of techniques, some of which include self-injuring behaviors. (The disruption of the development of an adequate self-boundary and related implications are addressed in more depth in Chapter 4.)

Many self-injurers describe the calm that follows self-injury. With this action, tension is released or significantly reduced and the survivor regains a sense of homeostasis. Cutting or gouging the skin may feel soothing. Repetitive head-banging may bring a sense of predictability and comfort. Sometimes reenactments followed by self-soothing return a sense of calm and homeostasis. One survivor reenacted the painful enemas she experienced in childhood, even saying the words her aunt said to her during the abuse, then comforting herself. After self-injuring in this way, she reported being more relaxed and calm than she often felt in her daily life.

Self-injury also provides a concrete, physical focus for the internal pain of some survivors. They describe a sense of relief that the pain is externally focused. As one man stated, "I feel less crazy then—I have an injury I can see rather than this crazy hurt inside that I can't get a hold of." Paradoxically, self-inflicted violence may also simultaneously serve to distract from the psychic pain as mentioned previously, providing a focus for the healing and organizing the survivor's internal experience, thus giving some relief from internal stress and a reduction of tension.

Another element of the purpose of self-injury as self-regulation is that it allows the survivor to regain a sense of control over free-ranging internal affects and sensations. One survivor said she felt a sense of freedom when she self-injured because she was gaining control over the intensity of feeling overwhelmed and out of control. Many survivors describe feeling trapped by their histories and memories, and finding a measure of freedom is attractive and helpful. This can also be contrasted, sometimes paradoxically, with feeling out of control with the self-injury itself, depending on the individual dynamics and style of the self-inflicted violence.

Self-injury can also provide a sense of groundedness. In addition to the experience of increased control and physiological relief, the constancy provided by the presence of self-injury in someone's life can meet the need for grounding in the body/self. As one woman explains, she finds the edges of the tears on her skin provide a comforting sense of her own boundary. She then feels more herself and is able to psychologically distinguish herself from her mother.

Management and Maintenance
of the Dissociative Process

Many survivors dissociate to some extent, as it is a highly effective and common way to cope with trauma as it occurs (Anderson et al. 1993, Briere et al. 1995, Chu and Dill 1990, Davies and Frawley 1994, Gelinas 1983, Marmar et al.

1994, Putnam 1985, van der Kolk 1996a). Over the course of time and throughout the healing process, survivors struggle to both maintain and change their dissociative responses. Survivors use self-injury as one way to achieve these ends. While recent research has made some effort to tease out the relationship between self-injury and dissociation (Brodsky et al. 1995, Zlotnick et al. 1996, 1997, Zweig-Frank et al. 1994a,b), we clearly need more research in order to better understand what we see clinically. Nonetheless, clinical experience and self-report studies provide us with some understanding of the use of self-injury in managing dissociative process.

Self-injury may serve as a toggle switch for some survivors. In other words, self-injuring may keep someone from dissociating or switching to another part of themselves, or, conversely, it may facilitate a shift in parts of self. Self-injurers describe both experiences. They find they sometimes self-injure in order to stay present and in their bodies. The pain can serve as an anchor to the present and allow them to avoid "going away." Other times, or for other survivors, self-inflicted violence either causes or coincides with a shift to an altered state, helping the person to disconnect from current distress or a trigger.

A related function for dissociating survivors is using self-injury to reassure themselves about being alive. One woman said that seeing the blood helped her to know she was indeed alive, in contrast to the intense dissociation and derealization she often experienced. Another survivor said that feeling the pressure on her skin as she self-injured helped her know she was alive. Ritual abuse survivors, in particular, may experience significant confusion about what it means to be alive and find self-injury grounding and reassuring.

A third use of self-injury in managing the dissociative

process is to regulate the degree of sensation. At the point of self-injury, flashbacks may recede, fade away entirely, or go into the background. Tension reduction may be a concurrent aspect, allowing the survivor to feel more able to cope with present life issues. Self-injury can also serve the opposite function, in allowing the survivor to feel sensation, as noted above (in reference to feeling alive).

Another meaning self-injury may have for highly dissociative survivors is that it represents an effort to communicate or an internal struggle between two ego states or personalities. One part may be trying to hurt or kill another part, without any awareness that he is self-injuring. It may be experienced as other-directed violence, rather than self-inflicted injury. One part may also be trying to interrupt or stop the actions of another part, or distract the system from a particular course of action. Any of the dynamics previously described as functions of self-injury may be operating for one part, with the self-injuring behavior directed at the perceived part-self, the body, or another part. A complex configuration of functions and meanings often exists for highly dissociative self-injurers (Alderman 1997, Mazelis 1991,Trautmann and Connors 1994), and separating the threads may be a gradual process.

Linda, who is highly dissociative, described the recurrence of the urge to cut herself after a period of several years without cutting. She felt compelled to cut, even though she wasn't sure why, other than that she felt for some reason she had to be punished. She reported that it seemed like the need to punish was coming from another part of her. With some exploration we discovered that a powerful child-part was very upset over the loss of her cat, and blamed the adult Linda for failing to care properly for the cat. The child-part was demanding that

Linda cut herself so she could be punished. Once we spent some time finding out what the child-part needed (to know that Linda also felt badly about what had happened to their pet and some reassurance that Linda would get another cat as soon as she could manage it), the child-part stopped pushing Linda to self-injure.

Similarly, Samantha found that one of her parts, a preschool boy who had no verbal language, would periodically bite her or one of the other alters when they were "out" (present in the body). Often, the biting left teeth marks and bruises; it was also hard to pry his teeth apart to stop the biting even though he was biting "from the inside" through whoever was out. As she developed a closer relationship with him, she learned that he bit her and the others to get their attention, without any overt intent to hurt. His communication skills were limited to extremely aggressive actions or sounds (like hitting or screaming). Within his repertoire, his biting was comparable to a tap on the shoulder. Once she realized this, she began to teach him some alternative methods for getting her attention, and the biting receded.

Overlapping Functions and Needs

These descriptions of the functions served by self-inflicted violence appear tidy and clear. In real life, there is much overlap in the purposes behind the behavior. Various needs are met simultaneously. Burstow (1992), in writing about the functions of self-injury, says, "A woman who engages in genital self-mutilation is almost inevitably a childhood sexual abuse survivor who is punishing herself. She is repeating the violation. This is partly self-punishment, partly compliance, partly resistance; it may also be an attempt to remember or to understand" (p. 193).

In the moment, some self-injurers have no idea why they are cutting or burning. They just know it helps them "get through." Others can state clearly what is going on for them and why they utilize self-injury. Like any conceptualization, this articulation of the functions of self-injury simply provides some guidance. Asking the self-injuring client what is going on is the best way to understand the purpose of the behavior. This may require some self-reflection and time, but ultimately it will provide the most useful description of the function and meaning of self-injury, and can help tease out the overlapping purposes.

The Addiction Model:
Does It Help Make Sense of Self-Injury?

Some self-injurers as well as some clinicians have utilized an addiction treatment perspective to understand the process and functions of self-injury. Similarities do exist between self-injurious behavior and substance abuse; both are actions harmful to the self intended to manage internal experiences that feel unmanageable, historical antecedents contribute to the current behavior, and emotional triggers can evoke the use of both self-injury and substance abuse. Certainly, by self-report, clients who self-injure experience some mood alteration as a result of harming themselves; regulation of mood is one of the reasons people self-injure. This supports the comparison with an addictive process. There is also some evidence that neurotransmitters released during some forms of self-injury may provide a physiological "rush" or serve to self-medicate, likening the biochemical process to the use of drugs or alcohol (van der Kolk

1989). In addition, some clients have found that the skills they gained in twelve-step programs to cope with their substance abuse have proven useful in managing their self-injury, since they experienced both as compulsive behaviors (Hyman 1999).

While all of these comparisons have validity, the differences between alcohol or drug addiction and self-injury also merit attention. Self-injury is not a mood-altering substance. Even though the biochemical aspect of self-injury may be operative for some people at certain points in time, it is not universal, as is the ingestion of alcohol or drugs. Anyone drinking alcohol or taking drugs feels the mood changes that result from ingesting a substance. The shifts in mood that may occur with self-injury may be likened to the effects of exercise on mood, or the impact of good cognitive strategies, a short shopping trip to the mall, or a hike in the woods. There are many ways we alter our moods without the use of substances.

Also, an active substance addiction significantly impedes useful therapeutic work. It is very difficult to work through related or underlying issues while clients are using substances, even if they are sober during the time of therapy sessions. The addiction process is more comprehensive than the actual time spent high or drunk; it includes an obsession with and focus on substances, and the clear avoidance of feelings and unresolved issues. Someone with an active addiction is not "present" and cannot be engaged in an ongoing therapy process effectively.

Someone who is self-injuring, on the other hand, can engage therapeutically. While the use of self-injury may wax and wane, often increasing as emotionally laden issues are explored, it often does not interfere with daily functioning at the same level as most alcohol or drug abuse. Some people who self-injure do describe a level of interruption in their day-to-day life as a result of their self-injury, and a small majority become obsessively fixated on injuring themselves (Hyman 1999). They are preoccupied with thoughts of self-injuring and organize their day around how and when they will harm themselves. The behavior and thoughts about the behavior become compelling.

Perhaps a reasonable approach to self-injury from an addiction perspective is to perceive self-injury on a continuum ranging from periodic use to regular use to compulsive or addictive use. This is comparable to regarding self-injury as similar to the *use* of substances, but not necessarily as the *abuse* of substances, all the while noting that it is not a substance. This comparison may be likened to the utilization of the chemical dependency or addiction model to understand compulsive behaviors such as gambling, the overuse of computers, sexual acting out, consumerism, and the misuse of food. This comparison is consistent with the belief that people who use substances to manage social anxiety, for example, are able to effectively utilize therapy without ceasing all substance use, while someone who is at the far end of the continuum in an active alcohol addiction probably cannot. (In my experience, this aspect of the comparison does not hold true with someone compulsively self-injuring. Such clients can still make use of a therapeutic process in helpful ways that lead to healing the underlying issues.)

It should also be noted that the physical addiction to substances probably plays a role in the obsessive and compulsive elements of drug and alcohol addiction, even if we cannot specify exactly how it works. Someone with sobriety is most likely to pick up where he left off if he relapses, rather than reverting to an earlier level of alcohol use. Experts in the addiction field would suggest that his "set point" has been raised to its current level by his prior substance abuse (Gorski and Miller 1986). Whether or not this is directly related to a permanent physiological change as a result of substances, rather than a neurobiological reaction to compulsive behavior, or a primarily psychological process related to obsession, is not clear. Separating cause and effect in such a way may not even be possible. However, the absence of mood-altering substances with compulsions such as self-injury or sexual addiction does denote a difference between chemical addictions and other addictive or compulsive processes. As Clemmens (1997) comments, care needs to be taken to discern this difference; the implications of different pathways to an addictive process may suggest differences in treatment or recovery needs.

The pull to utilize an addiction model can be strong for clinicians. It provides a framework within which to understand seemingly senseless behavior. This grounding and structure alleviate the clinician's anxiety and focus the therapeutic work. This model also provides some degree of useful explanation. However, since many people who self-injure are not at the addictive end of the continuum with their self-injury, and because no substance is ingested, this approach needs to be utilized prudently and with awareness of the differences. A simplistic implementation of an addiction treatment-based program or approach focused on behavior rather the person will miss the central issues underlying the self-injury and ultimately will not be useful. Conterio and Lader (1998) concur that while self-injury can be an addictive-like behavior, it is not an addiction; rather, its causes have emotional roots.

Alderman (1997) offers a nice conceptualization of the way addictive processes work to reinforce existing self-harm behaviors. An exploration of this model and the use of twelve-step program concepts for clients interested in intervening on their behavior is discussed in more detail in

Chapter 7. Both of these approaches have value when incorporated into a person-grounded therapy process or as one aspect of a self-help repertoire.

Anchoring Our Perception of Self-Injury in a Continuum of Self-Harm

One of our greatest assets in therapeutic work with people who self-injure is our ability to understand their self-injury as a sensible and practical coping mechanism. This understanding creates a bridge between clinician and client that is essential to effective work. Because human beings draw so heavily on context to make sense of the world around us, one of the ways we can get inside our clients' experience of self-injury is to consider our own self-harming behavior. Reviewing our own use of drugs and alcohol, television, the Internet, food, shopping, smoking, exercise, and overwork can give us a living, breathing sense of context.

This process of self-assessment may occur naturally for readers of this book, or through the course of clinicians' work with clients who self-injure. Figure 2–1, the Personal Self-Harm Spectrum Worksheet, offers a focused approach to aid your self-reflection as well. This tool was developed by Lois Arnold (1997) in the United Kingdom as part of a training packet designed to sensitize professionals about self-injury. Spending a few moments noting where we fall on the spectrum between self-nurture and self-harm along a range of life activities can quickly provide a context for better understanding self-injury. (This tool can also be utilized by people who self-injure to help them identify areas of their life where they self-nurture rather than self-harm. This shift in perspective may be helpful by highlighting strengths.)

Figure 2–1. Personal Self-Harm Spectrum Worksheet.

Below is a list of activities/aspects of life. These can all be carried out in ways which are more or less self-nurturing or self-harming. On the scale for each activity, show in a way that feels appropriate to you where you think you fall.

	Self-nurturing	Self-harming

Eating ....

Sleeping..

Working...

Exercising..

Leisure/relaxing..

Partner/sexual
relationships..

Friendships..

Family relationships ....

Alcohol/drugs ....

Spending ....

One other activity
of your choice ....

Arnold, L. (1997). *Working with People Who Self-Injure: A Training Pack.* Bristol, UK: Bristol Crisis Services for Women, p. 22. Reprinted with permission of the author and publisher.

The Basic Point: Self-Injury Helps

At its core, self-injury is an adaptive coping mechanism that makes a great deal of sense from the inside. It is a method born of necessity and, usually, a child's perspective of painful experiences and an inadequate self-boundary. Initial acts of self-injury may be reinforced by their effectiveness and become habitual, or become compulsive actions interlaced with substance, food, or sexual addictions. This repetition may add another layer to the complexity surrounding a client's efforts to change the self-injury, and require a range of treatment strategies. However, fundamentally, responses to self-injury—either by the client or by helping professionals—can only be useful if they are grounded in an understanding of the idiosyncratic and personal meaning attributed to and the functions served by this form of coping with unresolved trauma.

3

Trauma, Wounding, and Healing

Imagine two states of being for all creatures—perhaps all life—in our world. One state of being embodies movement and the flow of life current, while the other consists of a disruption of the flow, a stopping of life-giving energy. When we are "in the flow," things work, they feel effortless, glowing with an aliveness and creating an aura of positive energy. When we halt the flow, or when the flow is interrupted by an external event such as violence or an abrupt change in the environment, it feels as if the world stops: nothing is the same, the vibrancy of life pales, things become small or hidden or absent.

Such simplicity is, of course, overstated. And yet, at the core of this imagining, a fundamental truth is at work, and can offer us a way to understand how trauma (in the broad sense of the word) affects us. In his popular book, *The Seat of the Soul*, Zukav (1990) posits some equally simple but provocative and rich ideas in a similar vein. He writes that human beings operate from two basic feeling states or energy patterns: love and fear. Loving carries and elicits a lightness and radiance that harbor many positive feelings such as reverence for life, joy, caring for others, happiness, and delight. He suggests that negative emotions such as frustration, anger, jealousy, loss, resentment, hurt, impatience, pain, and irritation are all derivatives of fear.

The Power of Love

To love is a powerful act. When we stand in the place of loving, we know wholeness; it is where the "flow" moves without impediment. Love transforms our experience of almost everything. It permits us to see differently, to open to new ideas and possibilities, to reframe pain and wounding, to keep going in difficult times, to develop compassion, to let go of old beliefs, to accomplish things that seem impossible. As physician Dossey (1993) writes, "Empathy, compassion and love seem to form a literal bond—a resonance or 'glue'—between living things" (p. 111). The energy of love—a palpable, measurable thing—has more power than we may know.

Researchers at the Institute of HeartMath, a facility initially designed to study effective recovery methods for cardiac patients, have begun to test and demonstrate something that good clinicians and many clients believe: that caring makes a difference in the healing process. First, HeartMath studies have found that the energy generated by the heart (as measured by electrocardiogram [ECG] readings) varies depending on the mood or feeling state of the person (McArthur 1998, McCraty et al. 1998). When love is present, the heart generates a coherent wave pattern, with more power (amplitude) than the chaotic wave pattern generated by frustration or hostility. "The coherent wave pattern is the electromagnetic signature of love" (McArthur 1998, p. 35).

HeartMath researchers further posit that the heart is the strongest generator of electromagnetic energy in the body and can influence the other fields in the body in positive or negative ways (McArthur 1998). In subsequent studies they have explored the transfer of heart energy to another person via touch (McCraty et al. 1998). Their data show that the heart pattern of the sender is indeed picked up by the receiver's nervous system (as measured by signal-averaged waveform at electroencephalogram [EEG] electrodes).

The Power of Fear

This research also suggests, then, that we communicate our fear or frustration as well—or whatever emotion we are experiencing. Clearly, fear and its derivatives exercise power. Anger or fear or impatience or pain *can* be energizing and purposeful if acknowledged and used to move us to action that remedies the situation evoking the painful or difficult feeling. The pain caused by putting our finger on the stove burner, for example, generally impels us to remove our finger. The pain is a signal that something is wrong. In this way, fear or pain, when not overwhelming, can serve as a useful impetus for ongoing change and development. However, too much fear interrupts our sense of the "flow," disrupting healthy development.

The pattern of our lives often weaves to and fro in order to regain balance in the face of the disrupting effect of fear or related feelings. Ideally, we use fear and disruption to effect change, as we move back and forth along the change–stability continuum. It is when we become immobilized and stand too long in a place of fear that the natural flow of movement between stasis and change is disrupted. We then create a fertile ground for debilitating feelings and beliefs. Continuing to remain in the place of fear (or anger, pain, hurt) ultimately contributes to psychological and physical distress.

"When disease occurs, it is a signal that we are constricting the natural flow of life energy through our multidimensional bodies," writes Gerber (1996), a physician and author of a fairly comprehensive overview of energy-based approaches to medicine. He continues: "For good health to be enjoyed, one must have constant and unimpeded energy flow. . . . If we are blocked in some way and thus impair the flow of energy . . . disease results" (pp. 474–475). Hunt (1996), who began her work measuring human energy fields at Stanford in the 1970s, also writes that anticoherent energy patterns and the interruption of coherence contributes to dis-ease and illness.

Nonetheless, Dossey (1993) warns us not to let these sorts of discoveries create simplistic cause-and-effect theories of health and illness, or to blame the victims of disease for not having been loving enough. The complexities and variations that impact flow and blockage make the equation about health and illness a complicated one. Many factors impact individual people with various constitutions in idiosyncratic ways. However, with care, perhaps we can use this general framework to acknowledge both the influence of fear and distress on human functioning and the power of love to transform and protect.

Emotions as Players in the Mind–Body Experience

Various models describe the impact of emotions on health and functioning using alternative concepts and data. Pearsall (1999) delineates some of these models in his effort to describe the nature of cellular memories as they relate to heart transplant patients. These patients often describe "receiving" information about the heart's donor. Pearsall's own concept, based in part on work by cardiac researchers Schwartz and Russek (Russek and Schwartz 1996, Schwartz and Russek 1996), is that "L" energy—information and energy contained within the physical heart—communicates its imprint to heart recipients posttransplant. Some of the other models he notes are ones based on the communication capacities of neuropeptides, the electromagnetic connections between the brain and the heart, and the power of the heart as the organizer of energy frequencies throughout the body. He also lists the concept of morphic fields surrounding the body and connecting all living things (Sheldrake 1988), and psychic phenomena such as psychometry, spirit possession, and nonlocal consciousness as ways to explain cellular memory.

Others bring diverse interpretations of some of the basic science research done in the last twenty years, with some specific attention to the concept of energy (Benson 1997, Cohen 1997, Collinge 1998, Dossey 1993, Gerber 1996, Pert 1999). This work holds much promise for the mental health professions as we understand more about the intersections of emotion, behavior, biology, and belief. Current thinking points to more integration of data and models based on different windows into human experience, ranging from the electrical system of the body (Becker and Selden 1985, Wright 1988) and bioneurology (LeDoux 1996, van der Kolk 1996a–c) to energy fields (Gallo 1999, Gerber 1996, Hunt 1996, Wilber 1985), spiritual systems, and psychological paradigms.

Regardless of the frame of reference one brings to the phenomena explored by research scientists, spiritualists, and practitioners of both indigenous healing and energy medicine, the concrete experiences of the potency of love and fear are familiar to all of us. We know how good we feel when we operate from a loving place in our interventions with a client. We also recognize how it feels to interact with a client when we feel afraid or frustrated—from that small, narrow place where possibilities disappear. We

know intuitively that it is better (in all the ways researchers may yet document or discover) to operate from a place
of openness and wholeness, than the tight, closed place of
fear.

Movement out of Stuckness, from Fear to Love

Sometimes simply choosing to move out of the place of
fear is enough to unstick us when we have stood too long
in negative feelings. Let's assume we have agitated, un-
happy feelings about a person with whom we feel en-
tangled, or an old situation we continually relive, or a self-
defeating attitude we hold about ourselves. We can create
almost immediate change when we open our hearts toward
that person, situation, or attitude by imagining a sensation/
image of opened heartspace in the vicinity of our physical
hearts. When we do so, we sometimes relax and let go of
the agitated sensation. Something shifts inside us and we
are able to have a wider view of the painful or difficult situation and, as a result, act differently. We get free of negative feelings and related behaviors. I find this simple exercise a useful tool when I find myself getting momentarily
annoyed with a client. Shifting to an open-hearted place of
loving alters my awareness enough to refocus me and allow a different response to the client. It takes only a minute
or two.

Other times this simple shift doesn't work, or it works
temporarily but doesn't last. In the moment, we may be
relieved of our resentment and jealousy, only to return the
next day or the next hour to the old place of negativity.
Our grief may lift, only to descend upon us three days
later. Then, more exploration of what is attached to this
persisting negative feeling is necessary. We need to look at

the tangled strands of the roots, as they wind around deeply entrenched beliefs. Sometimes we can reengineer these beliefs, cognitively restructuring our understanding of this dimension of our worldview. We can employ positive self-talk long enough to give us time to logically convince ourselves of a new belief. The old beliefs give way and we feel free of the old negativity. We then return to the "flow" and a more balanced, positive experience of ourselves and the world.

And, sometimes, this doesn't work either. It is as if the fear or anger or pain is fed by an underground stream that keeps the root tendrils alive, with the vociferous capacity to grow new roots from a minute bit of plant material. It seems that no matter how much of the old stuff we tear out, it comes back to haunt us. This process is akin to the way plants called invasive aliens (nonnative species like crown vetch and loosestrife in the United States) relentlessly take over meadows and roadsides. Bamboo, another invasive alien, embodies the amazing ability to send up new shoots year after year, regardless of the gardener's belief that she has removed every last root and rhizome the previous year.

The Role of Balance

Just as when an endless proliferation of new leaves occurs, even after varied attempts at removal or modification, the gardener needs to shift her focus from the plant itself to the presence or absence of balance in the plant's environment, similarly we may need to ask, What is out of balance that allows the fear or hurt or rage to keep recurring? What environmental condition in our psyche permits us to return with such frequency to a state of rage, for example? Inva-

sive aliens grow like crazy when out of their natural habi-
tat because normally inhibiting factors in their home ecosystem, such as animal predators, soil acidity, or competing
plants, are missing. Oftentimes such a lack of balance per-
vades our internal ecosystem.

The return to balance can be a challenge. Many factors contribute to being out-of-kilter. External demands or
conditions can throw us off balance. Too much work and
too little play. Not enough joy. The wrong foods and lack
of sleep. Air pollution and dust mites. Excess alcohol in our
bodies. Infrequent exercise. Constant criticism or under-
mining by others. The stress of poverty. A lack of emotional
or practical support. All of these can keep us out of balance, making it difficult to regain a sense of equilibrium
and return to the "flow."

The out-of-balance state may also be due to a physical and psychological holding-on to past trauma. Trauma
is encoded in our cells and energy field, as is everything
we experience (Collinge 1998, Gallo 1999, Gerber 1996).
In ideal circumstances, we are able to process (in other
words, sort and file in useful ways) all the elements of any
experience. By processing, I am not talking about a conscious working through. I mean the split-second, out-of-our-
awareness processing that we do naturally as human beings.
When information is integrated, we return to a state of
balance. This return to balance does not signify stasis but
rather dynamic balance, where constant change is occurring (Benson 1997, Gallo 1999, Hunt 1996). We change
moment to moment as we incorporate new information as
simple as the temperature of the air around us or the
sound of a door opening, or as complicated as all the elements of a social situation involving a group of family and
friends. This integration process is an innate capacity that
enables us to maintain a sense of internal order, thereby

allowing information about a particular experience to be accessed consciously or unconsciously in the future as needed in useful ways.

The Impact of Trauma

If we are not able to process an experience immediately, due to an overload of sensory information, physical injury, confusion, psychoactive substances, or another overwhelming element, then we get jammed up. The event is perceived as traumatic by our energetic, electrical, and central nervous systems and things go haywire. Unprocessed traumas can be likened to computer-generated error files that encapsulate the unprocessed information. Sometimes we key into these error files inadvertently, as in a flashback that occurs with the right stimulus. But often the most potent effect of unresolved trauma is how it stops the cohesive energy flow in and around our bodies that we can't see (Gallo 1999, Hunt 1996). These blocks cause subsequent information to detour, or serve as dams, aggregating pieces of information that would naturally flow along a particular channel, thus impeding proper sorting and filing of other data.

When trauma occurs and remains unprocessed, sensations, feelings, and beliefs get entrenched, showing up repetitively in direct or disguised forms. Direct forms may be a nightmare about the traumatic event, expressions of anger and fear, panic attacks when triggered by stimuli similar to the event, or a belief that people go away if you get too close to them (for someone who experienced repeated loss in childhood). Disguised forms may be chronic low-level physiological irritation, a devotion to wounded animals, or feeling compelled to be a nurse in a critical care unit (for someone who struggled with ongoing helplessness in the face of her mother's alcoholism).

The traumatic event can be a simple, seemingly small event like being shamed by the second-grade teacher for chewing a pencil to a point instead of using the pencil sharpener, or falling down a flight of stairs. Or it can be a more obviously difficult trauma such as the loss of a parent or interpersonal violence or a car accident. Sometimes the small events create more powerful, in-the-fabric blocks to health and healing. By their very nature, they don't stand out, clamoring for attention and resolution; they are simply part of what is/was. (Recall the comments in Chapter 2 regarding invalidating environments and strain trauma.) Either way, if at the time of the trauma we are unable to process the experience and integrate it comfortably into our body/mind/psyche, then we will carry it with us until we find a way to free the block.

The blocks in our energy fields resulting from unresolved trauma can masquerade as inherited traits or temperament. The block may be likened to a chair sitting in a traffic path in the living room that we routinely walk around; even in the dark, we tend to be so acclimated to these blocks that we manage to avoid them. They become familiar. They start to feel as if they are just part of who we are, and in many ways, they are who we become.

Traumatic events that are adequately processed do not create blocks. On these occasions, our energy field does not become anticoherent or closed off. Our brains don't shift into trauma mode (more about the differences between normal and trauma-based brain functioning follows later in this chapter). We are able to integrate the trauma. We can describe and have some understanding of the event, we soothe ourselves or receive comfort from someone else, we express and release the feelings the event engendered, and we find acceptable meaning in the occurrence of the event. We are able to access cognitive, sensory, affective, and perceptual information about the event without feeling flooded or disorganized. Conversely, the event is not intrusive at unbidden moments. The effect of trauma, therefore, is not inherently permanent; traumatic events can be absorbed and integrated if the conditions are right.

The Presence of Fear and the Absence of Love: How Trauma Gets Stuck

What allows us to process traumatic events effectively some of the time? Why do we integrate some of our emotionally painful or physically injuring experiences and remain healthy, rather than getting stuck? What makes the difference? The complex of factors that may be protective and facilitate processing tend to mirror those that also allow healing long after the event: physical and emotional safety, a sense of control, adequate support, comfort and soothing, validation of feelings (normalization), and appropriate information. Many traumatic situations, by definition, disallow these elements. Traumatic events, even what we might consider little traumas, are situations that are overwhelming and out of our control. We feel unsure, unsafe. We don't know what to do, or simply cannot do anything. Often, fear underscores and coats the experience. We freeze. Overwhelming sensation and affect bombards us. Confusing thoughts and perceptions ricochet. We try to get internal control, but feel unable to do so. So we stop. We dissociate, shut down, go away, block things out. The trauma gets logged in our cells. Energy is jammed. Things stop.

When we are loved—in other words, held in unconditional positive regard by others—the energy begins to
move again. Sometimes the movement is slow, a gradual
thawing out. We talk again and again about what happened. We make sense of it over time, putting things in
perspective. We begin to look at the various elements of
the trauma, what actually occurred, what we thought and
felt, what scared us. Held in the safety of another's loving
presence, we gradually sort out what happened. We begin
to move on in an integrated, more whole way. We return
to a state of balance. Without loving presence, it becomes
harder to let the trauma—the stopping of life energy—
move on and pass through energetically, biologically, and
emotionally.

Context as a Regulator of Impact

The other key element determining the long-term impact
of trauma is context. Wilson (1995) and others working
with trauma survivors state that the significance of context
cannot be minimized. Our sense of the context surrounding a situation or event often dictates how we perceive and
subsequently process and store an experience. It frames our
efforts to find meaning in an event and grounds the experience. It orients us, helping us in that split-second filing process. For example, being able to say, "You know, we
always have hurricanes in September" helps one to cope
with the unpredictability of a severe storm and the related
losses or damage. The lack of context ("I had no idea he
was capable of this. I just can't believe it. It came out of
the blue."), or a confusion of context ("Why is someone
who loves me doing this to me?") makes it harder to find
a way to make sense of a traumatic event. Without appro-

priate context, we struggle to make sense of and ground the experience.

The extent to which loving presence and context can mold our experience of a painful event, even to the point of preventing posttraumatic stress, remains a question. Certainly, crisis intervention methodologies and programs operate from the premise that posttrauma support, debriefing, and help with finding meaning can prevent or minimize the long-term effects of trauma. These approaches offer interpersonal support and help build a context in the aftermath of trauma. Studies of resiliency suggest that the presence of a significant person, a spiritual framework, and positive self-regard (as well as a diverse repertoire of coping skills) in the face of adversity mediate the negative effects of trauma (Lam and Grossman 1997, Rutter 1987, Valentine and Feinauer 1993). (Resiliency studies also address the role of preexisting vulnerabilities in understanding the variability of stress reactions [e.g., Rutter 1999]; this is similar in intent to recent efforts to discern susceptibility to posttraumatic stress disorder [Bowman 1999, Ford 1999, Yehuda 1999b]. For more information about resiliency and children, see Anthony and Cohler [1987] and Dugan and Coles [1989].)

The 1998 Italian film *Life is Beautiful* grapples powerfully with the question of the mediating effect of loving presence and useful context. In this story, the father creates a fictional context ("We are playing a game and we have to do this [or that] to get points, so we can win the game") for his preschool-aged son as they enter and negotiate life inside a concentration camp during World War II. His love for his son is palpable as he constructs fictions to help manage the continual humiliation, privations, and losses of daily life in the camp. Did the father's love and provision of a developmentally acceptable context prevent some degree of traumatic stress for the son? Even though the son inevitably learned that his father's framing of camp life was untrue, did his passionate, loving efforts to make it bearable for his son reduce both immediate and therefore subsequent stress? Watching the film, one feels that the son's day-to-day life was easier than it might have been had the father taken a different approach; the long-term effects are unclear. Regardless, the question posed by the thesis of the film is an interesting and relevant one for trauma workers.

Brain Functioning during and after Traumatic Events

Research of the last fifteen years or so has helped neuroscientists articulate what seems to happen in the brain as we experience and process a traumatic event. Van der Kolk (1987, 1996b,c) has provided the most useful conceptualization by drawing on his own and others' research, and the neuroanatomy schemas developed by LeDoux (1996). Others have described the neurobiochemical processes and systems impacted by trauma (Charney et al. 1993, Chu 1998, Hartman and Burgess 1993, Saporta and Case 1993, Yehuda 1999a). The following summary attempts to translate into ordinary language van der Kolk's concepts about the functioning of the brain in conjunction with these biochemical reactions. My goal is to give a very general sense of the physical reality beneath the behavior we often see clinically because it has particular relevance to self-injury as a traumatic outcome. See van der Kolk's "The Body Keeps Score" (1996b) and "Trauma and Memory" (1996c) and LeDoux's *The Emotional Brain* (1996) for a more comprehensive and technical discussion of the mechanisms involved.

Brain functioning involves various processes, systems, and neurohormones that relate in complex ways. This simple summary is limited primarily to describing the functions of five areas of the brain: the thalamus, the amygdala, the hippocampus, Broca's area, and the prefrontal cortex. Under normal (i.e., nontraumatic) circumstances, sensate data such as an odor or an image travel from the sense organ (e.g., nose or eye) via the central nervous system to the thalamus. The thalamus's job is to send these sensory data in a somewhat more integrated form to the amygdala. The amygdala attributes emotional significance to the information and, when necessary, recognizes danger. If the amygdala perceives danger, then an emergency signal (i.e., the fight or flight response) is sent to the brainstem, triggering emotional and hormonal reactions.

From the amygdala, information is passed on to the hippocampus. The hippocampus's job is to organize the incoming information and integrate it with related, previously stored information. The hippocampus orients the incoming information against the backdrop of our existing schemas about the world, establishing a cognitive map with some temporal and spatial characteristics. The information is then sent to the prefrontal cortex and to other parts of the brain for short and long-term storage. The prefrontal cortex serves a further integrative function by grounding the information more firmly in time and space, and also provides feedback to the amygdala for future reference. Simultaneously, Broca's area is activated. This part of the brain, located in the opposite hemisphere, generates language to describe the sensory data, so one is able to verbally tell someone else what has been experienced.

Under extreme stress, the information from the thalamus enters the amygdala and is flagged as dangerous. How the amygdala codes the information has impact on how the hippocampus treats the information. Moderate arousal enhances hippocampal functioning; high levels of arousal in the amygdala (i.e., attaching high levels of emotional significance to the data) decrease hippocampal functioning. During a traumatic event, hippocampal functioning seems to decrease. It never gets to make meaning of the experience or put it in context. Heightened amygdala activity also depresses Broca's area, and thus the connection of language to experience is impaired.

The sensory data are thus stored as affectively charged memory traces, without having been completely processed. These bits of information are without context or words; in other words, they lack an integrated home in the brain. As a result, they are easily evoked when similar stimuli (or triggers) are perceived by the amygdala in the future. The fight or flight response becomes activated in moments that would not seem (to someone else in the external environment) to require such a response. For example, when a survivor of incest feels oppressive weight and heat on her body, which could occur while making love or playing sports, she may react vehemently with fear and anger, abruptly pushing the "offender" away. In her brain, the amygdala registers the weight and heat as dangerous, recognizing them as data similar to the data stored during the rapes by her stepfather.

One of the additional difficulties is that since the information is not sufficiently processed, it never adequately reaches the prefrontal cortex. This means two things: (1) the information does not get well situated in time and space (accounting for the always-in-the-present quality of traumatic memories); and (2) the prefrontal cortex cannot give useful feedback to the amygdala, providing a modifying function. So the amygdala continues to send out "danger, danger" messages, and the survivor continues to feel frightened, angry, and upset in the present, even when she cognitively understands what is going on (i.e., she is experiencing old feelings related to the incest). Van der Kolk (1998) has also mentioned the role of the prefrontal cortex in attaching the sense of "I" to experiences. The fact that the information about the traumatic event never gets to the prefrontal cortex supports the experience survivors often describe: "It feels like it happened to someone else."

Self-Injury and the Psychobiology of Trauma

This model of brain functioning under traumatic conditions provides a perspective on the internal experience of someone who turns to self-injury to regulate arousal and facilitate communication of internal experiences. Repeated occasions of intense affect and the concomitant neurohormonal changes flood the survivor, accompanied by intrusive imagery. No language exists in relation to these images and sensations. Unintegrated, nonverbal sensory data that feel frightening or overwhelming call for containment and calming. Words don't make sense. Enactment and physicality make more sense. Self-injury, as a nonverbal expression of wounding and pain, meshes neatly with trauma-based brain functioning. This neuroanatomical framework lends understanding to the comments self-injurers make: "Nothing is as effective as cutting." "I don't have words for it—I just need to do it when I get this feeling." "It's like I am compelled to hit myself." "It just comes out of nowhere." "I didn't even know I was triggered—it just happened." These comments reflect the potent triggering (without much cognitive processing) that sometimes precedes self-injury.

Neurohormones, particularly endogenous opioids, also play a role in chronic stress reactions and the physiologic pull to self-injury. Van der Kolk (1989) surmises that self-injury and other forms of self-destructive behavior release endogenous opioids, producing the experience of calm some people describe after self-injuring. This release, and its subsequent dissipation, may create an addictive-like cycle, prompting someone to seek the effect of the opioid release to regain a state of calm. Mazelis (1998), however, challenges the idea that most self-injury triggers this opioid release, since most wounds from self-inflicted violence are not severe enough. Also, this does not mean that self-injury functions fundamentally as an addiction, as noted in Chapter 2. There are other ways to achieve the sense of relief or calm (and certainly ways less evocative than self-injury and the responses it elicits), and the physiologic drive to self-injure can be mediated by insight and the choice to utilize other coping strategies. The possible role of endogenous opioids is mentioned here simply to acknowledge the underlying draw to self-harm some self-injurers describe.

Freeing Up Energy by Removing the Blocks in Our Energy Fields

Posttraumatic healing involves opening the blocked channels of energy. Removing blocks frees up energy that is trapped or stopped, permitting forward movement and change. This can provide access to information previously unavailable. This also allows the resolution of the trauma, resulting in calm, safety, understanding, acceptance, meaning, and relief from intrusive thoughts and feelings. Opening energy channels creates an environment in our bodies that permits physical and emotional healing.

Blocked channels in our energy fields are opened or cleared in many different ways. Some openings that allow energy to begin to move occur spontaneously. The acquisition of new information that propels us to change a fundamental cognitive schema, or a creative process such as writing a novel, or a genuine spiritual transformation that offers new meaning can be spontaneous occasions where blocks are removed and energy is freed. Chance events such as seeing a play about an evocative topic or news coverage of an assault or natural disaster sometimes offer access to the blockage. Similarly, subsequent trauma can actually provide an opening in which earlier traumas are opened and reworked, allowing for deep healing.

Other blocks clear as the result of specific healing efforts. These efforts can be deliberately designed to open energy lines, as in the case of acupuncture or thought-field therapy, or to balance energy patterns and flow, as with flower essences, meditation, or Reiki (a form of healing touch). Alternately, openings can occur in the course of work that is intended to heal the trauma but is not focused on energy per se. Examples of this might be a sufficient reworking of a traumatic event in talk-oriented therapy, chiropractic adjustment, an abreactive experience, prayer, cognitive reframing, massage, EMDR (eye movement desensitization and reprocessing), anger work, or art therapy. (A number of these approaches are discussed in greater detail in Chapter 9.)

Many methods are effective. Clinical reports and research have demonstrated the effectiveness of some methods; others are being evaluated, and still others have yet to undergo focused scrutiny. What we don't know is what methods are the most effective with whom under what circumstances. Perhaps what works cannot be delineated in a for-this-population-use-this-approach method. A particular client at a particular point in time with particular supports brings a particular need and set of vulnerabilities and skills to a particular therapist, who has an equally variable and changing set of characteristics. Finding the "right way" to go about opening blocked energy might change from week to week with any particular client–therapist pair, especially if we believe that energy patterns are always changing, in spite of embedded blocks and jam-ups from unresolved trauma. We and our energy fields are so much more than just our unresolved issues, and much does change daily even for the most "stuck" person.

Having a broad repertoire to choose from—along with some general knowledge about a range of approaches and a list of varied practitioners for referral—greatly assists therapists working with trauma survivors and those who self-injure. Appreciating the diversity of healing options and encouraging clients to pursue avenues that support healing for them matters more than a particular method or style. Fortunately, there is now a wealth of literature on the impact of trauma from various perspectives. See Briere (1992), Chu (1998), Davies and Frawley (1994), Herman (1992), Rivera (1996), and van der Kolk and colleagues (1996)— just a few of the recent texts available—for more detailed information about the sequelae and healing of trauma.

Self-Injury as a Beacon

The push to remove the blocks in our energy fields seems to be almost organically programmed. We continue to move toward wholeness and resolution in spite of ourselves. Weil (1995), in reviewing research on the body's ability to repair itself, states that "healing is an inherent capacity of life" (p. 75), even though highly complex and affected by many external factors. Blocked areas repeatedly malfunction or cause us distress. In this way, the blocked energy

channels are beacons guiding us to the specific points requiring intervention, so we can move more efficiently to
wholeness (Gallo 1999). Self-injury is a particularly bright
light, shining out on unresolved traumas. It can point to
fruitful areas to pursue therapeutically. Lack of useful attention and inadequate resolution cause the glow from self-
injury to return repeatedly until we are able to see more
clearly. Often, what we need to see, and sensitively attend
to, is the experience of the self, as described in the next
chapter.

4

The Incomplete Self-Boundary

The residue of childhood events such as abuse, inadequate parenting, and early loss creates fertile ground for the use of self-injury as a coping mechanism. Current events tap into old experiences and activate the internal, trauma-based worldview of the child. This schema elicits strong affect and sensation, and sometimes also evokes the use of self-injury as a coping strategy to manage this blend of past and present intensity. In addition to this triggering action, these childhood experiences play another role in relationship to self-injury. This role is the way in which childhood trauma and loss disrupt the development of the self-boundary.

With an incomplete or inadequate self-boundary, the repertoire of skills normally available to an adult to regulate internal sensations and mediate interactions with the external environment may be temporarily inaccessible. It is as if the combined intensity of past experiences and current events cannot be sorted effectively or contained (Davies and Frawley 1994, van der Kolk 1996a). The self-boundary operates inadequately, as people struggle to find some method to ground, sort, hold, and understand their experiences. Avenues to less self-violent means of coping can short-circuit, or become blocked, and self-injury becomes the regulator and communicator.

The distinction between the role of the past as the *activator* of a particular worldview or schema and the role of the past as a *disrupter* in the development of a boundaried sense of self may be arbitrary and artificial. Perhaps these two roles are the same, simply described differently in an effort to facilitate a conceptual understanding. On the other hand, perhaps the two roles are distinct but function interactively to create an inclination to use self-injury. Maybe the inadequate or incomplete self-boundary is the poor regulator that allows the internal worldview to be activated to such an intense degree, thus leading to the use of self-injury. It is not the presence of the old internal world-view or trauma-based schema that is problematic per se. Rather, it is that this worldview—which coexists with other worldviews within any survivor's consciousness—becomes predominant and moves into the foreground as triggered survivors try to manage an evocative or overwhelming experience. And the reason that this worldview becomes the focusing lens in a particular moment results from the presence of an inadequate or incomplete self-boundary.

Regardless, while only a conceptual framework, the role of the self-boundary is an essential element in understanding the process of self-inflicted violence. The metaphor of the skin as a physical manifestation of the self-boundary or sense of self has been described by diverse writers and thinkers (Anzieu 1989, Bick 1968, Freud 1947, Linehan 1993, McLane 1996, Strong 1998). Certainly, the skin features significantly in many forms of self-injury. Freud's concept of a body ego reflects the significance of the skin as a physical container for the self. (Strong [1998] offers a short summary of psychoanalytic thinking about how this metaphor of skin-as-physical-self-boundary specifically relates to self-injury.) Exploring the way in which the self-boundary develops and functions gives us better insight into the use of self-injury.

Basic Theory about Attachment and the Sense of Self

Developmental and object relations theories posit that, through a process of initial bonding or symbiosis with parents or caregivers followed by gradual differentiation from them, infants and toddlers develop a cohesive sense of self (Bowlby 1973, Fraiberg 1959, Hamilton 1992, Kaplan 1978, Mahler 1975, Spitz 1965, Stern 1985). This primary sense of self offers a solid ground upon which future developmental tasks can unfold and be resolved, leading to a reasonably healthy adult capable of interdependence and intimacy, autonomy and self-control, passion, self-esteem, and a sense of meaning, with access to affect and the ability to regulate that affect. This process of attachment, followed by gradual separation, eventually leads to an individuated sense of self, or the existence of a self-boundary. The provision of a "secure base" (Ainsworth 1982) by a "good-enough" caregiver (Winnicott 1965) who can tolerate and even invite both profound attachment and age-appropriate, child-initiated efforts at separation plays a major role in creating the biosphere necessary for a completed individuation process.

Many children develop adequately in spite of variable caregivers, changing environmental conditions, interference in the individuation process, or traumatic events. Some are fortunate enough to have made a substantial attachment to a parent in order to achieve a sense of self at around 3 or 4 years of age; this is considered normal or ideal. They then weather subsequent disruption with some strength. Others have inadequate or inconsistent attachments; some never attach substantially to an adult caregiver. Yet other children attach and separate adequately, but experience a severe trauma during or after the completion of this process, affecting their ability to sustain their sense of self throughout development, including adulthood. In fact, a number of clinicians and writers have noted that a significant aspect of the aftermath of trauma, particularly trauma related to interpersonal violence and loss, is the impact on the survivor's capacity for attachment and relational management (Barach 1991, Davies and Frawley 1994, Herman 1992, Saakvitne et al. 2000, van der Kolk 1996a).

Children who reach adulthood with inadequate, disrupted, or injured individuation may struggle with addiction, mood swings, intense and poorly regulated affects, distorted perceptions of self and other, inconsistent self-esteem, inadequate impulse control, overuse of projection, disturbed cognitive schemas, and self-injury (Cole and Putnam 1992, Davies and Frawley 1994, Hamilton 1992, Herman and van der Kolk 1987, Holmes 1998, Pearlman and Saakvitne 1995, Walant 1995). They may be diagnosed with personality disorders, affective and anxiety disorders, or dissociative disorders. The legacy of an inadequate self-boundary also appears in subsequent generations, as the inadequate self-boundary can impair the ability of parents to provide sufficiently supportive parenting to their children.

The Development of the Self-Boundary

When the attachment-separation-individuation process can be completed without disruption, the child develops a basic sense of self as denoted by the presence of the self-boundary. The self-boundary is an internal perception of a line dividing self from other, clarifying what is "mine" and what is "yours." It can be a barrier to other people's projections and demands, or a filter through which self can understand other. It helps regulate arousal, affect and perception by providing a container within which self—"me"—operates and finds meaning, a safe ground from which to process information and make decisions.

The self-boundary evolves gradually. The formation occurs over time as the child experiences the child–caregiver boundary as a regulator that she absorbs and incorporates. Over time, the locus of control of the regulation function shifts from external (caregiver as regulator) to being primarily internally based (self as regulator). By age 3½ or so, if no significant unresolved traumas have interfered, the child has taken the template provided by the child–caregiver boundary and determined her own boundary with its attendant regulatory and filtering capabilities. Like most new growth, it requires protection and support. New seedlings, for example, need to adapt gradually to the wind until their stalks can support them without breaking. Placing a tray of newly sprouted plants outside for a few hours at a time each day for a week allows the progressive development of enough strength to be transplanted into the garden. Similarly, children developing a sense of self require graduated experiences over time in which they increasingly learn to regulate the space where their internal and external realities meet.

In the best of worlds, infants experience a joining with their parents that is exquisite, vibrant, and enchanting. Parents fall in love with their babies, and dote on them, cooing and exclaiming and singing. Babies chortle back, thriving in the warm energy field created by this loving dyad or triad. The parents' deep desire to give to their babies fuels their ability to provide needed nourishment, tending, and engagement. When distressed, the babies receive tender soothing, contained by the parents' bodies and words and gestures and love. They sense a kind of rebalancing, a righting, and a return to homeostasis, and gradually incorporate self-soothing into their repertoire of behavior.

As babies become toddlers, parents marvel over the babies' capacities for basic skills like walking. They give the babies room to wander off, within a safe perimeter, to begin to define their own sense of the world. These wandering toddlers in time become both more independent and more aware that they are separate, triggering an anxiety response that makes them alternately clingy and argumentative. Good parents are able to allow this coming and going, responding to their growing children as the new regulators of their own experience. The children set the pace of attaching and separating. These parents are invested enough in the attachment between themselves and their babies to be present and engaged, but also secure enough to be able to let the toddlers become separate beings. Over time, the children develop their own edges, their own sense of self, creating a self-boundary that defines where they stop and another begins.

The repeated experiences of coming and going, of feeling both secure and anxious (but not too anxious), experiences of someone beaming back to them a sense of well-being and groundedness no matter what—these experiences allow children to develop the self-boundary. Whether understood as an intrapsychic structure, an energetic field, or a cognitive schema (or all three), an adequate self-boundary allows for flexible containment, permitting intimacy with others, comfort and ease in managing life's ups and downs, and a cohesive perception of identity.

Consistent soothing, positive mirroring, nonpunitive limit-setting, genuine affection, and the freedom to come and go support the development of the self-boundary. Further, a solid attachment with parental caregivers offers some inoculation against the damage of subsequent trauma (Holmes 1998, McFarlane 1988).

Figure 4–1 shows a conceptualization of a completed individuation process. The four sets of two circles represent a securely attached parental caregiver (darker circle) and child (lighter circle) who are then able to effect a separation and individuation process, leading to a solid but flexible self-boundary for the child.

For readers who are unfamiliar with attachment theory and interested in a further exploration of these concepts, I suggest Holmes's *John Bowlby and Attachment Theory* (1998), Hamilton's *Self and Others: Object Relations Theory in Practice* (1992), and Kaplan's *Oneness and Separateness: From Infant to Individual* (1978). I find them readable, useful, and relatively free of confusing or obfuscating jargon. Goldbart and Wallin's *Mapping the Terrain of the Heart: Passion, Tenderness, and the Capacity to Love* (1996) offers accessible information about the implications of early attachment patterns for adult relationships.

Figure 4–1. The attachment-separation-individuation process: development of the self-boundary.

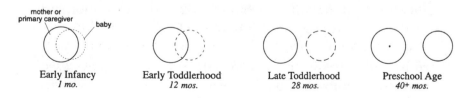

mother or primary caregiver baby			
Early Infancy *1 mo.*	Early Toddlerhood *12 mos.*	Late Toddlerhood *28 mos.*	Preschool Age *40+ mos.*

Disruptions in the Developmental Process

A range of events or conditions may interrupt this process. A parent or caregiver's psychological or practical limitations can disallow the process to unfold. A mother who is depressed, or a father who has a high need for control, or a grandmother who still longs for her own mother will all struggle with this process. They will have trouble being emotionally available and engaged, or allowing the child to set the pace of differentiation, or tolerating the separation themselves. Parents may struggle with unresolved issues from their pasts, including inadequate or hurtful parenting from their own childhood, or with other emotional vulnerabilities that preclude their ability to be present and available to their children.

Babies are sometimes born with physical ailments or dispositions that demand more of parents than they are prepared to give. Severe medical conditions or pain may interfere, either for babies or parents. Some parent–child dyads or triads are ill-matched; the parents have different temperamental styles and needs from those demanded by infants or toddlers. Practical constraints can also interfere. Caregivers who need to work long hours, have too many children to allow for availability to any particular child, or must concentrate on day-to-day survival generally experience the demands of the attachment-separation-individuation process as too great, and pull back from or avoid it.

It should be noted that there is a wide range of adequate conditions within which attachment-separation-individuation can occur. As Winnicott (1965) noted, a "good-enough" mother/caregiver is sufficient. One of the painful truths about trying to identify sufficiently adequate conditions is how idiosyncratic the needs of a particular baby are, and it is very hard to ascertain them with any specificity until it is too late, when the child is already struggling or distressed. What might be adequate for one child is inadequate for another. Temperament, family dynamics, and physical limitations all contribute to these idiosyncratic differences, as well as the particular match or mismatch between child and caregivers. As Linehan (1993) writes, "A system that may originally have consisted of a slightly vulnerable child within a slightly invalidating family can, over time, evolve into one in which the individual and the family environment are highly sensitive to, vulnerable to, and invalidating of each other" (p. 58).

Holes and Weak Links: The Inadequate Self-Boundary

Some children never attach to a caregiver. Many children seem to attach to varying degrees to available (or semi-available) adults or older children, but may not have the chance to form an attachment that is strong enough to support the individuation process. These children are at risk for impaired cognitive functioning, an inability to form emotional connections, and poor impulse control; they may be antisocial, aggressive, and without an apparent conscience (Levy and Orlans 1998).

More commonly, individuation is interrupted. Some degree of attachment occurs, but the separation and individuation process is disrupted, either by the adult's need to maintain the attached state with the child or by loss of the caregiver. The loss of the caregiver can vary from parental death to family traumas that cause the caregiver to become unavailable, from a bout of depression in a parent to the birth of another child who occupies the caregiver. The child may also experience a loss of the caregiver as traumatic events occur about which the caregiver has no knowledge, thereby being unable to provide protection or comforting.

When the child remains attached to the adult caregiver even as she herself develops into an adult, her self-boundary is incomplete; her sense of self—feeling grounded and okay and safe in the world—is dependent on the (at least psychic) presence of the other. As long as both adult caregiver and child (as an adult) are willing to remain in the attached state and maintain their connectedness, the inadequacy of the self-boundary may not be experienced as problematic. If and when the desire or capacity to maintain the ongoing intense connection changes, the child's sense of her self-boundary shifts to the latter case of a lost caregiver (even when the loss occurs in adulthood). When the child loses his caregiver, the child's incomplete self-boundary is more likely to then be perceived as wanting.

To conceptualize this in concrete terms, it is as if the place where the child was attached to the caregiver stays open. In either scenario described above, the child is left with a hole in the self-boundary. For the still-attached child with an engaged caregiver, this space may not be felt as a hole unless the caregiver becomes suddenly unavailable, such as with illness. For the child who has (effectively) lost his caregiver, a gaping hole remains, as the child holds it open so he can reattach to the significant adult at some point in the future and complete the process. The drive for completion and evolution, the relentless push of development, requires that the child wait so he can complete the process. Some children use a fantasy caregiver/parent in their internal attachment process, and hold open a space in a similar way. Their actual parents weren't adequate but they imagined an idealized parent who someday would come and make it all okay. So they hold open the space for the parent-who-will-come-someday. This may take the form of dreaming of a true love who will arrive in adulthood to fulfill these needs (Goldbart and Wallin 1996).

The space held open for the returning caregiver is not the only hole in the self-boundary. Traumatic events can rip the growing sense of self, slicing through a tender self-boundary. Repeated, low-level stresses can prevent the self-boundary from solidifying, leaving holes or weak places. A brittle, rigidly constructed boundary is likely to crack or fragment with any stress, even the stresses of ordinary daily events. More substantial losses or traumas at a later age can also strain the self-boundary, creating holes in subsequent years, perhaps even in adulthood. Some people may have enough ego strength to maintain a sense of self, except under extreme stress or following a new trauma.

Figure 4–2 is a representation of the inadequate or incomplete self-boundary of a traumatized child who is now an adult; the gaps or holes represent the disrupted attachment and the effects of unresolved trauma. The shadow

Figure 4–2. A conceptualization of the inadequate self-boundary.

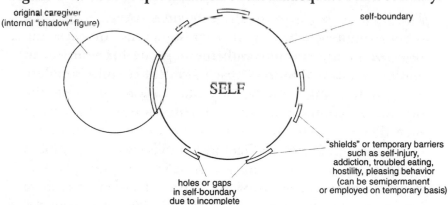

circle represents the caregiver to whom the child may still, at some internal level, be attached in spite of the gaping hole.

I do not mean to suggest that people with adequate self-boundaries are unattached to their parents and childhood caregivers, their spouses or partners, or other intimates. Attachment is a basic human need that remains important throughout the life span. Most of us utilize one or more people as a secure base, enabling us to function more comfortably and happily in our worlds (Holmes 1998, Pistole 1999). Rather, I suggest that an incomplete self-boundary creates a fundamental sense of unsafety or a lack of groundedness, sometimes with a concomitant over-dependence on another person. The resulting effect, as I describe shortly, is that the capacity for attachment from an adult position is often compromised by the incomplete separation from a "child place," and actually interferes with healthy adult attachments.

Operating with an Inadequate Self-Boundary: How It Feels

The hole or gap kept for the returning caregiver and the other wounds left by the intrusion of trauma or other unresolved events interfere with the capacity for intimacy in adulthood, as well as the capacity to regulate one's experience of the internal and external worlds. In short, the boundary defining self—normally functioning as a barrier or a filter or a container—is un- or underdeveloped. Because the self is not sufficiently boundaried, worry about being okay or a consistent but indefinable perception of danger creates chronic anxiety. This distress may vary from low-grade anxiety to more significant levels, even to panic.

People with an inadequate self-boundary live with a sense of being off-balance, of not being quite able to trust one's self or other people. This unsettleness colors daily experiences, particularly with regard to interpersonal connection and management of emotions.

Some people feel they simply cannot contain the intensity of their feelings, and will explode, disintegrate, or disappear at any moment if they don't keep them under constant check. Others may feel intact most of the time, and feel they fragment when highly stressed. The stress can be simply too much stimuli in too short a period of time, or rejection or criticism by others. The result is often an extremely low threshold for frustration; they may become sharp or aggressive when overwhelmed in an effort to regulate the flood of incoming stimuli and shore up the self-boundary.

Fear about another person getting too close and seeping in, or fear about losing one's self and seeping out, remains ever present, though often out of awareness. People with inadequate self-boundaries may experience merging and connection with another person. Often, the merging happens somewhat quickly and without conscious choice, and isn't noticed until sensations and affect suddenly feel overpowering. Alternatively, interpersonal interactions may tend toward the other extreme of avoiding intimate connections or actively deflecting contact with others. At this end of the continuum, the fear of engulfment is great enough to interrupt relatedness. Either way, someone with a self-boundary full of holes is inclined to stay away from the edge of the self. Contrary to the experience of someone with a sufficient self-boundary—where one can move all the way to one's edge and join with another without fear of getting lost in enmeshment—the lack of a solid self-boundary creates anxiety that keeps one not quite present even when engaged or enmeshed.

The Impact of Incomplete Individuation:
Self-Injury and Other Clues

The consequences of incomplete individuation can be described in at least two ways. One method involves observing the effects of living with a self-boundary with holes or weak places. "I don't feel whole" and "I'm doing so much better but there's something else here I haven't gotten to yet" are examples of comments made by people with incomplete individuation. These subjective perceptions are often bolstered by self-reports or observations of overreactions to others' behavior, by feeling caught up in craziness with another person, by illusions of responsibility for others' feelings and behavior, by disavowal of responsibility for one's own behavior and feelings, by feeling either victimized or excessively entitled, by being flooded with feelings, or by feeling disconnected from self and others.

To compensate for what feels like a lack of protection, people with an inadequate self-boundary develop shields or temporary barriers to shore up and guard the insufficient psychic boundary (see Figure 4–2). These barriers may take various forms. Self-injury or the use of chemicals can help someone with a frayed self-boundary to regulate sensation and contact (Calof 1995, Clemmens 1997, Davies and Frawley 1994, van der Kolk 1996a). Substance use and abuse, rigid roles and rules for relationships, a hostile personality style, avoidance of intimacy, and physical aggression toward others seem designed to keep the external world out, though they may also meet the need for containment of one's internal experience.

Self-injury often serves this latter purpose, by giving a concrete sense of the skin and the body to hold and contain the self. Hamilton (1992) offers this example of a physician who carefully cut herself when she felt her boundaries dissolve: "The slight pain and the sight of her red blood oozing through her white skin reminded her in a tangible way of her self–other boundary" (p. 155). Overeating and other troubled eating patterns may also be employed to fill the holes (thus providing both containment and deflection), as can other addictive patterns such as over-work, compulsive sexuality, and endless entertainment.

The second way to distinguish an inadequate self-boundary is to identify the attempts to complete the attach-ment-separation-individuation process that occur (usually) unconsciously and often problematically. Many people with an inadequate self-boundary find they alternate between intense intimacy with others, and disconnection and dis-tance. While some people remain primarily at either end of the intimacy continuum (enmeshed or disengaged), many vacillate between the two modes. This vacillation is driven by the longing to resolve and complete the inter-rupted individuation process. It reflects an attempt to at-tach, separate, and thereby define self. Such attempts tend to be highly charged with affect and based on strong in-ternal beliefs that may be in conflict with current, external-world facts.

Intimate relationships generally provide the arena within which the drive for completion of the individuation process occurs. Goldbart and Wallin (1996) suggest that our early relationships with caregivers create an inner map that we use in subsequent relationships to guide our traverse through our interpersonal present. They eloquently describe the refinding that emerges in adult intimate rela-tionships. "We often challenge ourselves by unconsciously choosing partners with whom the problematic past can be replayed. The opportunity in this refinding is to repair the emotional damage" (p. 201). However, refinding also en-tails the risk that all one's triggers are activated, and, depending on the level of awareness and self-monitoring skills, the potential for repetition (rather than healing) looms large.

Romantic or partnering relationships are not the only environment in which the drive for completion of the individuation process emerges. Sometimes these dynamics are activated within a supervisor–employee relationship, or another similar relationship wherein the roles echo the power differential present in the parent–child dynamic. Clearly, the nature of the therapist–client relationship strongly invites a reopening of the attachment-separation process for some people.

Ego States or Alter Personalities:
A Concrete and Sometimes Confounding Element

Survivors of childhood trauma sometimes develop a very concretized internal structure reflecting the fragmented parts of themselves. These parts can be quite distinct, autonomous, and without awareness of other parts of self (as with people who meet criteria for the diagnosis of dissociative identity or multiple personality disorder), or they can be more fluid embodiments of child and adult dimensions of self (as in ego states). As Watkins and Watkins (1981) suggest, we all perceive and express ourselves in different ways at different times depending on the demands of a particular situation, while still maintaining a connected, ongoing sense of self across these particularized expressions of self. For example, we might act one way with our boss at work, another way with a good friend at lunch, a third way in bed with our partner, and an entirely different way at a party. The differences might include variations in language, syntax, clothing, demeanor, and affect. For a relatively integrated person, all four of these selves is understood and claimed as "I." The person recalls the varied interactions and feels a cohesive sense of herself across all situations. This conceptualization of personality has been called normal ego state theory (Watkins and Watkins 1981).

People who have suffered significant trauma and loss sometimes develop more distinct and separate ego states as a way to encapsulate and manage traumatic events. Varying degrees of separateness and difference between parts may exist. For example, someone may feel like she is 2 years old when she gets upset and frustrated and hurt and unable to verbalize her feelings, but not lose her awareness of being an adult in the present; she might say she feels "taken back" to being a frustrated 2-year-old. Similarly, someone molested at age 8 may find he talks like an 8-year-old, or feels smaller in his body, when he is describing to his therapist the abuse he suffered—and at the same time know he is an adult and have a clear recollection of everything that occurred while he was "being 8." At the furthest end of the continuum are people with autonomously functioning parts of self who may be amnestic about the existence and actions of other parts of the self. Someone at this end of the continuum of dissociative personality structures may not remember when the 5-year-old part of her is out eating cookies by the fistful in the present or when the teenage part of her has sex with a stranger in the present.

The very nature of a fragmented sense of self suggests an inadequate self-boundary. Each part has a permeable and sometimes shifting self-boundary, and the person as a whole operates with an inadequate self-boundary. Many of the triggers or cues that evoke different parts to emerge are grounded in the inadequacy of the self-boundary to contain or filter experiences in the present. Further, highly dissociative people consistently struggle with strong needs for attachment and the provision of a sense of safety by an outside, caregiving adult—indicators of disrupted attachment. Some clinicians have even suggested that dissociative identity disorder is fundamentally an attachment disorder (Barach 1991, Blizard 1997). (See Davies and Frawley [1994], Kluft [1985], Putnam [1989], Rivera [1996], Ross [1989], and Watkins and Watkins [1981] for more information about dissociative personality structures.)

The presence of personified fragmentation in someone's approach to the world (a dissociative personality structure) can complicate the efforts to heal and rework the self-boundary. The self-boundary in this case is multiple rather than singular, existing in different layers with different parts of the self. The attachment process occurs with layered intensity, as the pure (i.e., undiluted) affect of young parts who long desperately for a good parent is more directly accessible than is generally true for nondissociative clients. Ambivalence is apportioned to different parts, often with fairly strong dissociative boundaries between the parts, again adding to the undiluted strength of powerful affects. Extensive trauma has occurred in the past, contributing many holes to the fragmented self-boundary. All in all, the presence of significant dissociation adds to the complexity of issues related to self-boundary functions. The frequency of self-injury among highly dissociative trauma survivors reflects this dilemma (Chu 1998, Coons and Milstein 1990, Rivera 1996, Zlotnick et al. 1996).

Implications for the Therapeutic Relationship

Clients with an inadequate self-boundary often bring particular needs to the therapeutic relationship. Given that intimate relationships offer a rich ground for the reemergence of incomplete attachment-separation-individuation processes, the therapeutic relationship is one arena that often solicits this reemergence. As noted, intimate relationships that echo the parent–child power dynamic are especially evocative. The therapeutic relationship, as a controlled and intimate space designed to provide care, lends itself even more readily, particularly when a traumatic history exists (Ehrenberg 1992, Elkind 1992, Herman 1992, Maroda 1998, Pearlman and Saakvitne 1995, Peterson 1992, van der Kolk 1996a).

The attachment and separation process may or may not be in the foreground of the work between clinician and client. For many clients, this activation of unfinished issues and the hope of reaching a more satisfactory and complete resolution exists outside their conscious awareness. Each therapist–client pair addresses this attachment—the connection between them—in different ways. (Varying styles and methods of working with these issues are explored in depth in Chapter 8.) What is important to note here is simply the potency of reenactment in the therapeutic relationship for clients with an incomplete self-boundary, and how this highlights the centrality of relationship in the therapeutic process.

What has been called traumatic attachment or trauma-bonding (Carnes 1997, Dutton and Painter 1981) can enhance the intensity of the reenactment in the therapy relationship. "According to attachment theory," Holmes (1998) writes, "a frightened child will seek out their [sic] attachment figure, and if he or she is also the traumatising one a negative spiral—trauma leading to the search for security followed by more trauma—will be set up" (p. 192). Thus, reenactment can take the form of the client working to elicit a rejection or other painful action by the therapist, while simultaneously seeking the protection and com-

fort of the therapist; this reenactment mirrors early deprivation or abuse (Davies and Frawley 1994, Herman 1992,
Miller 1994, Pearlman and Saakvitne 1995). Ross (1997) has
described this as ambivalent attachment to the perpetrator,
and states that these issues often contribute substantially to
the complexity of therapeutic issues for highly dissociative
clients (also see Blizard and Bluhm [1994]).

One client, for example, found that she wanted to
demand physical holding from me by literally pushing up
against me and, in her word, "invading" my boundaries.
She felt she needed to break through my therapist demeanor to the real me and get a reaction. She realized that
she was trying to re-create the actual scenario she experienced repeatedly with her mother as a young child, by
approaching her mother and reaching out for connection,
only to be verbally dismissed, physically rejected, and sometimes beaten. Fortunately, in this case, the client was able
to verbalize her impulse rather than entirely act it out.
Nonetheless, it illustrates the potency of such needs, and
one of the ways they are brought to us as clinicians.

The nature of reenactment can be painful and complicated for both therapist and client. From the therapist's
perspective, the client's needs related to attachment and
individuation may make perfect sense, but nonetheless feel
emotionally and intellectually demanding. The level of
engagement required to negotiate a new outcome for the
client asks that the therapist be highly alert to nuance, and
be responsive and respectful amidst conflicting feelings.
Sometimes the therapist may feel that the interaction asks
for more than she can offer. Sometimes the client feels she
(herself) is too dependent, vulnerable, and out of control.
The emotional reactions of both members of the therapeutic relationship speak to the power of reenactment and how
fiercely these issues demand resolution.

Borderline Personality Disorder or Inadequate Self-Boundary: What's in a Name?

As mentioned earlier, the most common diagnostic label utilized currently for people who self-injure is borderline personality disorder (BPD). Over the last fifteen years, various clinicians and writers have discussed the relationship between trauma and the diagnostic label of BPD (Briere 1993, Bryer et al. 1987, Burstow 1992, Chu 1998, Davies and Frawley 1994, Gunderson and Sabo 1993, Herman and van der Kolk 1987, Johnson et al. 1999, Miller 1994, Ogata et al. 1989, Zanarini et al. 1989). Some have even suggested that BPD is simply or primarily a posttraumatic outcome (Briere 1993, Burstow 1992, Herman 1992).

Certainly, the proposal that survivors who self-injure (among other diagnostic criteria) would be better served by a diagnosis of posttraumatic stress disorder (PTSD) makes sense. Such a shift does help to link prior trauma to current self-injury, chronic difficulties with affect regulation and intimacy, the presence of anxiety and anger, a fluctuating sense of self, and experiences of emptiness and alienation, thereby providing a more helpful therapeutic ground. A trauma-based perspective on BPD also raises an interesting question about the role of dissociated ego states or fragments in the abrupt mood changes and labile responses to intimacy in this group of people. Which common behaviors and emotional experiences might be the result of rapid, undetected shifts among young ego states?

A diagnosis of PTSD is also less pejorative. Most people diagnosed as borderline know what it means functionally to be called borderline—that many professionals see them as demanding and manipulative, hard to work with, chronically impaired, and irritating. Such a perception does not aid the development of a supportive therapeutic relationship or positive self-esteem in the client. Thus, using a diagnosis of PTSD—when a diagnostic label is required—benefits both client and therapist.

However, people have a range of different reactions to stress and trauma. Not everyone who is a trauma survivor meets the criteria for PTSD. Even those who do meet the criteria may be more different than alike. This has led to several new diagnostic conceptualizations in an attempt to distinguish among posttraumatic reactions, such as complex PTSD (Herman 1992), and DESNOS (disorder of extreme stress not otherwise specified) (Pelcovitz et al. 1997, Roth et al. 1997). Neither is a codified diagnostic category at this point (American Psychiatric Association 1994), but rather these suggestions reflect a desire to better identify and understand different reactions to similar stressors.

Relatedly, researchers and thinkers are working to discern biological and other vulnerabilites to the development of PTSD (Bowman 1999, Jones and Barlow 1990, Yehuda 1999a,b, Yehuda and McFarlane 1995) in order to clarify different trauma reactions. Further, researchers continue to assess what predicts chronic PTSD (Freedman et al. 1999) and to tease out the complexity of posttraumatic reactions (Ford 1999, Ford and Kidd 1998, McFarlane 1999). All of these efforts suggest complicated and interesting variations, and flesh out the simple notion that trauma can produce long-lasting effects. As Wilson (1995) has noted, future diagnostic frameworks will most likely list posttraumatic disorders as an entire category, with detailed subcategories reflecting varying patterns of effects.

The best reason to use diagnostic schemas is to better understand what is going on. In this light, I would suggest that it is the lack of an adequate self-boundary in particular that creates the picture often named BPD. The inadequacy of the self-boundary may be a primary factor in permitting or facilitating the development of complex PTSD or DESNOS. Research by Ford and colleagues (Ford 1999, Ford and Kidd 1998, Ford et al. 1997) supports this general idea. The concept of the inadequate self-boundary may help to delineate why some people with traumatic histories don't meet criteria for a diagnosis of BPD or PTSD. This may explain how some people are able—in spite of a history of significant trauma and related sequelae—to maintain a sense of equilibrium and a cohesive sense of self under stress, avoid the use of self-harm as a coping mechanism, and integrate a traumatic experience with some success.

Regardless of the diagnostic label applied to people who self-injure, identifying the lack of an adequate self-boundary as well as the role of early loss or trauma can be quite useful. It provides a conceptualization that is less pejorative than borderline personality disorder and more descriptive than posttraumatic stress disorder, thus offering a framework within which to work therapeutically, pointing to possibilities for healing.

Summary

This chapter concludes the first part of this book. These introductory chapters sketched the basic framework within which to understand self-injury. Getting a glimmer of the "felt experience," getting inside the symptom, usually helps us begin to perceive what is going on for someone else, no matter the presenting issue. From here, we can then ask the question, "What can I do to help?" That is the focus of the next part, Responding to People Who Self-Injure.

II

Responding to
People Who
Self-Injure

5

Therapeutic Goals and the Role of Compassionate Presence

Mental health and other helping professionals usually become aware of their clients' self-injury in one of three ways: they observe self-injury or its remnants (e.g., scars); their clients directly disclose past or current self-injuring behavior; or they are told of the client's behavior by other professionals, family members, or friends. Regardless of the form of the disclosure or discovery, once the professional knows the client self-injures, the question of how to respond comes up. How central should the issue of self-injury be in the therapy process? Do the clinician and the client make working on issues related to the self-injury the primary goal of the therapy, a secondary goal, or no goal at all? How does the therapist respond to the client about the self-injury? What is useful both in the moment and throughout the course of the relationship?

Therapeutic Goals Regarding Self-Injury

The psychotherapy process with clients who self-injure generally encompasses a wide range of issues and tasks. The self-injury is frequently not the presenting concern, and the client and therapist may determine specific goals for their work together that do not address the self-injury directly in

121

any way. Managed care limitations or other insurance constraints may dictate that the work focus on decidedly concrete and measurable goals, further removing any focus on
the self-injury. On the other hand, the self-injury may be
identified as the pressing problem. Occasionally it is so
named by the client; more often, others in the client's life,
such as family members or a mental health professional,
have focused their concern on the self-injuring behavior.

Regardless of the relative importance given to the self-
injury at the time of initial contact with the therapist or at
the time of disclosure, the task facing the psychotherapist
is to work with the client to establish therapeutic goals that
meet the client's needs. These may or may not focus on
the self-injury itself. Over the course of their work together,
they may shine a spotlight on issues related to the self-
injuring behavior from time to time, and then refocus on
other issues. Rarely is it useful to concentrate solely on the
self-injury. If a client struggles with self-injury, a host of
other issues also clamor for attention, and to focus solely
on self-injury does the client a disservice.

Underlying this flexible approach to treatment planning, however, three therapeutic goals regarding a client's
self-injury can be conceptualized (Connors 1996b). The
first and most important goal is to encourage communication about self-injury as a relevant aspect of the client's life
that has some relationship to his past and other issues of
concern. Working consistently to achieve this goal allows
the client to address the second and third goals when they
are salient for the client. The second goal is to improve the
quality of the client's life as it relates to self-injury. This
might include reducing shame and isolation, receiving adequate medical attention to the self-injury when needed, and
decreasing self-criticism for injuring. The third goal is to
significantly diminish the use of self-injury as a coping skill.

The phrase "when they are salient for the client" in the preceding paragraph is a key element in approaching goal-setting about self-injury in the therapy process. Mental health professionals, particularly when pressured to produce measurable outcomes or when uncomfortable with their own reactions to the self-injury, tend to leap to the third goal (diminishing the use of self-injury), either ignoring the first two or simply using them as stepping stones to the third. While the role of nonblaming, affirming communication about a client's experience of self-injury does indeed facilitate the approach to both improving the quality of the client's life in the context of self-injury and potentially reducing the occurrence of self-injury, working toward these latter goals needs to be the client's agenda. Only when the client desires to make changes regarding her behavior about self-injury should the second and third goals become central or even relevant to the therapy process.

Three Levels of Response

Therapists and other helping professionals can respond to clients who self-injure at three levels (Connors 1996b). By levels of response, I mean a quality of engagement with the client, and to some extent, what kinds of details are emphasized in the therapist's focus. The word *level* may imply a hierarchy of preference, suggesting that a higher level is more important. This is not quite accurate. All the levels matter, although the first level of response is a prerequisite and the most critical. Each serves a different purpose and is loosely parallel to the therapeutic goals outlined above.

The first level or quality of response is to simply be present with the disclosure of or subsequent discussion about clients' self-injury. This response is fundamental, and essential for effective work with clients who self-injure. The second level is to help clients intervene in their self-injury when the clients have asked for help in changing their self-injuring behavior. Presence still matters most and must be incorporated into problem-solving approaches. Chapter 7 discusses this level of the work in specific detail. The third level of response is to work toward resolution of the under-lying issues that elicit self-injury. This work may encompass many issues and is addressed further in Chapters 8 and 9.

Professionals may find their responses (their actions, words, and postures) operate at all three levels simulta-neously. Clearly, sustaining a supportive presence is a pre-requisite to the subsequent responses. However, specificity about the intent of our responses is very helpful in more effectively tailoring interventions for individual clients, and, ideally, emerges from an informed assessment of what will be most useful at a given point in time with a particular client. Each situation requires a conscious decision on the part of the professional. The best response at any juncture will depend on the professional's sense of what the client is needing in the moment, thereby informing the intent behind the response. The potency of pacing and joining the client where she is cannot be overemphasized.

For example, listening attentively and without judg-ment or comment to a client's description of punching herself may be the best way to enhance communication. For some clients, any verbal response from the therapist at this point may feel intrusive. Clients who tend to need a lot of control over their process and the conclusions they reach may be most helped by this approach. Therapists who are uncertain about what to say can also serve their clients well by at least listening attentively though silently. For other clients, asking an open-ended question might fit better: "Is there more you'd like to say about punching yourself? It's okay if there's more you want to say." This question allows for the client to feel in control about how much she says, but at the same time more directly expresses the therapist's interest than simple attentive listening does.

Or, a clinician may feel the more useful response would be to engage even more directly, and say, "I'm glad you told me about that. I'm sorry you hurt yourself and I also believe it helps you somehow. We can talk more about it again if you would like to." Some clients need to hear the particular interest and concern expressed in such a statement. This may be especially true for clients who were neglected or criticized consistently as children. Regarding what she needed from a therapist about her self-injury, one woman said she needed this direct invitation. "Sometimes I have a hard time talking to my therapist about stuff unless she asks me . . . because I'm so embarrassed about it I assume that she doesn't want to hear about it" (Hyman 1999, p. 154). Also in this intervention, the possibility of talking further about the self-injury is offered, while still allowing the client to set the pace of disclosure.

At another juncture, or at a later time during the same session, I may ask the client if she is looking for ways to cope differently, or if she understands how hurting herself helps her. These questions provide a vehicle for the therapist to gauge the client's hopes and needs in their work together. Questions of this nature shift the level of response in a way that further invites the client to pace the work and inform the therapist about what would be helpful, while overtly increasing the options about the scope of the work.

A next step might be to make an observation or ask a question about the link between the self-injury and previous trauma. Some clients will make this connection readily, depending on their perspective and what opportunities and support they have had in the past in usefully addressing their self-injury. For others, this will be a new idea. In making the following comment, the level of response shifts once again: "I'm wondering if how you burn yourself is connected to what your stepfather did to you in any way, since it involves the same part of your body that he touched." Another example would be this question: "Has working on what happened when you were 5 made any impact on the cutting?" Clearly, these interventions need to be well timed and fit the context of the relationship. I would be cautious about raising these possible connections with a client I just met, unless he indicated either directly or indirectly that he has some glimmer that his past is related to his current self-injury. I would want to first have some sense of his support network, his style and skills in coping with potentially intense issues, and current life stressors and functioning.

All three levels of response need to occur within a working therapeutic relationship. Why the relationship is so central, and how therapeutic presence helps, is addressed further in this chapter. But first a few cautions about interventions *not* to employ.

Unhelpful Responses

A range of common practices regarding self-injury are not useful in achieving any of the three goals outlined previously. Unfortunately, the prevalence of these interventions gives them the patina of appropriateness, when in fact they augment the shame and despair of people who self-injure. Three particular practices will be addressed here, though any interventions that violate the client's sense of self-control are likely to be unhelpful (Connors 1996b), as is discussed in depth in the next chapter.

Isolating self-injuring behavior from the person's history, sense of self, family experience, and the social context within which the person lives is not helpful. The degree of disconnection with which many people, especially trauma survivors, live is already profound (Herman 1992, Saunders and Arnold 1991). Viewing self-injury as a (particularly problematic) symptom apart from someone's history and internal experience compounds the sense of disconnection and often evokes the use of further self-inflicted violence (Hyman 1999). At times, focusing primarily on the self-injury in therapeutic work can serve to isolate this behavior if the work is not grounded in the larger context of the person's past history and current life situation (Wise 1989). A common reaction that also serves to isolate self-injury is to perceive it as manipulative behavior (the meaning and dynamics of manipulation are discussed in the next chapter).

Hospitalizing solely because of the presence or anticipation of self-injury is similarly unhelpful and excessive. It not only participates in a cycle of reinforcing self-injury as a way of securing involvement with service providers (something neither clients nor professionals find satisfying). It also maintains an external locus of control for the client in relation to her self-injury and her healing process. The act of involuntary hospitalization further confuses power and responsibility issues, and interferes with the client's development of an internal locus of control. (The next chapter offers a detailed exploration of issues related to power, responsibility, and locus of control.)

Self-injury may coexist with significant suicidal ideation or gestures, thus necessitating a good risk assessment and

possibly a hospital stay. But most self-injury does not require hospitalization per se, as it is not life threatening. Just
as clients are not hospitalized for smoking even though it
is clearly harmful to them, hospitalizing for most self-
inflicted violence does not make sense. This common practice functions essentially to comfort professionals, rather
than provide short- or long-term help to the person self-
injuring. Unfortunately, recommending hospitalization is
often a knee-jerk reaction to the disclosure of recent self-
injury. One woman said it was least helpful "when a therapist wants to immediately put you in the hospital when
sometimes it's not needed—it's just a temporary crisis that's
going on. They don't talk to you, they just say 'go to the
hospital.'"

In fact, in many cases, hospitalization based on self-
injury actually harms the client. This harm occurs by creating complicated and unfruitful power struggles between
patient and professional, by prompting reenactments of
inappropriate control over the patient's body through the
use of chemical and physical restraints, and by setting up
a template for all involved about how to manage crisis. A
much more efficient use of resources would be to help the
client manage her crisis in another way, rather than insti-
tuting the first of what too often becomes a series of hospitalizations. Further, psychiatric hospitalization is stressful in
and of itself, adding to the distress with which the client
is contending and can actually create posttraumatic stress
effects (Morrison et al. 1999).

These negative effects are also compounded by the
fact that hospitals are not, particularly these days, in a
position to provide help for self-injuring clients. As sites of
short-term stabilization, they are ill-equipped to provide
patients with the kind of connective exploration of the issues underlying self-injury that will ultimately facilitate heal-

ing. In an unusual setting with aware and sensitive staff, some inpatient units may be able to address the first and second therapeutic goals listed above (encouraging communication about self-injury and improving the quality of the client's life). However, this is rare.

A third practice not helpful to clients is setting a requirement that clients not self-injure if they are in therapy with us. This action also confuses power and responsibility issues, setting up a difficult dynamic that will impede the therapeutic process in the long run. Although there may be situations when a therapist feels unable to participate in a therapy process if she knows the client is self-injuring, most of the time this criterion is not useful for the client and serves primarily as a way to manage the therapist's anxiety. The likelihood that the client will violate the agreement is great (not intentionally, but because the underlying causes are complex and intense), thus inviting the experience of failure for both client and therapist. If a therapist cannot tolerate the distress she experiences due to the client's self-injury, then referral to another therapist is preferable.

People living with self-inflicted violence report many unhelpful responses from professionals in addition to those practices listed above. As one woman said, "I wanted my therapist not to get angry with me, to pay attention to the fact that something was wrong, and help me to find out what was wrong since I wasn't in touch with my feelings. A few times, my therapist got really upset with me when I cut, and I would leave there feeling so ashamed that I'd go home and cut again" (Hyman 1999, p. 154). Criticism, disgust, unreasonable demands ("Just stop it!" or "Don't you think it's time you quit?"), shaming ("So you're back here again for cutting"), and other negative reactions obviously do not facilitate recovery. This chapter and the following one offer suggestions on how to create a supportive, inviting environment for people who self-injure by the simple and valuable gift of human presence.

The Centrality of Relationship
in the Healing Process

As Herman (1992) states, trauma is about internal and external disconnection. The sense of disconnection from one's self, one's history, one's family or peer group, or one's community can be quite strong. Therefore, a central element in healing trauma is reconnection at many levels. This is particularly true when the source of the wounding occurred within the context of a relationship, as is the case with interpersonal violence. Even if the perpetrator of the violence is a stranger to the victim, it remains an interpersonal (between two people) event. Rogers (1995) writes, "What has been wounded in a relationship must be, after all, healed in a relationship" (p. 256).

The therapeutic relationship can be one of the healing connections for survivors of trauma. It can provide a container within which other reconnections can occur, such as memory processing and integration, reworking of trauma-based beliefs, and expression of split-off feelings. Freyd (1996), in discussing the trauma resulting from the profound betrayal that occurs when someone is victimized by a person on whom he depends, suggests that therapy provides an environment within which the client can integrate social information processing mechanisms. "The potential for healing is dependent upon the relationship between the therapist and client, suggesting that a focus on the nature of the therapeutic relationship is paramount" (p. 168).

For people who have experienced interpersonal violence, the relationships they experience with helping professionals—even short-term contacts—reverberate power-fully. The act of betrayal occurs in a social context, and the next layer of social context—the responses of others to the act itself—also impacts the victim's experience and subsequent processing of it. Research supports this idea. How others respond to victims has been correlated with how well they cope with the aftermath of an assault. Rape victims experienced fewer negative effects such as depression when they felt supported by their partners (Moss et al. 1990). Similarly, victimized children coped more successfully when their parents or caregivers were supportive and nonblaming (Cohen and Mannarino 1998). Adult survivors of childhood abuse had better relationships, more positive self-esteem, and less depression in adulthood when their childhood disclosures were supported by nonoffending parents and others (Palmer et al. 1999). While most of the research has focused on the responses of family and significant others, it logically extends to others with whom survivors discuss their victimization experiences. In other words, what we do and say as helping professionals makes a difference, positive or negative, with trauma survivors.

Transforming Shame by Listening: The First Step

The capacity to be present with and listen to someone disclosing information that can be difficult both for clients to tell and professionals to hear is integral to an effective response to self-injury. This is similar to the attentive, nonjudgmental listening trauma survivors require when disclosing traumatic events (Herman 1992). "Perhaps the crucial factor for recovery is that the abuse survivor have a relationship (whether with a therapist or someone else) in which the truth can be told without recrimination, a relationship in which the survivor can trust that the truth will be heard and believed without the listener's subsequently abusing his or her power" (Freyd 1996, pp. 172–173). Such presence and listening meets basic needs self-injuring clients often bring to the helping relationship.

Sometimes we underestimate the difficulty clients have in disclosing self-injury, and concomitantly underestimate the power of simple, genuine listening. To be met and received with acceptance occurs infrequently for many of us in daily life. Coming to a therapeutic setting in particular, clients often long for such a reception, but fear this need won't be met. For many, the fear extends beyond what won't be there to what might be there—verbal or nonverbal judgment, or even actions that remove a client's sense of control (e.g., involuntary hospitalization, behavior contracts, physical restraint). These concerns tend to be even greater for clients who self-injure. Clients who have previously disclosed their self-injury often have a concrete basis for their fears.

Even when fear does not predominate, clients may avoid disclosure due to shame. The sense of shame directly or indirectly related to self-injury can be profound (Alderman 1997, Burstow 1992, Davies and Frawley 1994, Mazelis 1992, Wise 1989). This shame may be sparked by a number of reasons. Many feel keeping the secret about their self-injury creates shame in their present day-to-day life. Others may be ashamed because of the conflict between their self-inflicted violence and a cherished value of nonviolence. Clients may have been shamed by other professionals at previous disclosure or discovery. Some people describe the sensation of feeling out of control in their bodies, or overwhelmed by the strong impulses or feelings that trigger the injuring behavior. Most people feel shame as a result of feeling so out-of-control, particularly in reference to body experiences. Other sources of shame are unresolved traumatic events or the globalized sense of inadequacy or "badness" some people carry.

Some clients, as a result of numerous hospitalizations or other involvements with service providers, have disclosed and discussed their self-injury with some frequency. This doesn't mean they have no shame, or feel at ease in talking about their self-injury. Often, their feelings about their behavior are complicated, veiled, and heavily shame-laden. They have simply learned that they are supposed to tell or talk, and so they comply. They may even appear to exhibit some pride about their scars. I believe that for most, if not all, people who injure themselves, under that bravado of pride is deep shame about being so out of control and doing something that is socially unacceptable and, in some circles, may be perceived as crazy.

Isolation and disconnection often accompany survivors' self-injury (Burstow 1992, Hyman 1999, Miller 1994). Many people who self-injure do not disclose their behavior to friends or family, often due to shame and/or anticipated criticism. Some do not know anyone else who self-injures. The links between current self-injury and past events may be obscured, further enhancing their sense of disconnection, not only from others but from themselves and their own history. Some people feel different from others because of the self-injury, creating disconnection in a social context. In *Women Living with Self-Injury* (Hyman 1999), Meredith says:

> I think that one of the biggest things [self-injury] does in my life is it makes me different and separate from other people. My time and my energies are focused on trying to keep myself safe as opposed to normal everyday tasks and concerns. . . . Other people when they

get dressed in the morning don't have to worry about
dressing so that they cover up their scars, or they don't
have to worry about what might happen if they start
to bleed and ruin their clothes. It's not an issue for
them. [pp. 70–71]

Marcy, the woman quoted in Chapter 1 who inserted
needles into her clitoris, says she even feels different from
other self-injurers. "I still have a lot of shame because of
how I hurt myself. Even though there is more information
about self-injury, most of the books are talking about cutting. There's a separate sense of shame that is different
because it's not talked about much. What I did isn't what
everybody else does."

Supportive listening in and of itself alters many
people's sense of disconnection, isolation, and shame. Repeatedly, when asked what would be helpful, people who
self-injure list compassionate, nonshaming listening, and
calm interest (Alderman 1997, Hyman 1999, Wise 1989). As
Kaufman (1985) notes, shame disrupts the "interpersonal
bridge" between people. By consciously working to rebuild
the bridge in the face of a potent issue about which people
feel shame, we offer clients a chance to lessen the shame
and isolation. Such modeling can also facilitate the client's
efforts to communicate more in general about their self-
injury. They may feel encouraged to share their experiences
with supportive allies, talk with others who self-injure, participate in a group for people who self-injure, and read
respectful materials on self-injury, thus further countering
the isolation and associated shame.

Our capacity to respond without blame or shame, either direct or implied, is fundamentally connected to clients' willingness to engage with us further about their self-
injury. Although some people will continue to raise the

issue of self-injury even if we fail to offer a safe and respect-ful environment, we can enhance the likelihood of further discussion if we do act in a caring, nonshaming manner. Such engagement is important, because without open and clear communication about the self-injury within the thera-peutic relationship, our ability to respond effectively at any other level is severely limited.

Presence as the Heart of Intervention

When we speak about the therapeutic relationship, we mean many things. Different approaches value different qualities and styles of interaction. The focus or context of the therapeutic relationship can be quite variable, impact-ing the nature of the interaction (e.g., is the focus on re-actions to medication, or identifying cognitive coping strat-egies, or exploring an aspect of the client's past?). The degree of task orientation also varies, as do the social rules governing how the conversation between client and thera-pist unfolds. The setting within which clinician and client meet impacts how they perceive each other. Individual characteristics, prior history with other therapists and cli-ents, and a range of other factors contribute to different experiences for both people in the therapeutic relationship. However, at the heart of any therapeutic relationship is an interaction between two people. And this quality—of two people meeting each other in order to help one of them—is at the heart of what many clients, especially survivors of trauma, are seeking.

Most of my clients, and I believe this is generally true of clients who pursue psychotherapy, have not had many, or at least enough, sustained experiences with a present and engaged other. For survivors of severe and repeated interpersonal trauma, the need for the availability of the therapist as a person who is present in her body, mind, heart, and spirit is great. Working to mend the shattering and disconnective effects of trauma often requires a sense of wholeness from the outside, from someone else, who then is accessed through interpersonal connection. The sense of wholeness is lent to the other, creating enough collective energy to make a space within which the trauma itself and its aftermath can be sorted out and processed. Watkins (1995), in a lovely little piece on the importance of therapist presence (or "emotional 'withness,' rather than countertransference which is an 'againstness'" [p. 1]), says it simply and eloquently. "As the therapist resonates with the patient's pain, the patient resonates with the therapist's ego strength; together they can accomplish what patient alone might not" (p. 6).

Part of what is healing to my clients is my willingness to make my self, my being, available for use in their heal-ing process (Connors 1998). Sometimes this is as a person who can be attached to, prodded, and poked (not physically, usually), observed acutely, and questioned ("Why are you wearing your old glasses so much these days?" or "You look tired—are you okay?"), loved and cared about, and raged against on occasion. Someone who is *there*. Someone who is willing to be engaged and involved. In other words, I have to be able to tolerate close and intense psychic or energetic engagement, to let this person into my heartspace and be willing to care about her and understand her worldview, so I can help her find new ways of organizing and transform-ing her pain. Sometimes I am the screen for her projections of herself or others in her life, past or present. Sometimes she engages me in enacting old dramas, so we can know them and let them go. But most of the time, my task is to be myself with as much presence as I can bring.

The challenge of being present is greater than it first appears. So many things interrupt our ability to be present. Fear, longing, pain, hurt, stress, and anxiety interfere on a regular basis. Distraction can be as simple as thinking about a phone call I need to make or as complicated as old issues being activated for me. Being tired makes this quality of engagement a little more of an effort. Sometimes, as therapists, we are preoccupied with an event in our personal lives, and just need to be able to withdraw in general. Staying sufficiently engaged with clients can be hard day after day. Over time, we need enough quiet spaces in our lives for both disengagement and replenishment, as well as adequate intimate relationships of many kinds so we can be nourished outside our work with clients. But if we can sustain such therapeutic intimacy, even in short-term relationships with clients, we offer an invaluable opportunity for their healing.

Intimacy Implies Mutuality: What Does That Mean in Therapy?

True presence with another person creates intimacy. Such intimacy is inherently mutual. To be intimate means both people reveal themselves, care about the other, risk wounding, tolerate a certain openness to the other, among other things. From a therapeutic perspective, it means establishing a collaborative relationship that is real, even as it is constrained. What are the implications for such mutuality? What are the limitations to mutuality in a therapeutic context? How much mutuality is reasonable, possible, or helpful?

Inevitably, an exploration of mutuality involves a genuine consideration of the role of power. The next chapter looks at power relations between therapist and client in depth. But first, let's look at how a few authors frame their thoughts about mutuality in the context of therapy relationships. Linehan (1993) discusses mutuality from a cognitive-behavioral perspective. In reviewing communication strategies, she talks about the power differential common to therapeutic relationships. She states, "The intent of reciprocal communication is to rectify such [power] imbalances more skillfully, and to provide an environment that holds the patient within the therapeutic enterprise. It is also intended to model . . . how to interact as an equal within an important relationship" (p. 371).

Miller, Jordan, and others at the Stone Center (Jordan et al. 1991) articulate a theoretical understanding of women's experience that is relationally based and emphasizes the salience of mutual engagement and connection. In speaking about mutuality and boundaries in the therapy relationship, Jordan (1991a) writes, "[in therapy] there is a contract that puts the client's subjective experience at the center, and there is an agreement to attend to the therapist's subjective experience *only insofar as it may be helpful to the client.* The therapist offers her- or himself to be used for healing" (p. 95, italics mine). This frame incorporates the presence of both the client's and therapist's experience, but outlines the fundamental constraint on mutuality: the basic contract underlying the therapeutic relationship dictates that the client's needs must be the focus.

Surrey (1991), also of the Stone Center, acknowledges that the therapy relationship has "a relatively fixed structure, an economic basis, certain power inequities and legal constraints" (p. 10). Nonetheless, she continues, "when the therapy relationship is working well, client and therapist come to a sense of shared purpose, a 'working together' which implies commitment and emotional investment in the relationship as an arena for growth and change. . . . For the therapist, mutuality refers to this way of being in relationship: empathically attuned, emotionally responsive, authentically present, and open to change" (pp. 10–11).

In *The Shining Affliction,* her exquisite articulation of the nuances and conundrums of the therapeutic relationship, Rogers (1995) writes about mutuality:

> The psychotherapy relationship is two-sided, whether we acknowledge it or not. Each person brings to that relationship whatever is unrecognized, unknown, and unapproachable in her or his life, and a wish for knowledge of truths and wholeness. Since one cannot thrive on memories, on a relationship with projections, what keeps alive the hope of wholeness is an interchange of love, longing, frustration, and anger in the vicissitudes of a real relationship. Such an interchange is part of the fragility of this relationship; with openness, one is vulnerable to hurt and to loss, on both sides of the relationship. However, the therapist must, of necessity, understand the vulnerability of both persons involved. [p. 319]

Elkind (1992), writing about impasses between clinicians and patients, talks eloquently about the complexity of the therapy relationship. She views the therapist and client as relational partners whose roles may shift as areas of primary vulnerability and wounding are accessed for each. The interplay between clinician and client is continual, as old relational patterns recur for both partners. Davies and Frawley (1994) articulately portray the textured interplay between clients dealing with trauma and their therapists. They write that all the reactions of both partners in the therapeutic relationship "are threads in the tapestry that is woven by both participants/observers to form the relational matrix within which and through which the therapy unfolds" (p. 5).

In short, some degree of mutuality in the therapy relationship exists in lovely and satisfying ways, and in potentially painful, evocative ways. Both people are changed as a result of knowing each other, sometimes in small ways, other times in powerfully transformative ways. We are never the same as a result of our work, if we let our hearts be engaged. Acknowledging the presence of mutuality—this genuine exchange between two people—is not license for therapists to satisfy their own needs for intimacy, power, and healing through their clients, though that may occur as a side benefit. It is the clinician's responsibility to safeguard the relationship to ensure that the mutuality and engagement between therapist and client serves to create a place of healing for the client. This means valuing and paying attention to the interpersonal interaction. Regulating our self-disclosure and the management of other boundary issues constitute much of the substance of thoughtful enhancement of mutuality in our relationships with clients. These issues are explored in the next chapter on the therapeutic relationship.

The Crux of the Work

Providing a holding environment, containing and transforming affects, empathizing, titrating the closeness, and focusing on the patient's value as a human being are all aspects of the personal relationship within the psychotherapeutic interaction. Yet, when one tries to teach these "real" aspects of treatment, they suddenly seem insubstantial. Primarily, attitudes are under discussion, not behaviors. [Hamilton 1992, p. 202]

The core of our work is just this: cultivating a loving, valuing attitude that supports the client's own healing process. And this is not insubstantial, as Hamilton fears. When we join with a client, allowing ourselves to be moved by and to bring compassionate witness to another person's pain, something real happens. Clients may or may not comment, or even focus, on what is happening between us. The relationship may simply be a steady part of the background, creating enough safety and substance to contain the work. Other times, grappling with the nuances of what is happening between client and therapist may occupy center stage in the therapy process. Regardless of the overt content or discussion, what matters is that something real and loving and connected occurs.

For people who self-injure, this compassionate presence is the most important quality we can bring to our role as helpers. It is our willingness to engage in a complex, emotionally charged relationship with another person in order to help her heal that makes all the difference. While such engagement demands much of us, it also holds the promise of change for our clients.

6

A Therapeutic Posture to Support the Healing Process

Given the significance of relationship to people struggling with self-injury, clarifying and defining a way to interact that is helpful to clients makes sense. The way we position ourselves in any setting has relevance to the outcome. When we choose to buy or sell shares of stock contributes to the loss or gain we receive. How we frame a complicated situation plays a role in how we feel about it. The extent to which we bend our knees when lifting heavy objects can determine how much stress we experience in our back. When doing therapy, how we are with clients contributes to what kind of outcome our clients achieve.

To talk about a therapeutic posture suggests that we position ourselves in our work with clients. This posture is both conscious and unconscious, and stems from who we are and what we believe about human beings, need, the developmental process, pain, strength, change, and other values. Being as thoughtful as possible within reason about what posture to assume allows us to maximize our impact as change agents and support clients to make useful gains in their work with us.

One way to approach the concept of what kind of posture we embody in our work is to assess our interactions with clients based on how power is managed in the therapeutic relationship. This chapter views the therapeutic relationship through this lens by considering power in a relational context, power as it is reflected by language, interpersonal boundaries as an expression of power, and the particular importance of attending to power in the context of loving presence.

The Role of Power in the Therapeutic Relationship

Attending to power dynamics in a relational context is crucial to effective work with trauma survivors (Briere 1992, Burstow 1992, Freyd 1996, Herman 1992). This follows from the understanding that traumatic events, in general, involve a significant lack of control for the victim. More particularly, interpersonal violence, by definition, involves a misuse of power over the victim's body. Regaining control is central to survivors' capacity to recover, thus underscoring the need for professionals to attend to the power dynamics in the helping relationship.

The need or desire for power, however, isn't limited to trauma survivors. Maintaining a sense of power and control over ourselves and our immediate environment is something we all appreciate. We generally have less anxiety and feel more confident when we know what to expect, and feel we can set the pace and style of an interaction, regulate the degree of intimacy and disclosure, and make choices about ending the interaction. Feeling our own power augments our ability to act and care for ourselves.

This is not to say that many don't feel anxiety also about having power. Many people in Western and other cultures have few opportunities to see power modeled well, that is, with respect and a sense of duty to fairness. Too often, those in positions of responsibility and leadership misuse their power for unfair personal gain. One conclusion some people come to is that claiming their power will somehow propel them into misusing it. They then avoid conscious access to and use of personal power, creating a ripe opportunity to develop the very thing they fear: the misuse and abuse of power. When we relate unconsciously to interpersonal power dynamics, we lose our capacity to think and choose, and we leave ourselves open to acting out our unresolved relationship to power.

The particular danger for clinicians is that we can too easily re-create the old abusive power dynamics our clients have experienced with others. Most clients, whether they identify specifically as trauma survivors or not, have perceived others—most frequently their childhood caregivers—as quite powerful and in some ways abusive or controlling in their use of power. I do not want to re-create these dynamics in my work with them. To do so impedes healing and can cause further harm.

Just because I work to minimize my unfair use of power with clients doesn't mean that clients do not bring their side of the unresolved issues about interpersonal power into their relationship with me. Some clients' primary method of resolving the victim–victimizer dynamic, of working out the painful aspects of those early relationships, is to reenact the issues with me. I am then cast in the role of power-abuser. Perceiving me in this light is, of course, the job or task of these particular clients. This is what brings them to therapy (Maroda 1998). My job is to allow the reenactment and then help provide a different ending to the old, familiar story. I can best do that if I remain alert to how I am using power in particular, in addition to making thoughtful choices about other interactional elements such as intimacy.

As psychotherapists, our task is to move toward an equalization of power in the relationship. The effort is in

the *movement toward.* Striving to balance power in the therapeutic relationship is not an achievable goal. The power
cannot be equalized between professionals and clients by
definition. Therapists determine when and where we see
clients, when the session ends, when we go on vacation,
what clients pay, and sometimes even where the client sits.
In many ways, we have the upper hand. Social status, client vulnerability, and professional duty all dictate a genuine power differential.

This is not to say that clients have no power in the
therapeutic relationship. Clients have considerable power,
and not just in the domain of their power to wound their
therapist's narcissism. Clients can choose not to engage in
therapy, which topics they address, and whether to even
speak at all. However, they are at a disadvantage in that
their need renders them vulnerable to desiring the relationship, even when it feels unhelpful or untenable for some
reason. This imbalance of need creates an imbalance of
power. And this imbalance of need is central to the helping relationship. In other words, working to balance the
need contradicts the very nature of the relationship. So
working to balance the power is the viable option.

The Particular Relevance of Power
in the Context of Self-Injury

The issues of power, control, and responsibility are quite
salient for people who self-injure. Self-injury is the embodi-
ment of a survivor's struggle to control her own body. The
early experiences that give rise to self-injury as a coping
mechanism were beyond the survivor's control. Self-injury
expresses the effort to regain control of one's bodily responses and sensations, one's internal affects, and one's

perception of reality. If the survivor is highly dissociative, it may also be an overt power struggle between parts of the self. The themes of power and control weave throughout the use of self-injury as a means of coping and expression.

For clinicians or health care professionals to enter this power struggle over who is going to control the patient's body defeats the ultimate purpose of healing. Resolution of the issues depends on the client coming to terms with her wide range of feelings and experiences, particularly those that are highly conflicted and of strong intensity. When we take on one part of the struggle for control, we deprive the client of the chance to know all of her own experience, and impede her movement to wholeness.

Fundamentally, the interventions suggested in this book are predicated on the belief that it is the client's responsibility to manage her own behavior and the helping professional's responsibility to assist in that process through various noncoercive means. It is not the professional's responsibility to control the client's body (nor is it entirely possible in most situations) (Burstow 1992). It is not a clinician's responsibility to stop the client's self-injury overall. There may be moments when the clinician intervenes, or works with client to make a change. These situations are addressed in subsequent chapters. The fundamental point here is that as helpers we need to maintain clarity about where our power and responsibility rest.

Claiming Our Own Power to Benefit the Client

It is essential that as clinicians we stand in our own power in our work with clients. Working to avoid re-creating "power-over" interactions doesn't mean we give up our power and accede mindlessly to the client's power. This simply flips the victim–victimizer roles; it doesn't shift the basic dynamic. Instead, we need to recognize and accept our inherent power in our position as therapists and use our power thoughtfully and specifically to aid in the client's recovery and healing.

The task we face is placing our power and responsibility in the right places. Too often, as therapists—either due to training or lack of awareness, or because we really want to help someone—we use power unfairly and take responsibility for things that aren't ours to manage. Or, conversely, in an effort to respect clients' power, we may abandon clients to their struggles and pain by *not* using our power or taking responsibility in ways that can help the client more effectively heal or change.

Here is an example, from the end of a therapy session, of a therapist's taking responsibility to manage what isn't his to manage:

Client: I don't think I am going to do very well this week. Already I feel like I am going to have to hurt myself tonight.

Therapist: Do you mean cut yourself?

Client: Yes. The pain just feels too great. I know we have worked to put away some of the feelings and I don't think there is anything else I can do right now. I just have that strong feeling that I might need to cut.

Therapist: Do you think you need to go to the hospital?

Client: No, I'm not saying that. I just needed to tell you. It sometimes relieves the pressure.

Therapist: Well, I'm concerned. It's hard to hear that you might cut yourself. What can we do to stop you from cutting?

Client: I don't think there's anything you can do. I just needed to tell you. I thought you wanted me to tell you if I felt the urge.

Therapist: I do. But I feel a responsibility to help you stay safe. What can we do about this?

Client: (*starting to get angry*) I don't want you to do anything. You're not going to put me in the hospital, are you? Forget I said anything.

Therapist: No, I don't want to take you to the hospital. But I think we need to come up with a plan so you won't hurt yourself.

In this example, the therapist is concerned and acts from a well-meaning place. However, he has an unbalanced sense of responsibility. He believes he is responsible for controlling the client's actions toward her body. With the therapist operating from this position, the interaction is likely to escalate into a greater power struggle between the therapist and client, who is already overloaded from the work done in the session and the emotional pain she is feeling. Let's look at an alternative interaction:

Client: I don't think I am going to do very well this week. Already I feel like I am going to have to hurt myself tonight.

Therapist: Do you mean cut yourself?

Client: Yes. The pain just feels too great. I know we have worked to put away some of the feelings and I don't think there is anything else I can do right now. I just have that strong feeling that I might need to cut.

Therapist: I see. That must be difficult.

Client: Well, yes. Well, I just thought I should tell you.

Therapist: Did you think I needed to know for any particular reason?

Client: Uh, I don't know. I just thought I should say something.

Therapist: Okay. I hope you take care of yourself.

Client: Oh, I will. I always do. There's no one else who can, really.

Therapist: Well, ultimately, you're right. It does come down to that, even though we can sometimes get help from others. We are ultimately on our own.

Client: Well, okay. I'll see you next week.

Therapist: Take it easy.

This therapist has taken the opposite approach. He may care about how the client is coping, but he is much less engaged, so it is harder to know if he is concerned about the client. He doesn't seem to feel responsible for ensuring that the client doesn't cut herself, but he also doesn't seem to feel responsible to help the client with her pain or to find alternatives either. He has stepped to the other extreme of professional disengagement. Let's look at a third interaction, again starting from the same place:

Client: I don't think I am going to do very well this week. Already I feel like I am going to have to hurt myself tonight.

Therapist: Do you mean cut yourself?

Client: Yes. The pain just feels too great. I know we have worked to put away some of the feelings and I don't think there is anything else I can do right now. I just have that strong feeling that I might need to cut.

Therapist: Hard place, huh? (*client nods*) We did a lot today. I know we have talked in the past about other alternatives. Do you want to talk more about what might be helpful, another option?

Client: I don't think there is anything else to do right now. I still have the list we came up with about things I can do if I feel I need to cut. You know I am always careful when I cut. I will have bandages and towels and Neosporin ready. I will be safe. And I don't want to do it. I really don't. It's been about six months since the last time. I think I just needed to say that I might. It sort of relieves the pressure just to say it.

Therapist: I hope you don't have to cut. I am glad you told me about feeling like you might have to, and I do hope you can find other ways to manage. I'm sorry you are in so much pain. Is there anything else you need from me before you go, anything that might help?

Client: Not really. I guess it just helps to know you care. Sometimes that makes a difference and I am able to remember that when I feel I just *have* to cut.

Therapist: I do care, and I believe things can be different in the future. Please take care of yourself.

In this example, the therapist's concern is also directly stated (as in the first example), but it is not overlaid with the therapist's anxiety about managing the client's behavior. In this example, he accepts that the client may cut. He does not feel impelled to stop her. He is then able to help the client hear his caring, which she states may make a difference. At the same time, he is also able to stay engaged, takes responsibility to explore the client's need to discuss alternatives to cutting and other things the client may feel would help, and offers hope about the future being different in terms of pain. Most importantly, in the long run, he preserves the sense of caring and respect within the relationship. He stays appropriately engaged with the client. This will enable the client to heal the underlying wounds and get relief from her pain.

Finding the Right Balance

Organizational consultant White (1992) once described these varied interactions in the context of the dilemmas we face in maintaining appropriate boundaries, one expression of power dynamics. In addressing the degree of engagement and intimacy we allow in the therapeutic relationship, he sketched therapist–client interaction on a continuum ranging from abandonment to enmeshment. Figure 6–1 is a graphic representation of this continuum. Not surprisingly, the two extremes of this continuum reflect the two types of countertransference errors Wilson and Lindy (1994a) identify as common to therapists working with trauma survivors: type I is described as detachment and withdrawal, and type II as enmeshment and over-involvement.

In the center is the safety zone where we are least likely to cause harm. There, we don't risk enmeshment or abandonment. This safety zone may also be so safe that the necessary tension required to help the client make a shift in his way of perceiving the world is absent. We may decide to move into the danger zone in either direction (to-

Figure 6–1. The continuum of intimate contact in therapeutic relationships.

ward enmeshment or abandonment) in order to heighten the tension, thereby engaging the client's issues with some potency. For example, a client who has a hard time believing anyone cares about her may never be able to shift that schema as long we remain in the safety zone of neutral, pleasant professionalism. She may need us to be personally connected, expose some part of who we are, and demonstrate that she exists as a person to us. Sometimes this shift is made by a simple statement like, "I thought of you the other day when I saw the PBS program on lighthouses. I wondered if you saw it. I know how much you like them. Some of the footage was beautiful." This communicates that she exists for me outside the therapy hour and is therefore a person (not "just" a client) and is someone who could be liked. Other times, the shift may be more dramatic. We may need to address clients' direct questions about liking them, or respond to their wondering about who we are as a person.

However, the risk we take by entering either danger zone is moving too far inadvertently into the end zone of abandonment or enmeshment. We may feel pulled into clients' reenactments too readily, become overly identified, or try to protect clients from their losses. In the preceding example, if I moved too far and became enmeshed, it might look like this: every time I see a lighthouse I think of my client, make a point of telling her I have been thinking of her, bring her a tape of the program, or a small lighthouse whenever I travel, and ask if she feels that I like her. In doing all these things I have crossed the line and entered into an enmeshed position inside her struggle to be likable. I am not allowing enough space for the client to grapple with her needs. I am then working to "fix" the client, rather than offering her a place to do her own reparative or transformative work. Whenever we operate at either end of the continuum, we are misusing our power as helpers and detracting from the possible healing value of the relationship.

The key is finding the optimal degree of proximity, where I am engaged and present at my edges, but not slipping over the line into the client's internal experience, or trying to rescue her from her internal dilemmas, or working to get my own needs met at the client's expense. Ehrenberg (1992) describes this as the "intimate edge," where the quality of the contact is the essential element. As clinicians, the challenge is to walk that delicate line where we engage significantly enough so the client begins to change her experience of "other," thus increasing trust and safety, but not engaging to the extent that we prevent the client from grieving earlier losses and deprivation, or attaining a realistic view of caregivers and others. The complexity of this challenge is heightened by the fact that the optimal level of proximity varies with the client. There is no set line.

Defining a Way to Relate

Setting out a general framework within which to conceptualize our relationships with clients can ground us, allowing a greater ease when facing more complex decisions about power. By general framework, I mean some fundamental values and parameters that define the character of how I interact. This framework holds and contains my interactions with clients, allowing me the freedom to be present and engaged.

I work to create a relationship that is real, clear, clean, and honest. This counters the dynamics and qualities of an abusive relationship that can be described as, at some level, unreal, confusing, dirty (particularly for survivors of sexual abuse), and tricky. (The element of trickery is always at least covert in abusive relationships, with things not appearing as they really are, often with someone who is a caregiver engaging in hurtful behavior. Sometimes the trick is overt: "If you keep this secret, I'll get you new clothes or give you candy, or let you go out with your boyfriend.")

Being real, clear, clean, and honest means, in a nutshell, two things: a willingness to be highly engaged and intimate within specific boundaries or limits, and a willingness to be direct about these limits with honest, caring affect and a validation of the client's needs. Clear limits about what I can and cannot do or tolerate gives me the room to be highly engaged. If I anticipate the client will need more from me than I can give (as is often the case), and I am unaware of this anxiety or cannot comfortably tolerate saying no to someone, then I am likely to pull back and maintain an interpersonal distance as a general stance. If I am clear about where I start and stop, and know how I will manage certain requests or needs, then I don't have to spend energy on anticipatory anxiety, with the resultant disengagement from the client. If I am honest, own my limits, and acknowledge the reasonableness of the client's need, the client is much more likely to be able to accept the limit and move to another solution in meeting his need.

Let's say a client is distressed at the end of the session. I ask her what would be helpful in grounding her until we meet again. She replies, "If I could talk with you every day, I would feel better. I just need to be in touch with you." There may be rare occasions when I believe it would be helpful for a client to have daily contact with me. For the most part, though, I don't think that kind of dependency is useful. It communicates that I am the person who keeps the client safe and grounded, and it shifts the responsibility for the client's process to me.

At the same time I recognize the legitimacy of the client's need to have someone be there for her, based on her childhood of inconsistent caregivers and isolation, and that asking for contact with me is a big risk for her. She is asking from a "child place." I need to honor and respect her need, while I simultaneously support and encourage her adult capacity to care for herself, as well as respect my own boundaries and needs in the situation. Further, I know that if I agree to talk with her every day I would begin to resent it. (As an aside, resentment is a sign that something is out of balance. It signifies to me that I have somehow slipped in my effort to keep responsibility in the right place, or that I am overwhelmed and not attending in a larger way to my own needs.)

So, my response to this client might sound something like this: "It makes sense to me that you feel calling me every day would help. It might—in the immediate moment. But, you know, I guess I worry that it probably wouldn't be good in the long run because I can't always be there. And there are days when phone calls are hard for me to manage. So, how about this. I'm wondering if it would help if we checked in once before our next session. Would that be useful? [client assents] And let's also make a list of what other things might help. Is there someone else you could check in with to get grounded? What about your friend Mary? What else do you think might help?"

These statements need to be said in a straightforward and kind tone of voice, and paced to allow for the client's nonverbal (or verbal) response. I blow it if I say the above and it sounds like a canned intervention, or I come across as condescending, or I am emotionally disengaged. My genuine affection and respect need to be present in my demeanor and my voice. For some clients, I might also acknowledge that I realize they took a risk in asking for what they needed, and I really appreciate their willingness to risk.

Generally, if clients feel heard and acknowledged in their need in a way that is nonshaming, and they sense I am being honest with them, they are then able to mobilize themselves to work to identify other options. If they don't trust that I am real and clean in my dealings with them, they are likely to have a harder time shifting gears and letting go of their request. They may persist, seeking validation of their need by demanding action on my part. This is a situation ripe for escalation into what often feels to therapists like manipulation. Caring, direct communication, as well as clarity about responsibility and limits, helps minimize the likelihood of escalating into a power struggle.

Supporting Clients to Be Responsible for Their Own Process

The healing process is the clients' journey. They are in charge of how it happens, how quickly it happens, where they go with it. To claim ownership can be frightening. For some clients, it feels absolutely overwhelming to be responsible for making things different. These clients need education about this concept, verbal support that they have the capacity to be in charge of and for themselves, and concrete help in identifying manageable therapeutic tasks. They then can begin to see that the process is their own, not something I am imposing from the outside.

Our clarity as clinicians about where responsibility lies is crucial in helping clients develop and/or maintain a sense of responsibility for themselves, their healing journey, and their life choices. We acknowledge their responsibility when we support clients to be the ones to make healing-related decisions such as whether or not to attend a support group or how frequently to come to therapy. This is also reinforced when we support their life decisions such as where to live, who to live with, and whether or not to take an offered but stressful promotion. It is not our job to make decisions about the client's life or decide what should happen next. It is our job to be very present and engaged, tracking what the client is telling us and sharing information, observations, concerns, and possible solutions. This helps the client make more informed decisions.

For example, I could outline a plan for a client to help him address his current self-injury of burning himself after engaging in sexual contact and to recover from the sexual abuse in his past. I might say he should (1) come to therapy weekly, (2) keep a journal and identify his feelings, (3) attend a support group for male survivors, (4) tell his partner to let him initiate all sexual contact between them for six months, and (5) write a therapeutic letter to his uncle who abused him. I might be "right" in that all of these interventions or approaches may have value and could be useful in his healing process. However, by dictating this treatment plan I am presuming to know what is best for him. This tells him that I am in charge of his recovery. It gives him a message that he is a passive recipient of my healing powers or professional experience.

After an initial consult, or when clients are in crisis, this avenue might be comfortable or feel appropriate for us as therapists. It might be what we feel managed care and insurance companies are requiring us to do. The danger, however, lies in setting up a dynamic in which the therapist becomes responsible for the client's process. This can come back to haunt the therapeutic relationship when clients are working on issues related to personal power, assertion, and locus of control. How can we expect clients to operate from an internal locus of control, assert themselves, or exercise appropriate personal power if we don't encourage this behavior and perception in our relationships with them from the beginning?

Instead of taking charge (i.e., taking over), I can be responsible and powerful in how well I listen to the client's concerns, share resources and information, and ask good questions. Returning to the previous example, I could share with him that I think coming to therapy every week might be useful right now, even though I know money is tight, because I sense that he is in a lot of pain and needs support. Or I could say that I think negotiating with his partner to feel more control regarding sexual contact might help him feel less triggered and overwhelmed. I could suggest any of the other ideas as possible approaches for either now or later. I could ask him what he thinks would feel most helpful today, or what he needs right now. I could ask him what he feels is his next step. I could ask him how he would feel most supported, given the options we discussed. All of these possible interventions or responses offer a direction and help (thereby fulfilling my professional duty), but also communicate that the process is his and he is the one who will decide what he needs to do.

A central element in our job as helping professionals is to ask good questions and not get caught feeling we have to have the answers. Our job is to ask the questions and support the client to generate possible answers, letting the client know we believe he can make a good decision. Such an approach embodies the belief that the process belongs to the client. In most situations (barring some forms of psychosis and extreme danger), clients do make good decisions if they have enough support and adequate, accurate information about their options and themselves.

Concretizing Trustworthiness

One way we can implement a consciousness about power in the therapy relationship is to be trustworthy. This demonstrates a fair use of our power by displaying a sense of stewardship about the relationship. It also communicates respect, one element of expressed interpersonal power.

It is unusual for clients to enter therapy trusting the therapist, particularly if they were wounded in childhood. They often have good reasons *not* to trust others. Simply because they tell us intimate things, rely on us, and ask for advice doesn't mean they trust us. We should not confuse need with trust, as need often drives the client's willingness to risk disclosure or ask for help.

Even if clients don't trust us, that doesn't obviate the need for us to be trustworthy. In fact, being trustworthy is the most effective method we have of helping clients develop the capacity to trust. How do people learn to trust? We have consistent experiences with others who are dependable and predictable. We interact with others who display by their behavior that they are worthy of our trust. We learn over time we can count on them, that they are reliable.

Being dependable in concrete ways communicates trustworthiness. This means we need to follow through on commitments. If we offer to copy an article for a client, we need to do so before the next appointment. We return phone calls within a reasonable time. Not returning a call sends a message that the other person doesn't matter, even if this is not the actual reason for the belatedness. Some clients conclude that we don't want to talk to them when we don't return calls. If indeed we resent the call or don't want to talk with them, then we need to figure out what is going on for ourselves rather than act it out by not returning the call. Are we simply on overload? Is this a client with whom we aren't suited to work? Does our resentment suggest some unfinished business from the last session, or an underlying issue in the therapy? We need to address the issue with ourselves first and then, if necessary, with the client in an appropriate manner.

An additional way we can concretize trustworthiness is to be on time for appointments. Setting an appointment time is an agreement. Lateness is a betrayal of that agreement. By being late, we communicate that we don't mean what we say. It suggests that whatever kept us from being on time is more important than the appointment with the client. If we are unavoidably detained, as happens in real life, common courtesy requires that we apologize, simply but genuinely. And we work to minimize future tardiness.

Answering Honestly

Another aspect of being trustworthy is telling the truth when asked a direct question. This does not mean disclosing everything related to the client's question. (A subsequent section in this chapter addresses boundaries and self-disclosure.) This does mean answering honestly both the literal or concrete question as well as the spirit of the question without overwhelming the client. A guiding perspective is to stay honest within the context of what is helpful to the client, including an acknowledgment of our affective responses. An example of this:

Client: (*somewhat resentfully*) I felt you were mad at me last
week. (*Silence*)

Therapist: Did you? I didn't feel mad.

Client: It was the way you said the stuff at the end about
wanting something my mother never gave me. It felt like
you were mad at me.

Therapist: I didn't feel mad, though I think I may have
sounded short or irritated.

Client: I knew it. I knew you were irritated with me. Was
it so bad that I wanted that stuff I never got from my
mother? I really was just talking about you and me. You
always tell me to say what I need and so I did and then
you didn't like it.

Therapist: You know, you're right. I do encourage you to
ask for what you need and I am glad you did. I think I
was tired and it was the end of the session and I felt I
couldn't get into all of what I thought was happening,
so I got irritated and short. I'm sorry. I didn't mean to
be irritated.

Client: (*silent for a moment*) Okay. (*Less upset*) I just didn't
understand. It seemed to me that talking about what I
needed is what I should be doing. I know you can't give
me everything I didn't get as a child. Sometimes I just
need to be able to say it, you know?

If we can honor and acknowledge what is real and
true in our interaction, we afford our clients a better
chance to identify what aspects of the interaction comes
from old sources. If I deny my irritation in the example
given above, then two things happen. First, I reenact with
the client a relationship in which she is unable to know
what is really happening for me (within the context of our
relationship). This perpetuates her difficulty with the sorting process of mine and yours. The other person remains

an enigma, someone who is unknowable and emotionally inaccessible.

Second, I am likely to provoke (understandable) frustration at my denial and what feels at some level like a lack of help. This frustration often leads to an escalation of a struggle over who is right about what really happened. The therapist becomes focused on her belief that what is going on for the client is about the past (which it *is* to a large extent in this example) and getting the client to see and acknowledge this. The client is similarly focused on trying to get the therapist to see and acknowledge the therapist's behavior, and has no room to look at the past. A power struggle ensues and both end up feeling like they are fighting with the other and don't know why it has to be that way.

Central to this level of honesty is the qualifier "within the context of what is good for the client." Again using the above example, what might be true is that the demands of the client evoke an old feeling of not being good enough for the therapist, a feeling with roots in her own childhood of criticism and parental alcoholism. She (the therapist) then reacts shortly, her irritation at a request occurring in the last five minutes of the session covering her sense of helplessness about not being able to ever respond effectively (she feels). Telling the client all of that is not useful. This is not really what the client is asking. What the client wants is to know is if the therapist was indeed upset or did she imagine this. Most clients do not want to know the therapist's process; they just want to know they can count on the therapist to sort and own her stuff, and be present and available to the client.

Strean (1999) discusses the importance of engagement by the therapist in modeling the disclosure of negative feelings. These responses are not only honest and validating, but serve to build a more solid therapeutic alliance, particularly with clients who struggle with interpersonal relationships.

> When the format of the therapy changes to a two-person psychology wherein the patients emotionally perceive that they have an obvious impact on the therapist, their self-esteem rises and they feel less hostile and more friendly toward the practitioner. Observing that the practitioner emotionally reacts to them and sometimes quite strongly seems to induce in these patients the feeling that they are indeed a "somebody" and, as at least four of the patients stated or implied, "You really care" (p. 137).

Asking for Feedback

One of the most informative and powerful ways we can shift the power dynamics in therapeutic relationships is to ask clients to let us know when something isn't helpful. My goal as a helping professional is to be helpful. If I am doing things that don't help, then I want to know so I can make some changes in how I approach this particular client.

When clients tell us something we have done or said is unhelpful, then we need to listen and find a way to be more helpful. This may mean exploring more about what was unhelpful and why. What was the client's experience of a certain comment or interaction or suggestion? Was it the content or the style? Often, the manner we say something communicates a disregard for the client's perceptions or experiences. Did it feel out of context? Did the client simply not understand the intervention?

Here is an example of where I made a mistake and the client's feedback was crucial to my understanding:

> A client mentioned at the end of the session that she felt that she would have to go home and self-injure. I responded by saying, "Well, you could do that. Or you could do something else." I felt she wanted me to somehow step in and save her, or talk her out of injuring herself, so I took a low-key, pulled-back position in an effort to avoid a power struggle or a reenactment of her desire for rescue (a recurring theme). I could tell by her body language that she was hurt by what I said, and we talked a little about what I meant and what she needed. I felt a little unsettled but knew we were out of time. I also trusted that she would bring me feedback if we needed to do more in sorting out the interaction.
>
> At the next session, she told me that she thought I misperceived her intent with the comment about going home and injuring. She was trying to let me know how bad she felt in that moment and her comment was the best she could do; she felt at a loss for words. What she needed was for me to be empathetic, acknowledge how bad she was feeling, and offer some support. Clearly, in retrospect, I was reacting from my own feelings of helplessness in that moment (it was the end of the session, and talking about the pull to self-injure and other coping options was something we had done on more than one occasion). I felt helpless in that moment, and so I reacted to part of what was going on (she *did* want to be rescued) but ignored the main thrust of what she was trying to tell me. We had a conversation about how I feel helpless sometimes, I apologized for misreading her comment, and we talked a little about how we can have different interactions in the future.

Modeling Positive Uses of Power

As noted earlier, the victim-victimizer power dynamic remains the most familiar model of power for many clients
and for many therapists. In this dynamic, one person has
power and uses it to take advantage of someone who does
not have power (or has substantially less power). This frame
is simplistic but deeply engrained for many people. Related
to this is the concept of limited power: "If I have *this* much,
you can only have *this* much. If I take it all, you have
none."

One of the ways we can help clients shift their understanding of power dynamics is to teach and model positive
uses of power. The concept of expanding power—the idea
that there is enough to go around and we can both have
some—can be overtly taught and modeled. If we demonstrate power that is assertive, nonvictimizing, and respectful of boundaries, we offer clients a different experience of
personal power. When combined with encouraging clients
to claim and express their own power, we create a model
within the relationship that embodies the concept of expanding and shared power.

Another way of describing this dynamic is to operate
from the position or attitude of "power-with," wherein both
the client and I can feel and use our power in appropriate ways for her growth. This is in contrast with a frame
that endorses either limited power ("If I have it, there's
none for you") or "power-over" ("Let me tell you what you
need and how to change your life").

Such an approach can be conceptualized as a mutual
collaborator model. Various theoretical approaches espouse
the value of collaboration. Burstow (1992) specifically suggests the idea of the therapist as "co-investigator" or "co-
explorer" (p. 192) when working with self-injuring clients

to understand the meaning and history of their self-injury. The key to genuine collaboration lies in the therapist's capacity to bring mutuality, shared power, and respect to all interactions, and be willing to be a teacher with the client about collaboration, as well as a student who learns from the client about what works best.

Encouraging and Respecting Clients' Choices

Earlier in this chapter I mentioned the importance of respecting clients' choices as a method for communicating client ownership of the change process. The potency of encouraging choice-making is often underestimated. Directly supporting clients to make choices and decisions is a strong behavioral message about their own power and capacity to make changes in their lives.

Such encouragement in the context of the therapy itself is a valuable tool. We can invite clients to sit where they prefer in the office or counseling room. We can tell them they are free to walk around or sit on the floor if that is helpful to them. We can ask them what time of day or what day of the week is best for appointments and try to accommodate their schedules. When applicable, we can let them decide what they want to do with artwork they produce in the session ("What would you like to do with your picture? Would you like to take it home? Do you want me to keep it here?").

We can be overt in encouraging them to make choices in the session. These statements and questions offer clear communication about the client's right to choose and to set the pace: "This is your time—how do you want to use it?" "What would you like to do today?" "You don't have to talk about this now." "What do you need today?" All of

these interventions support the client to increase his awareness that this process is his and he is determining what will
happen next.

Relatedly, we need to be real about choices clients
don't have and empathize with their feelings about the
lack of choice. Clients have no choice regarding when I
go on vacation, or when and where I move my office, for
example. I can, however, provide space for their feelings
about these matters. Waiting until the end of a session
to tell a client who is currently struggling with difficult issues in therapy or who has significant anxiety about loss
that I am going on vacation in a few weeks is probably not
a good decision. I need to let such a client know about
my vacation earlier in the session so there is time for her
to recognize and express her feelings, and for us to process the meaning of my being away in the context of her
work.

Support for clients' choices is also communicated
when we value the choices they do make in their lives,
even if we don't, at first glance, see their choice in the
same light they do. For example, we may believe that a
client living with her parents and brother will function
better if she moves out on her own. After discussing her
options in the previous session, she comes in and says she
has made an important change: she told her brother that
she is not going to wash his clothes any more. If we are
focused on our belief that she needs to move out, we are
going to miss an opportunity to support her in her choice
to set a limit with her brother. She *is* making choices for
herself and effecting power in her relationship with her
brother, even if she is not electing to move out at this
time. In the long run, being able to join with her in her
decision making and encourage her choice is going to
help her make whatever other changes are in her best

interest. Sometimes this means we have to reframe our clients' choices so we can see them as our clients do, in all the fullness of their meaning.

The Hard Part of Respecting Clients' Choices

Sometimes clients make choices we don't like. I am not talking about simple preferences in taste or style. I am referring to decisions like choosing to remain with an abusive partner or in a job where she is underutilized and mistreated. These decisions are ones where I may have to work hard at giving up the notion that I really do know what is best for my client. This doesn't mean I can't or don't share my opinions, even when they are quite divergent from my client's perspective. Or that I don't share concerns for safety and well-being. If I simply accept what my client says is her choice, I fail my client. It may appear that such acquiescence and acceptance is support, but in fact I do clients a disservice if I simply agree.

Such moments offer a chance to use my power in a responsible and clear manner, drawing on my knowledge and being direct about my difference of opinion. Communicating my concern and difference of opinion noncoercively and with heart can be a challenge. It is tempting to try to convince someone to change her mind when we feel much is at stake. The most responsible thing we can do, however, is be direct. Again, in the big picture, this is much more useful for my client because I offer her real information free of a hidden, semiconscious investment in wishing she would make a particular choice. This is modeling positive power. Then, once I have said my piece, I have to let it go and truly offer the best support I can.

Not surprisingly, in fact, when I am able to offer additional information or a perspective clients haven't considered, they sometimes change their decision. The key is to share honest concern directly ("I am having a hard time with your decision because I am worried about your safety") and real information in a way that clients don't feel shamed, inadequate, or coerced ("As you know, many women find that although their partners intend to change, violent behavior is ingrained and change only happens if he really wants to change. I hope Frank is able to do that."). The element of respect is central. This paradoxical approach loses its value if it is used as an approach devoid of genuine interpersonal relatedness. We must truly believe that clients know their circumstances best, and remind ourselves that they are indeed the ones who will live with the consequences of their choices.

Sharing Therapeutic Dilemmas

Another way we can work to balance the power in the therapeutic relationship is to share therapeutic dilemmas with the client directly, without blaming. Impasses, conflicts within the client that are enacted within the relationship (e.g., wanting help and not being able to accept help), and conflicts between client needs and system needs are all opportunities, if managed with care. Identifying these as problems for the client and therapist to collaboratively solve in a way that feels nonblaming can be very fruitful and satisfying, avoiding a power struggle that feels unsettling to both. In bringing such dilemmas to clients, we as therapists appropriately take responsibility for raising an issue without taking undue responsibility for finding the answer or solution, and maintain a respect for the client's capacity to solve his own problems.

A classic example of such a dilemma occurred in an inpatient setting:

Amanda, a patient with significant self-injuring behavior, suicidality, and complicated relationships with staff, was scheduled to leave the hospital on a day pass. Two nights before she was to go out for the day with her husband, she told John (a staff person she liked) that she planned to attempt suicide while out on pass by taking pills—and asked John not to tell anyone. John brought this information to the treatment team meeting the next morning and we discussed how to manage the situation.

The team was aware that Amanda would feel betrayed and set up if told she couldn't go out on pass, and, at the same time, knew we could not legally and ethically permit her to leave the hospital the next day without a solid safety plan in place. Prior history with Amanda (this was not her first hospitalization here) suggested that being told to do a safety plan would also prompt a strong reaction from her that she was being punished, and was not trusted or supported by staff. We also anticipated that she would state she felt betrayed by John for telling the treatment team about her plan.

We wanted to avoid a power struggle. And we wanted her to be able to go out the next day, but needed reassurance that she would be safe. So, our approach (John and I did this together) involved sitting down with the patient and telling her directly that John had told us about her plan to take pills. I stated that John did the right thing, because we all wanted her to be safe and that we believe she did too and that is why she told John about her plan. We said we didn't know what to do, because we really wanted her to be able to go out on pass, but we were in a bind. The hospital policy and our own sense of ethics dictated that we had to be sure she would be safe, since she was in our care. What did she think should happen?

Amanda looked at us, seemingly surprised that she wasn't getting yelled at for splitting staff and causing trouble, and said, "I really do want to go out tomorrow. How about if I work on a safety plan today and we can discuss it?" She said she wasn't upset with John for telling, and that she understood our responsibility. She was scared about leaving the hospital but she really did want to try going out. She was also scared about the pills she had stashed at home. She then spent an hour or two on a safety plan. She listed the need to give her husband the pills as soon as they got there, her plan to be in the same room with him at all times on the visit, and her idea to tell him about her fears and former plan with the pills in a meeting with the social worker at the hospital when he came to pick her up. She also incorporated several ideas for managing her feelings and staying grounded.

We couldn't have come up with a better plan ourselves. And, best of all, she felt successful and less fearful. She was directly asking for the kind of help and support she needed. She went out on pass and followed her plan. She had a good day with her husband. Her interactions on the unit after that were more direct and self-initiating, especially when specifically supported and complimented by staff for doing so well in making behavioral shifts.

Being able to sit with the dilemma and not force a solution is central to effectively collaborating with clients. We are often tempted to find a solution, either to relieve our own discomfort or because we feel pressed for time. The actual problem solving that occurs is more significant than simply resolving the current dilemma. Usually, such dilemmas are representative of common, recurrent issues for the client. Even if the dilemma is unique and not representative, it is an opportunity for clients to improve problem-solving skills and embrace self-responsibility within the context of a supportive relationship. Such conditions bode well for enhancing self-esteem and internalizing a realistic locus of control.

Being Overt If We Agree to Act as an Authority Figure

There are times when clients may need us to take specific responsibility for tracking something or encouraging them to address an issue they tend to avoid. If this occurs at the client's request ("Would you please help me stay on track with this issue about my mother over the next month or so? I really want to resolve it."), it is clear that we are agreeing to manage a process element for the client. Often, clients' desire for this kind of help is not as direct or obvious as a simple request. They may consistently bring up an issue at the end of the session and say they are frustrated about not getting to it sooner.

One intervention we can employ is to ask if they would like our help remembering to bring it up earlier in the session. If we just take on the responsibility without directly clarifying this role, we covertly shift the power dynamics. We take on the task of managing the client's process without agreement. If we offer to help, and make the help explicit, we maintain a respect for the client as the one in charge and serve as a helper to the client. This subtle difference matters, particularly when it is repeated over time and becomes part of the fabric of ongoing interaction. Again, responsibility rests in the right place, thus allowing change to occur.

A simple example:

A client consistently raises a concern, at the end of the sessions, about her uncle's treatment of her. The third time it happens, I make a comment about how I noticed that this issue tends to come up just before she is leaving. She smiles, and says, yes, she is aware of that but it feels too hard to bring it up earlier. She says she really wants to talk about her feelings regarding her uncle because she will be seeing him next month at a family gathering. I ask her if she would like me to remind her about it earlier in the session next time. She says, yes, that would help because she really wants to talk about it. I agree to do so, and make a note to myself so I won't forget. The following week, I will wait for her to set out the issues for the session, giving her a chance to bring up the topic of her uncle herself. If she does not do so within the first ten or fifteen minutes, I will then remind her that she wanted me to mention the issue of her uncle while there was still time to address it.

Asking my client if she would like me to remind her next week communicates that it is her choice and I am here to help. If I ask her if she wants to talk about her uncle next week, and then simply remind her without having the interchange about her desire for me to remind her, I create a precedent where I am the one who is responsible for determining what she needs to address in therapy. I have missed a chance to reinforce the idea that the work we do together is *her* process. Also, if I jump in right away as soon as we sit down, I also preclude her having the opportunity to introduce the topic on her own. In my experience, once we have made an agreement that I will bring up something the following week, many clients actually feel supported enough to remember on their own.

Reframing Contracts

Some people find contracts useful as a way to manage their own behavior. I tend to be careful with contracts specifically regarding self-injury because of the likelihood that the self-injury will recur until the underlying issues are resolved, and to contract to not self-injure may create more shame when the person "fails" (i.e., self-injures). The complexities of contracts regarding self-injury, and some parameters for their cautious use, are outlined in Chapter 7. The issue addressed here is about the importance of noticing power and responsibility in the context of contracts in general.

A behavior contract is a contract the client makes with herself. She is agreeing to do or not do something because she believes it is in her best interest. Talking it through, clarifying the terms, writing it down, and even signing it with her therapist present may be a crucial aspect of setting the contract in place. However, the therapist needs to be aware that the contract is not between the client and the therapist—rather, the therapist is a witness to the client's contract with herself. Contracts are only between the therapist and client when each person is agreeing to a certain code of behavior or something interactional that they mutually decide. If the behavior the contract is describing is relevant only to the client, then the therapist need not be a party to the agreement, but instead should offer to be a witness.

Sometimes an informal contract occurs in a simple, spontaneous way. For example, the following interaction occurred after a discussion of the client's behavior in Alcoholic Anonymous meetings, and her desire to stop being so triggered in meetings:

Client: Okay. I promise that I will pay attention to my reactions in meetings when I get the impulse to just walk
out. My goal will be to stay longer than I have in the
past, and try to track what is triggered for me. I'll take
my little notebook and write things down. I am making
a commitment to do this at every meeting I go to this
week, and I will plan to go to four meetings. Agreed?

Therapist: Does that feel right? If so, I support you and I
will be a witness to this deal you are making, because you
are making this with yourself, not me.

Client: Well, I was making the promise to you. But I guess
I see what you mean.

Therapist: I know you felt you were making the promise to
me, but really, I think it's yourself you want to promise
to. You want to do this for you. That's what is important
—it's really not about doing it for me. Even though I
agree with you that what you're proposing would probably be a good idea and I support you.

Client: Okay, it's a deal.

Attending to Our Language:
A Powerful Indicator of Beliefs

As stated at the beginning of this chapter, how we position
ourselves, what stance we take, and how we are with clients
reflect our fundamental beliefs about therapeutic work.
These beliefs inform, create, and mold all of our interventions. Awareness of our underlying beliefs gives us greater
choice and flexibility in our behavior with clients. One of
the ways we can increase our awareness of our underlying
beliefs is to listen to our language. The words we use directly with clients—as well as the words we use in reference
to clients in reports, in discussions with colleagues, and in

our thoughts about clients—communicate these values and beliefs, including our attitudes about power.

How we introduce ourselves to clients (e.g., Dr. Connors, Robin, or Dr. Robin) communicates something about title, position, and power. Exactly what it communicates will vary with each person, each setting, each client, and the speaker's accompanying demeanor. But it says something, and we need to be certain that we are indeed communicating what we want to be communicating. How we describe the therapy process, how we articulate limits, and how we let clients know our general procedures all tell clients things about how we view power. This is not problematic. It just underscores the need to bring awareness to our language, since the use of words is generally our primary therapeutic vehicle.

In the mental health field, there are an array of commonly used words and phrases that communicate blame (unintentionally, one assumes) to clients. Blame ensues from a one-up power position. It says, "I know what's true here and it's your fault/responsibility that . . ." Or, "If you would just do this, then your life and symptoms would improve." We don't consciously intend to blame. More often, the implication of blame is the result of professionals' unconscious management of our own feelings of helplessness. (This dynamic is explored in more detail in Chapters 10 and 11.)

A common example of blame-to-allay-helplessness is the casual comment, "She's so borderline." Generally, when this is said about a client, it is because the speaker feels or anticipates feeling overwhelmed by what he believes this client needs. It may also be because the client's interactional style, combined with intense or fluctuating affect, telegraphs her wounding and unmet needs. Anxiety about these clients, commonly expressed in jokes or warnings, ripple through mental health settings, often before a worker even has a chance to develop a relationship with the client.

The use of pejorative language is a power act, an effort to regain a sense of control (via blaming) when feeling out of control or overwhelmed. Though perhaps different in magnitude, the act is still a power act such as that utilized by abusers. Batterers and child molesters are doing the same thing—trying to get control over feelings of powerlessness by taking advantage of or physically controlling someone else (Dutton 1995). Our seemingly casual language of blame re-creates the same abuse dynamics within the therapeutic relationship.

Manipulation: A Popular Word

Other words and phrases float around mental health settings to create a less than conducive environment for clients, often alienating them at a subtle level and interrupting or precluding a good therapeutic alliance. At times, these words and the accompanying unconscious use of power can be directly insulting or work counter to stated therapeutic goals. One example is *manipulation*. Manipulation is simply getting needs met in an indirect manner. Because the method is indirect, the person expected to meet the need often feels tricked and feels the interaction was unfair. It probably was. What we as clinicians need to remember is that this person apparently has not developed other effective methods for getting her needs met. As Burstow (1992) says when speaking of women who self-injure, "If their direct communication of neediness had been taken in throughout their lives and been responded to caringly, they would not now be communicating indirectly" (p. 195).

Helping such clients learn more direct ways to get needs met is part of our job. One of the skills we can bring to this process of teaching new skills is to be as direct, clear, and nonshaming as possible when giving feedback about our interactions with clients. When people feel shamed, they are less likely to feel they have enough room to change their behavior. A shame-filled space is not one in which any of us generally feels able to embrace our inadequacies and adopt new behavior. So when we tell a client that we had a hard time with how they asked for contact, for example, we need to be direct but kind, and manage our tone of voice well. In so doing, we provide good modeling of assertive power and clear communication.

This example comes from a session after a brief phone call the night before:

Therapist: I had a hard time with our phone call last night The answering service said it was an emergency, but when I reached you, you said you just needed to talk with me. I'm confused. What was going on?

Client: I guess I just needed to hear your voice. I felt sort of panicked, and I didn't think you'd call me back if I left you a message on your answering machine asking you to call, since it was a Sunday.

Therapist: Well, I don't check my machine frequently on the weekends, but I probably would have at some point in the day and I *would* call you back if you asked me to directly.

Client: Really? Would you really, even if you were busy and it wasn't an emergency. I mean, I wasn't suicidal or hurting myself or anything.

Therapist: If you just talked a bit on the machine and said you were having a hard time but didn't directly ask me to call you, I probably wouldn't. But if you asked me to call you, I would, unless I was out of town or didn't get your message until really late. I guess I count on your being able to let me know when you need me to call you back. I try to be clear as well when I leave you a message to change a time or something, if I need you to call me or not. And maybe we should talk about how late I can return a call—I don't know when you go to bed or if calling would be disruptive to your husband or kids.

Client: I can't believe you'd really call me back. That's amazing. I mean, I don't want to bug you, and I really don't expect you to call me all the time. It just helps to know that you really would return a call on the weekend if I really needed it.

Therapist: I really will. And I agree with you. I don't think it's good if you are counting on me on a regular basis to be the person you call for support when you're upset. But I *am* here, and I will be here. I think it's about some kind of balance. When you *really* need me, I'm here. But I'm not like a friend who you can just chat with.

Client: (*bristling a little*) I know that. I wouldn't expect that. I just need to know that you are there.

Our Ongoing Struggle with Resistance

Resistant is another word often used to describe a client with whom we are feeling helpless. The underlying process involved with what is called resistance is fundamentally about power—who will control what is happening and at what pace. Being resistant is one way clients choose to regulate the work and the change process. Frequently, the presence of resistance indicates ambivalence, which bears exploration as well.

Most people are ambivalent about change. On the one hand, the desire for change drives us to seek help; we want our lives to be different. On the other hand, change is frightening and unpredictable. It requires that we relinquish what is familiar and discover something new. It involves risk-taking. The outcome is uncertain. As clinicians, our job naturally puts us on the side of change. We are employed to help people change.

Sometimes, in the course of supporting clients to change, we slip into "taking up all the space" on the side of change, leaving the client with the other half of his ambivalence—the side that pulls toward maintaining the status quo, the part of himself that resists change. We then embody the "I-want-things-to-be-different" half of the client's ambivalence, and the client embodies the "no-I-can't-change" half of their experience. It is much more useful for us to step back and help the client to sit with both sides of his experience. He then can grapple with this conflict and reach resolution, rather than feeling locked in a power struggle with us.

Clarifying the Locus of Control

Another good example of working counter to stated goals is the inconsistency between belief and practice that often exists regarding the locus of control. While many professionals believe an internal locus of control bodes well for clients' mental health, their behavior suggests otherwise. Clients are perceived as uncooperative or resistant if they say no to their therapists' suggestions (an example of an external locus of control, from the client's point of view). Clients are expected to accept treatment recommendations as determined by others (the word *treatment* implies an external application of something to another person, rather than internal change process).

Further, many systems and institutions seem to operate in order to maintain themselves, rather than from a ground of commitment to client needs and individualized approaches. Forms, procedures, and policies appear to be grounded in what works for the system, rather than what is best for the client who is to be serviced. These systemic dynamics and the accompanying language tend to reinforce an external locus of control. We can shift this effect somewhat by, again, viewing professional–client interactions through the lens of power, and let this view inform our interventions and policies.

Managing Our Boundaries

Our own boundaries are the only ones we can control. We may set boundaries that in effect limit our clients' behavior, but fundamentally we are establishing the lines within which we will operate within a particular relationship (Connors 1998). Regulating our boundaries mindfully and honestly provides us with a potent method of demonstrating assertive, nonvictimizing interpersonal power. Such modeling can be extremely useful for clients both in their relationships with us and subsequently in other relationships. Such teaching is invaluable for clients who have experienced trauma.

Physical and interpersonal boundaries can be described as the parameters within which we come to understand our internal and external worlds. They help us define self, others, situations, geographic locations, roles, and other discrete entities. In the context of therapy, Peterson (1992) writes, "Boundaries are the limits that allow for a safe connection based on the client's needs" (p. 74). Knowing what the parameters are contributes to a sense of safety, thus freeing up energy for therapeutic process and change. Further, in a slight reframe, Jordan (1991b) states that often "'boundaries' are defined as a means of protection rather than as channels of meeting, exchange and communication" (p. 4). In other words, she suggests we might consider boundaries to be useful avenues wherein client and therapist interact, the place of joining. Considered together, these concepts suggest that boundaries function as a conduit—a clearly defined pathway that allows for the stuff of therapy to flow between client and clinician within specific limits.

Boundaries are fluid by nature, adapting to shifting circumstances and the people on either side of them. A clinician may decide that certain limits always make sense, and stay clearly within a certain parameter, such as never getting sexually involved with a client or former client. Other limits may change over time, depending on the nature of the relationship, the client's needs, and the therapist's needs. For example, when a therapist is going through an intense personal experience such as grief over the loss of a parent or partner, she may feel she needs more solid, impenetrable boundaries for a period of time to avoid "leaking" into the client's work.

One of the difficulties in discussing the management of boundaries is that we are talking about a multidimensional phenomenon. Discussions about boundaries tend to focus on a verbal or written delineation of behavior. This is the most concrete and accessible way to conceptualize boundaries. Since we rely so heavily on language, this makes sense and is necessary. However, to more substantially consider the perception of boundaries of self takes us into realms of experience that do not lend themselves as readily to words. I imagine many clinicians know what I mean in the previous paragraph in referring to "more solid, impenetrable boundaries for a period of time to avoid 'leaking.'" There are times when we may feel the need to be more guarded or protected, because we are vulnerable and raw, inside our own experience. We put up a psychic barrier, or psychically insulate ourselves a little more than usual. Conversely, we may know the internal sensation of opening that allows clients to really attach to us and join with us. We experience a sense of welcoming spirit and presence; we have room for all they bring. In these experiences, we are not talking primarily about behavior, though behavior tends to follow from these internal perceptions or sensations. Rather, we are talking about the subjective experience of the self-boundary discussed in Chapters 4 and 8.

A Process, Not a Set of Rules

Boundary-keeping is a process, rather than a set of rules, requiring regular, consistent attention (Herman 1992, Pearlman and Saakvitne 1995, Rivera 1996). Part of our job as clinicians is to create an environment where conversations about boundaries can occur as we or clients feel the need. This includes a willingness and capacity to acknowledge boundary violations when they occur. Generally, practicing therapists have some guidelines they adhere to with some consistency. Some may be strictly maintained, such as striving always to keep the client's interest paramount in the relationship, and not becoming sexually or romantically involved with clients. Many harmful boundary violations entail a breach of one of these two parameters so essential to therapeutic work, particularly in work with trauma survivors. However, a range of other boundaries (a few examples of which include disclosure of personal information by the therapist, physical touch, out-of-session contact, and payment of fees) may be handled with less rigidity, provided care is taken.

Perceiving boundaries as a process rather than a set of rules enables us to become more competent at tracking interactions relevant to boundary issues. This means we are able to stay present to any changes in our own behavior as well as the client's expression of her boundaries. For clients with a history of boundary intrusion (as noted in Chapter 2, this includes most people who self-injure), attentiveness to boundaries as an ongoing process is an invaluable opportunity. Monitoring and discussing changes in boundaries can be instructive and transformative. Honing this kind of awareness also serves as a protection against more flagrant, clearly harmful boundary violations.

Sometimes a seemingly quite small shift in a boundary can be significant.

Several years ago I walked out of my office building with a client after a session. We were leaving at the same time and walking out together occurred in a natural and spontaneous way. I was aware that this was a new experience for both of us in that we had not done such a thing over the course of the three years we had worked together. It felt like a shift in a boundary that we had established by default; I simply never left when she did.

We talked about this shift in the next session. The client found it disconcerting at first, but said she also thought it was helpful. As she described it, she had put me in a box. I only existed in the therapy room at some level, even though she knew otherwise and actually had some facts about my life. This opened up a whole discussion of her interactional style—how she makes rules by which to guide her behavior with others in order to avoid rejection and punishment. She had constructed a rule that said she shouldn't think about me outside the office. She based this rule on a statement I made early in the therapy about how she and I would not become friends in the future, in an effort to clarify some questions she had about the parameters of our relationship. We discussed the implications of this further, which led into a range of intimacy issues for her. Had we not discussed this apparently slight shift in a boundary, both of us would have been left with a tinge of discomfort, and my client would not have had the chance to open up the issues that emerged.

Determining and Communicating Boundaries

Central to our task of consciously managing our boundaries with clients is our capacity to contain two seemingly contradictory elements: to be consistent and dependable, *and* flexible enough to sort and respond to each situation. This means that we hold the frame steady *and* we try to meet the client where he is. Peterson (1992) cautions against shifting the boundaries, because it allows for ambiguity, and "ambiguity is often experienced as an intrusion into the sphere of safety" (p. 74). Changes in boundaries, therefore, need to be done carefully and with thought. Since boundary violations may not be perceived by the client until they have escalated to some level of harm, we need to exercise special caution when we deviate from our standard practice.

The following list of questions is offered as a guideline in the process of discerning and maintaining appropriate and workable boundaries:

1. What are my fundamental boundaries with clients?
2. Do these make sense with this client? If not, why not?
3. Why do I want to change this particular boundary?
4. Can I think of two colleagues I can discuss this with? What do or would they think?
5. Is my changing a basic boundary or limit in the interest of the client in the short run? In the long run?
6. What are the potential risks? What are the potential benefits? How do I decide if it's too risky?
7. How does the client feel about it? What do I know about how my client perceives safety? Will this change create any sense of danger?
8. How do I feel about it? What are my gut reactions and what are my limits in making a change?

Generally, this sorting process occurs out of the session and is not discussed in detail with the client, or even with the client at all. Other times, a frank conversation about the potential risks and benefits concerning a possible boundary shift can be utilized effectively, even if the end decision is to not act on the change.

A shift in the therapeutic boundary regarding touch is a common example that may arise in working with clients who self-injure. The potency of physical contact for clients with abuse or neglect histories cannot be overemphasized. Touch offers many possibilities for healing, as well as many possibilities for further intrusion and harm. A number of authors have explored the impact (good and bad) of touch by therapists with trauma survivors (Burstow 1992, Courtois 1988, Pearlman and Saakvitne 1995, Sakheim and Devine 1992); the complexity and nuances of this issue demands thoughtfulness and care. People who

harm their own bodies often find that physical touch communicates acceptance and presence more effectively than
many other modalities. The desire for safe, respectful touch
can prompt a client to ask for physical contact that is outside the therapist's normal boundary, creating the need to
explore a possible shift.

I generally do not touch clients beyond an initial
handshake unless we have an explicit conversation about
physical contact, almost always at the client's request. On
a rare occasion I may ask if I can touch a client's hand
during a particularly distressing moment, or place my hand
on their arm or shoulder as they leave the office after a
difficult session. These occasions generally do not occur
unless there has been a previous opportunity to discuss
touch and an agreement to make a shift. The desire for
physical contact is usually expressed as a wish for a hug at
the end of the session, or for me to sit with the client on
the couch and/or hold her hand. Sometimes the request
is for me to place my hand on the client's back to facilitate awareness of sensation or provide a sensate experience
of support.

When a client asks me to touch him in some way that
seems reasonable (i.e., not overtly sexual or physically
harmful—examples of touch I would simply refuse and
then subsequently discuss), I might ask how he thinks my
touch would be helpful. I want to know more about what
he needs and what he thinks about the act of touching. I
try to explore any possible sexual elements that would be
likely to make the touch confusing. Sometimes I ask this
directly ("I wonder if holding your hand would feel sexual
or confusing to some part of you") or indirectly ("How do
you think it might feel if I held your hand? Would there
be any confusion or discomfort?"). I ask myself (silently)
how it would feel to hold his hand or place my hand on

his back. I mentally review our history together, including the issues we have addressed and the nature of our interactions, and try to assess how touch might resonate with what I know about him. I might raise a concern based on a specific issue from the past ("I wonder how it would be for me to touch you in light of the ways your babysitter touched you when you were small").

I also consider whether meeting the client's expressed need is more useful at this point than helping him process the underlying grief or other feelings about not getting the need met. Determining when need-meeting is more transformative and healing than holding the space so the client can process and understand the origin of the need is not tidy or straightforward. I might explain that struggle to the client, asking him to consider what will be more helpful overall. This is sometimes a conversation we have over a period of months.

In general, I try to ask myself the questions listed above, and engage directly with the client when it seems useful or necessary. Sometimes we might conclude that we need to wait and see what we think in the next session. Sometimes we might decide that touch makes sense, but choose the next time it comes up *not* to touch. Different responses at different points in time can be healing.

This sorting process may continue beyond the session in which it was raised. On these occasions, I might seek consultation from a colleague. Other times, the process is relatively quick and focused; to belabor the issue would make more of it than what the client is bringing up. It is hard to provide definitive guidelines about when it is necessary to engage in a longer discernment process, and when a more rapid decision makes sense. I believe that my own intuition and gut feelings are the best guides when the issue is not clear-cut (i.e., clearly harmful or clearly beneficial). If I am connected to myself and aware of my own issues, I am more likely to be tuned in to potential problems, as well as potential benefits, and in the best position I can offer for discernment.

What to Do When Boundaries Are Violated

We all violate our clients' boundaries at times, either unknowingly or because we make mistakes. This human act occurs in all relationships; it can be expected to happen in the context of therapy because the nature of the relationship is so sensitive and because complex issues, often ones that directly involve boundaries, are being addressed. Briere (1993) commented once that clients have a sense of safety with us when they know where we make our mistakes. Similarly, Rogers (1995) quotes her therapist as telling her "'There are probably reasons not to trust me entirely, and we will find them out as we go, right? Once you find them, then you'll know exactly how much to trust me'" (p. 135).

Ideally, we make our mistakes in areas that don't create lasting or substantial harm. Accepting our vulnerability as people who err means that we monitor our interactions, acknowledge our mistakes or boundary violations when they occur, and remedy the problem as soon as possible. It means we listen when clients feel violated or dismissed or controlled or intruded upon. We make every effort to see the situation through our clients' eyes. We may not always agree there has been a boundary violation. But we must try to understand the interaction or behavior from the client's perspective in order to keep the relationship intact.

A good place to start to remedy the situation is to apologize. A direct statement, such as "I am sorry I was thoughtless; I didn't mean to be hurtful," goes a long way toward rebalancing the sense of respect and caring in the relationship. The next step may involve an actual change in behavior or a reassertion of a boundary; this may require further discussion as well in order to clarify the nature of the violation more precisely. Perhaps there is a level of work for the therapist that involves shifting the internal experience of her self-boundary without saying anything more to the client. Sometimes it is useful to seek supervision or consultation, particularly when we are uncertain about how to best remedy the situation.

Peterson's (1992) clearly written book, *At Personal Risk: Boundary Violations in Professional-Client Relationships,* serves as an excellent guide to understanding the potency of boundary violations as well as guidelines for repairing relationships. Her analysis of the power differential between professionals and clients, her focus on the "ethos of care" as a standard of practice, and her numerous examples serve to create a valuable text for practicing clinicians. Relatedly, in *Resolving Impasses in Therapeutic Relationships,* Elkind (1992) offers a rich exploration of confounded boundaries, misused power, and failed empathy from a slightly different perspective. Both ground the issues that so often trip up therapists attempting to permit a real, mutual, and connected relationship with their clients.

Self-Disclosure by the Therapist

One of the most common forms of boundary violation— or at least boundary *confusion*—is in the area of therapist self-disclosure (Pearlman and Saakvitne 1995). Determining the amount of personal information to share with clients can challenge even seasoned therapists who are willing to engage in case-by-case decision making about boundaries. Part of the complexity of such decisions emerges from the variability of client need.

Some clients are not particularly interested in their therapist beyond that person's background, credentials, general approach, and willingness to engage with them. How we interact matters, but facts about who we are as people are not relevant to them. For others, especially those who struggle with early deprivation or abuse and carry the scars of an incomplete attachment process, who we are is often a regular part of the foreground. The therapist's words, demeanor, choice of clothing and jewelry, values, or personal history can be important to clients who are striving to define their own sense of self and need to use a relationship with a therapist as part of that process.

Self-disclosure is a potent, important element that I attempt to use carefully in the therapy process. Information about me can be alternately useful, confusing, overwhelming, clarifying, supportive, painful, threatening, or somewhat unimportant. I disclose more to some clients than others, depending on my assessment of their needs and their capacity to take in or use such information at a given point in time. What a specific client needs with regard to who I am, whether it's knowing if I am a lesbian or a Christian, or if I have ever been victimized, or if I grew up poor, or if I have children, can be quite idiosyncratic. A determination about disclosure needs to be made on a case-by-case basis, and can only include aspects of self that I am comfortable revealing.

What clients need to know about me can also vary with time. At one point in the therapeutic relationship, a client may not feel the need to know much about me, or even feel able to experience me as a person. Some clients need me to provide a safe, neutral place and not inject my self into the foreground. For the same client at a later point in time, asking me about myself may matter more as, for example, she begins to explore her developing sense of self. Or the situation might be reversed: early on, having a sense of me as a person may make all the difference in a client's ability to begin to enough trust me enough to talk about his internal world. Later in the work, that same client's focus on me and who I am in my life may have little charge or interest for him.

I work from the guiding principle of answering what clients ask and not offering more, though I sometimes decide otherwise. I may make a decision that it will be helpful to someone's change process to let her know a specific fact for a specific reason—something she did not directly ask me. For example, I may volunteer that I am the oldest of seven children and know what it's like to be part of a big family, if this theme comes up and I perceive that with an increased level of joining on my part she may be able to more fully express what she is feeling, or talk more candidly about what she needs. Or I may decide to tell someone about my own experience in grappling with an issue she is struggling with—in only enough detail to communicate empathy and the possibility that things can be different. Again, my choice to do so is based on my assessment that this disclosure will facilitate her movement through a difficult juncture or allow her to see more options for change.

Other times, I am very cautious if I suspect that knowing certain information about me might be difficult or complicating. I take care to explore with a client if or how it would help if I told her something about myself, or to ask if she really wants to know what she has asked. Sometimes just being able to ask without criticism or interpersonal withdrawal by me is more important than the answer.

I try to discriminate what makes sense when and with whom. While this discernment process can be influenced by my own needs for intimacy and connection, I try to base it on what I think will support this person to take the next step she wants to make. Timing and sensitivity clearly matter, as well as the client's specific issues.

An example:

A client once asked at the beginning of a session why I didn't live with my partner (a fact she had already ascertained). This young woman raised the question with some hesitation and said she hoped I wouldn't be upset with her for asking something personal. I reassured her that it was fine to ask me questions, and said that I could give her a brief explanation, but first I was curious about why she wanted to know and how she thought hearing my answer would be helpful to her. She said she was trying to make sense of primary relationships and is unsure if she wants to live with her boyfriend.

We discussed whether she really wanted information about me or if she wanted to focus on the issues involved in such a decision. She realized as we talked that what she needed to know was that I was okay with my situation (i.e., not hurt or in pain about living alone), and that she and I could discuss her wishes and concerns about her next steps with her boyfriend. I reassured her that I was fine with my circumstances and we went on to talk about what she needed to explore about her own situation. Had I simply gone ahead and told her some of the reasons my partner and I had made the decisions we had made, I believe she would have felt overwhelmed and uncomfortable knowing things about me that felt too personal, and we would not have spent the time focused on what she really wanted to discuss. Asking if

I was hurt or in pain was her way of surfacing her own fears and concerns.

Power and Loving Presence

Many clinicians, at least in private moments with people they trust, acknowledge the presence and significance of love in healing work. I know my willingness to allow the presence of loving feelings, and my capacity to articulate those feelings of care and concern at the right time and with the right words, play important roles in the change process. If I open and enter heartspace, if I value it as a place to sit with clients, then I permit love to flow through me. This does not mean falling in love, having sex, or pursuing friendships outside the therapeutic relationship. Nor does it mean abandoning standards of care, failing to intervene when a situation so dictates, or protecting clients from their pain. It does mean that I let clients matter to me, that I try to hold their trust and vulnerability tenderly, that we make a space where hard truths can be spoken— whether about the client's past or about my observations of her current life or about how convoluted our interactions have become, and that I make a heartfelt commitment to be there consistently and kindly.

Such willingness to allow love to enter the equation in therapeutic work also requires responsibility and a heightened awareness of power in the relationship. When love becomes part of the picture, I need to be even more attuned to my use of power. It's too easy to feel loving in a particular moment, and then pull back or withdraw when it's too much or when I feel how big the client's need is, or when it feels inconvenient. I try to remember that it makes perfect sense that when I enter this loving space with a client, her old unmet needs and longings will emerge fully and fiercely. While not frightening, this experience can be demanding and intense. It may push at the edges of my boundaries and the constraints of the therapeutic relationship. However, I find that when I can respond from a loving place, clients actually get some of these old needs met, and are therefore strengthened to be able to grieve the bulk of the needs and longings that can never be met.

Amidst efforts to stay consistent and present in my lovingness are the limits of what I can offer. Promises of false intimacy are not useful, nor are attempts at regular contact outside session time. Rather, the substantiality of our connection inside the therapy room sustains clients in deep, internal ways between sessions. The validation of their needs in a kind and nonblaming manner coupled with clear and overt limits about what I can or cannot provide helps clients begin to own and contain the immensity of their needs and feelings. These moments of modeling both acceptance and limitation provide a concrete experience of recognition and containment of intense internal experience, contributing to the development of a more whole, integrated self. Such interactions are augmented by insight about the source of the need or pain as well as practical help in the holding and regulation of strong affect.

I strive to be myself in all my power and all my tenderness with clients. The more present I am with me, the more present I can be with them. As Satir (1987) says so well, "I have learned that when I am fully present with the patient or family, I can move therapeutically with much greater ease. I can simultaneously reach the depths to which I need to go, and at the same time honor the fragility, power and the sacredness of life in the other" (p. 23). Even if I sometimes vary in my ability to be present and engaged, I also know that this variability, as long as the range isn't too great, is a good reality experience for clients. I communicate and offer a model that says real people in real relationships vary in their ability to be connected.

One client, a survivor of early and chronic deprivation, neglect, and abuse with whom I worked for some years, said to me once, "What has happened here is that for the first time I found a place where I could really be myself without judgment. I didn't even know who I was. How you have been with me has let me find out who I am." With respect, kindness, power, and love, it is this gift we offer clients, as they sift through the past and move into finding out who they are and who they want to become. We offer *ourselves*—our sense of self—so they can journey to a more whole, integrated self for *themselves*.

7

Helping Clients Address Their Self-Injury

One of the elements involved in therapy with people who self-injure is helping clients learn more about their process of self-injury. This aspect of the work may involve efforts to prevent, interrupt, or lessen the self-injury. However, interventions at this level are not necessarily or predominantly focused on stopping the self-injury. The goal is to enlarge the clients' knowledge base about their own experience of self-injury and increase their capacity to manage or live with their behavior. Some clients may set an initial goal of wanting to interrupt the self-injury, or find that this goal emerges over time; for others, stopping the behavior never becomes a primary goal, but simply occurs as a by-product of their efforts to heal.

Still other clients feel that an exploration of the underlying functions and needs associated with the self-injury is valuable, but don't believe that intervening in the behavior is necessary. These clients and their therapists believe the behavior will diminish in time as core issues are resolved. They generally have a high capacity to tolerate the presence of self-injury (and do a periodic check to ensure a tolerable level of harm) and recognize that the self-injury may persist or reemerge in times of stress or with difficult therapeutic work. For these therapist–client teams, there may be less focus on interrupting the self-injury or finding alternatives, with more focus on the long-term resolution of the underlying issues as discussed in Chapters 8 and 9.

Mindful of the basic concept that someone who self-injures is responsible for choosing to intervene or not intervene on her own behavior, this chapter explores some concrete ways someone might do that. The mental health professional can be quite active in this process, and some guidelines and suggestions are offered to facilitate an engaged role defined by clear boundaries regarding responsibility. Appendix A can be used in conjunction with this chapter, as it offers specific questions a therapist might employ when helping someone explore and address her self-injury. The focus here is on information gathering and generating new ideas—an open-ended and creative process. This attitude in and of itself can invigorate the therapeutic process.

Burstow (1992) frames this approach as "co-exploration." Such a collaborative perspective offers affirmation of the person who is injuring, and also provides a ground for helping the client learn more about her process.

> Co-exploration serves many ends. It defines the self-harm as something purposive and meaningful, as opposed to something meaningless or crazy. It helps counselor and client truly appreciate self-mutilation as a valid means of coping. It allows a woman who is not understood and who thinks she is not understandable to receive and take in understanding. Clarity around purposes [of the self-injury] combined with acceptance additionally gives the client the possibility of exploring alternative avenues for meeting these ends. [p. 193]

Identifying Patterns

One way to begin increasing clients' knowledge base is to identify patterns of self-injury. This often includes taking an inventory of self-injuring behavior at a pace that fits for the client and in a manner that feels supportive and exploratory. This might mean simply asking the client to tell us more about how she hurts herself, and then following where the client goes with this response, not trying to nail down specific details. Further exploration of what the client does when she injures might occur six or eight sessions later. The information as a picture is often pieced together over time. Some people will be quite relieved a clinician is interested in some of the details, while others may be reticent, embarrassed, or unsure of our intent in asking. They may need to gradually tell about their experiences with self-harm. Following the client's lead while taking some responsibility to initiate conversation about the self-injury reflects the delicate balance involved in such explorations. Expressing both interest in talking about the self-injury and respect for the client's pace of disclosure and discussion is the therapist's task. A statement such as "I am interested in hearing more about how you cut if you can or want to tell me about it" communicates both interest and a respect for pacing.

A number of areas of discovery can be co-explored over time. These might include some basic information about the different forms of self-injury the client engages in and when she first self-injured. Daily or seasonal patterns may exist; asking the client about what time of day, or what time of the year she tends to self-injure can help her become more aware of these patterns. The client may be able to describe a set sequence of actions regarding her self-injury that includes information about specific current or past events, or environmental or interpersonal cues. This can facilitate more awareness about feelings and sensations present before, during, and after the self-injury, and help with the identification of triggers that elicit strong emotional responses.

Two resources may be particularly useful in helping clients explore the patterns, associated feelings, and functions of their self-injury. One is the workbook Kristy Trautmann and I developed, *Understanding Self Injury* (Trautmann and Connors 1994). It provides a self-directed format for identifying patterns, making connections, and understanding the functions of self-injury, which the client may choose to explore on her own or within a therapy process. This workbook also lists many suggestions for alternatives to self-injury as they relate to functions. The second resource is Tracy Alderman's book for people who self-injure, *The Scarred Soul* (1997). She offers a wealth of information about self-injury, as well as many exercises that clients may find useful in clarifying their process. She also notes alternatives to self-injury and other resources for clients.

Describing Feelings and Triggers

Some clients have quite a bit of information about their feelings related to their self-injury. They can delineate triggers likely to contribute to self-injury. Others may only be discovering this information. All clients tend to learn more over time if they are working with a therapist who is willing to tolerate the presence of self-injury and invite conversation about the injuring. Such support offers clients more space within which to understand their process. It also helps clients increase their ability to put words on feelings, to link body sensations to these words, and to express those feelings through various means.

This cognitive mastery of emotionally potent triggers can be useful in helping clients feel more grounded and less at the mercy of flashbacks and intrusive memory states. (See Dolan [1991], Finney [1992], Matsakis [1994], and Napier [1993] for concrete suggestions in managing flashbacks and triggers.) Such work can decrease the frequency and intensity of stressful triggers and thus decrease the likelihood that self-injury will be employed, or that any significant coping mechanism will even be required. This kind of awareness and mastery also increases the client's sense of control. For clients who utilize self-injury to regain control, simply knowing what they are feeling and being able to intervene to some extent regarding triggers can be stabilizing.

Looking at the Elements of the Self-Injuring Process

Describing how her self-injury occurs can be informative and useful to a client. How impulsive is it? What sets her off? Does she plan it in detail or not? Are there rituals involved with harming herself? Does she gather instruments with care, or does she use whatever is available? Does it feel like an addictive process that feeds on itself? Is she hearing someone inside (a dissociated part) telling her to hurt herself? Does she feel like some other part of her is doing it to her? Being able to more clearly discern the details affords not only understanding, but, for some, the chance to insert a few seconds in the process the next time it occurs. For people who want to stop self-injuring, those few seconds can be valuable. In those moments, they may be able to remember other options and recall resources for support.

Alderman (1997) provides exercises to help people more clearly identify and describe their process of injuring from several perspectives: an addiction-like process, operant conditioning, and observed learning. These models are not discrete; in other words, there may be addictive elements as well as learned behaviors. The focus, again, is exploration, not a diagnostic or definitive label. Alderman also offers exercises that address the role of trauma and substance abuse in someone's self-injuring process.

Making Connections to Past Events

By describing feelings, patterns, and elements in the process of self-injuring, clients often mention or discover a link between their self-injury and past traumas and events. They may say, "I started doing this after I was abused in seventh grade," or "I think somehow this is related to what happened when I was a child, even though I'm not sure how it's connected." Some people may have clear ideas about how their self-inflicted violence serves to manage the feelings they have about past traumas, or to show what they have experienced. They may have always known or have made the connections prior to their work with us. Others will not see a link until they learn more about their process of self-injury. In the course of talking about and working through old traumas, some clients spontaneously identify the functions and needs self-injury meets.

These connections are very important, because they offer a path out of what can feel like a maze. They help clients create a cohesive understanding of their histories. The links to the past can seem somewhat obvious once recognized, as with some reenactments. The use of harmful enemas, for example, was utilized by one woman who was traumatized by medical procedures that always involved enemas as part of the prep. Sometimes the link is not so obvious; the client just has an intuitive sense that there is a relationship between what is happening now and something from the past. Over time, with support but without directive questioning, the client will discern what fits for her, what she believes are the connections in her own life.

Assessing the Functions of Self-Injury

At the heart of helping clients intervene in their own self-injury process is their exploration and identification of the functions self-injury serves for them. Understanding how self-injury helps them cope can allow clients not only to reframe their behavior as essentially functional—even if it is not as functional as they would like—but also to create a foundation for subsequent brainstorming about alternatives to self-injury. Such awareness also builds clients' knowledge about their self-injury, providing a richer database for their work on the underlying issues, and increasing their sense of control over their own process.

Initial explorations of functions can be as simple as open-ended writing or verbal conversation in answer to questions such as "How does this [the self-injury] help you?" or "What does this do for you?" When the inquiry is framed in this nonjudgmental and inviting way, some people realize they have, and can explicate, a fuller understanding of the functions of their self-injury than they previously thought. A more focused exploration can be done using a checklist of possible functions (see Appendix B). For some people, a checklist is useful because it gives language to sensations and feelings they may not have felt able to articulate previously.

Bringing the connections about function into awareness can be potent; this information alone may shift the behavior by interrupting old patterns. As stated earlier, clients may find they gain a few crucial moments between the impulse to self-injure and the actual hitting or cutting, thus introducing a window wherein alternatives become possibilities. Also, such exploration and discovery within a relational, nonjudgmental context begins to erode the wall of shame surrounding the behavior. This lessening of shame frees up energy for the client, who may then be better able to think through an alternative response to the impulse to self-injure.

As noted in Chapter 2, self-injury can serve a range of functions. Sometimes this is because the self-injurer engages in several forms of self-injury that serve different purposes: she may burn her breasts when she feels aroused in order to punish herself, and hit her legs and head when she is frustrated and overwhelmed. Or the same act of injuring may meet several needs at once: cutting her arms helps her know she is alive because she sees the blood, and it may also give her something on which to focus her anxiety as she cares for the wounds during the following week. Also, a client's understanding of how self-injury helps her is likely to change with time. As shame lessens, more information about her process is available. Awareness of the elements of her process and the working through of traumatic aftereffects will alter her self-perceptions, adding layers of insight about her self-injury.

For example, a client might initially say she cuts herself because she is bad and has to punish herself. As she talks more about her process and feels increasingly comfortable with a therapist, she might add that seeing the blood helps her know she is alive and has feelings. The blood represents her tears and unexpressed grief. As she works through early incest experiences and shifts her perception of responsibility for the abuse to her godfather, rather than placing it on herself for wanting to spend time with him, she might feel that cutting is less about punishing herself for being bad. She might then say that her cutting is about her rage at having been so needy that she put up with his behavior. Later, she might add that her rage is at her godfather for taking advantage of her. These changes may occur over a period of two years or more. Whether the function of the self-injury actually changed over time, or whether it was about her increasing awareness of her feelings, is probably not going to be clear to either the client or the therapist. What is important for us as clinicians is that we give our clients room to let their process and awareness unfold in all of its complexity and nuance without feeling we have to capture it into a tidy box labeled "functions."

Finding Alternatives

Some clients will spontaneously generate alternatives to the self-injury once they understand its function(s). For example, if they realize that their self-injury helps to calm them, they may say, "You know, I guess I could hold myself when I feel like I'm going to fly apart and just sit in the rocking chair for a while." For others, developing alternatives will be a more deliberate, problem-oriented task to take on with a therapist or friend, or alone in a quiet moment. Fostering a spirit of brainstorming and maintaining the belief that other methods *can* meet the needs currently served by self-injury are key. It helps to frame the discovery of alternatives as an ongoing creative process.

Finding alternatives essentially consists of identifying not previously considered ways to meet a function or need.

Sometimes this means actually learning new skills in the areas of problem solving, self-soothing, relaxation and anxiety reduction, organizing and grounding, information processing, and other aspects of self-care. Other times it involves thinking about current skills or coping strategies in new ways. For example, someone who uses gardening when anxious or overwhelmed may find she can also use gardening to express anger by doing heavy tasks.

Alternatives to self-injury need to fit the function. If particular self-injuring behavior serves several functions, a mix of alternatives may be most effective. Developing a list of alternatives tied to specific functions or needs can be initiated during a period of relative calm, in or out of the therapy session. Sometimes ideas will occur in moments of crisis, or following an occurrence of self-injury. If the client and therapist have established some degree of comfort communicating about the self-injury, they can utilize this fertile opportunity to access information about the real needs and generate new solutions. Keeping a list of alternatives handy can be useful, as many survivors self-injure under stress when they may have trouble remembering alternatives (more on list making and state-dependent memory follows in this chapter).

The following list of possible noninjuring alternatives has been gathered from clinical practice, informal interviews with survivors, and colleagues. This list is just a start; the best ideas come in response to a particular situation involving a specific person, with a clear link between the function and the alternative. For example, someone who needs to see the blood may find it is helpful to mark on his skin with a red marker as an alternative to cutting. These alternatives are listed by type of alternative behavior; as a group they may or may not link to certain functions. Different options will meet different needs for different people at different times.

- Nonharmful symbolic enactments: draw the "blood" or marks on paper, injure a toy or stuffed animal, cut a box, make marks with red marker or crayon on your skin, punch a punching bag, insert things into or cut off parts of a doll.
- Physical awareness/sensation: breathe, do a body scan by attending to each part of your body, stroke your arm or leg, stomp your feet, drink hot water, brush hair, take a bath or shower, place ice on your skin, snap a rubber band on your wrist, give yourself or get a massage, use relaxation techniques
- Distraction: read a book, watch a video, do a puzzle, walk around the mall, promise yourself to wait 5 to 10 minutes before self-injuring, go to a movie, get a task done on your to-do list, play with a pet, look at a favorite object of beauty.
- Interpersonal contact: call a friend, talk out the impulse to self-injure, talk about something else altogether, listen to tapes of a friend or therapist talking, call a support group member, leave a message for a friend or support person saying how you feel.
- Imagery: imagine the self-injury, imagine directing the impulse to self-injure elsewhere, fantasize (rather than acting out) sexualized self injury, create a safe place where you are free from self injury and other forms of violence.
- Physical activity: exercise, do yard work, dance, use a hammer, play a physical game, shred tissue or other paper, play drums or other percussion instruments, use exercise putty (or hand-held stress ball), walk or hike.
- Creative process: draw the feeling or need or memory, write about your internal experience, create a clay sculpture that expresses your feelings, play

a musical instrument, write a letter to your abuser or your parent(s) or another significant person, compose a poem, write about wanting to self-injure, draw the ways you have self-injured.

- Expressive anger activities: hit or punch safely, break old crockery or glass in safe ways, throw ice cubes, smash aluminum cans, scream, rip up old phone books, pound pillows, rant and rave into a tape recorder.
- Self-soothing: rock yourself, wrap up in a blanket, take a bath, eat a favorite food, play comforting music, meditate.
- Grounding and reorienting: visually scan the environment, describe the environment out loud, use notecards with reminders about how to stay in the present, hold transitional objects that link you to people and events in the present, use physical awareness or self-soothing techniques such as breathing or meditation.

Highly Dissociative Clients and Self-Intervention: A Complex Task

For clients who are dissociative, working with parts of self and other aspects of their dissociation is an integral aspect of addressing self-inflicted violence. Sorting and clarifying the complex relationship between a client's dissociative process and her self-injury will take time and needs to be grounded in the larger frame of good psychotherapeutic work with the dissociation and many related issues. Sometimes the internal resources of a dissociative client can be shifted for crisis management of self-injury (Putnam 1989).

One approach might be asking the multiple-personality client who else inside can come out when one part is preparing to self-injure, or exploring who else can help that part get what he or she needs (e.g., comfort, distraction, or movement to another location inside). For example, if one part punches walls when she is mad, or another head-bangs when he is overwhelmed and feeling alone, it may help to find ways to meet their needs internally and/or safely rather than have them be out in the body and harming it. Maybe the angry girl needs a safe place inside where she can express anger and be supervised by an older or adult part, so she is not alone with her anger. Or the boy who head-bangs needs to have a comforting adult pick him up and rock him when he feels overwhelmed. One woman with a dissociative identity structure had a part named Cutter whose job was, not surprisingly, to cut—either herself or others. The other parts insisted that Cutter stay inside and not be allowed near knives, scissors, or razor blades. Fortunately, in this case, Cutter was not a strong or well-developed part and the others were able to manage this most of the time.

While the development of specific alternatives may be useful to individual parts and provide some respite, making sense out of the system dynamics as they relate to self-injury is even more crucial to the sorting process, and often more helpful in the long run. West (1999) provides a good example of this systemic approach with dissociative clients. He describes how he and his therapist worked with his internal system of alters to understand and intervene when a child part was repeatedly cutting their body. This part—an enraged, deeply hurt 8-year-old boy—was gallantly serving the purpose of expressing the anger and frustration of West's whole system that felt internally locked up. (Focused on completing his Ph.D., West didn't allow time for the others to be out.) Once this was understood and heard by everyone in the system, they all expressed their desire to stop the self-injury, and worked out collaborative ways to meet their various needs. This meant several things: asking the primary personality to agree to some "body time" each day for the alters, helping him decrease his denial about being dissociative, acknowledging and praising the child part's desperate but effective efforts to draw attention to the needs of the system, and providing comfort (via other alters) for this child part. Working separately with the child part on his anger would not have been as effective as focusing on what was going on inside for the whole system.

Assessing and Managing the Level of Harm

One of the areas of exploration that may be reassuring to both therapists and clients (in different ways) is to assess the level of harm resulting from the self-injury. For therapists, knowing the extent of the harm is, in most cases, reassuring, because self-injury is generally not life threatening or even seriously harmful to muscle tissue or organs. Knowing in some detail the extent of the harm can alleviate some of the therapist's concern about inadvertent death or serious injury. Such information gathering needs to be done sensitively and respectfully, so clients don't feel they are being interrogated. Some assurance and clarification may need to be given about the therapist's interest in knowing these details, in order to allay fears that the therapist is trying to collect evidence to use in an involuntary commitment of the client to a psychiatric unit.

For clients, looking at the level of harm can be reassuring because it can help them feel more choice about the degree of harm they experience. Working to manage or reduce the level of harm without actually stopping the self-injury appeals to some clients. Some clients find that although they are scared about an escalation in their self-injuring behavior, they don't want or feel able to stop at the moment. Focusing on reducing the level of harm offers a comfortable avenue for change.

Burstow (1992) notes several ways to approach safety issues and a reduction in the level of harm. Safeguards include not sharing instruments with others, being sure instruments are clean, caring well for wounds, and seeking medical care when the wound cannot be managed alone or with help from friends. Reducing or managing the level of harm is enhanced if the person who thinks she might injure refrains from using drugs or alcohol. Choosing to injure less severely, or for a shorter period of time, or deciding to keep a certain area of her body injury-free might also help lessen the degree of harm.

Tolerating "Failure"

Clients may need reassurance that they are not failing and encouragement to keep trying if the alternatives don't work as well as the client would like. As in changing any habit, effective methods vary and take time. Both clients and therapists gain from viewing this work as an ongoing process of skill building and increasing tolerance for difficult affect and painful memories. This is one of those times that it is very important for the therapist to be self-reflective and work to manage any overinvestment in the client's ability to use alternatives. An unconscious or unspoken desire for the client to be able to use alternatives can interfere by placing pressure on the client to change; it is likely that the client is already placing too much pressure on himself. If the client really wants to stop or lessen his self-injury, and he gets support for working on the underlying issues, the self-injury will change in time. Both client and therapist need to remember that different approaches work at different times for different people. Developing flexible and comprehensive lists of alternatives that try to account for a range of potential situations can help maximize the chance for incremental change.

Making Lists: A Way to Manage the Limitations of State-Dependent Memory

One of the difficulties many clients experience in changing habitual responses is that they forget or can't access the new ideas they have come up with in therapy, for example, when they need them. Under stress, they have a harder time locating and using information they have stored while in a calm, relaxed state. This dilemma of state-dependent memory is one of the difficulties of trauma survivors since they may reexperience highly charged affective states with some frequency, or live with dissociated parts of the self (Davis and Frawley 1994, Dolan 1991, Putnam 1989, Rivera 1996, van der Kolk 1996c). Many survivors find it difficult to remember current external (e.g., other people) and internal (e.g., creative ideas) resources in moments of upset when they are most likely to self-injure.

Using concrete organizing strategies, such as list making circumvents these limitations to some degree. Reading a list is often a more manageable task in those moments when remembering seems impossible, overwhelming, or unavailable. Using lists to recall information and new coping skills can provide initial success in making changes, and gradually facilitates an incorporation of the broadened repertoire. Strategic placement of these lists—such as on the refrigerator, in one's journal, by the bed, or on one's desk—can increase access across fluctuating emotional states by making the information available in the locations most likely to be seen. This limits the task of remembering what to do under stress. The list serves as a reminder that something besides the distress the person is experiencing in this moment does indeed exist. The simple act of reading the list may help reduce anxiety or shift the affective-physiological state, thus assisting access to further recall of and the ability to use other coping skills.

List making can take many forms and have varied foci. A list of alternatives to self-inflicted violence is one option. Other lists might include ten things to do when angry, or twenty images of beauty a person appreciates, or five people to call for support (noting the specific kind of support each person can offer, e.g., having a cup of coffee or calling in the middle of the night). Appendix C offers a number of ways to organize information that clients may find useful under stress, when suicidal or lonely, or when they feel the need to self-injure.

A more comprehensive version of list making is to create a self-care package. This bundle, stored in a special place, can include a list of alternatives to self-injury, small objects of beauty or meaning, telephone numbers of key resource people, comforting audiotapes of either favorite music or someone reading stories (children's stories or poems may be especially helpful), and reminders about comforting foods or activities. People can keep these care packages in places they are likely to find themselves when stressed or anxious, such as near a favorite chair or by the bed. Some people find they can make a small bag or pouch for their self-care package (or a miniversion) and wear it, or carry it in a briefcase, purse, or backpack.

Helping Clients Talk to Others

As mentioned previously, shame often accompanies and supports self-injurious behavior. Countering and ameliorating shame occurs every time someone who self-injures talks with someone else about his self-inflicted violence and he is received in a caring, nonjudgmental way. Since shame tends to be crippling regardless of its origins, working to reduce shame is advantageous and healing. One of the primary ways people who self-injure can reduce shame is to talk with other people about their experiences. Opening the conversation also adds another resource to the list of available alternatives, if someone is able to actually say to a support person, "I really want to cut right now."

Earlier chapters have addressed the importance of acceptance and respect on the part of the clinician when a client discloses self-injury. The task here, in supporting clients to intervene on their own behalf, concerns the client's move to tell others about his self-injury. This might include friends, family members, health care providers, other therapists or support people, colleagues and co-workers. Just the idea of telling some of these people may feel incredibly risky to some clients. "Outing" oneself, regardless of the issue, often feels dangerous (Signorile 1995). It involves telling a fact that has been a secret for some period of time, during which the secret has gathered all sorts of affective charge. Fearing the responses of others combined with shame about who one is can be a powerful deterrent to disclosure. Selective and thoughtful self-revelation can be equally powerful and often very healing.

Suggesting the possibility that a client might want to tell someone about her self-injury can be a useful intervention by the therapist. It is most likely to be met with disagreement—that telling a certain person would not be a good idea. However, discussing the pros and cons of telling may, over time, allow the client to begin to imagine telling her best friend or her sister—someone close to the client who is inclined to be supportive and nonjudgmental. (Helping the client think critically about who to tell and in what context, especially for a first-time disclosure, enhances the likelihood of a positive experience.) Other clients will have already told some people over the course of their lives or people in their current network, but have the need to talk with someone in particular, and be struggling with how and when to do that. Each disclosure may evoke particular feelings, some more difficult than others. Working through the fears and exploring the possible benefits may be an ongoing discussion over a period of time.

The benefits of telling about the self-injury include reduced shame and reduced isolation. Most clients can't imagine these outcomes if they haven't disclosed previously. The potential benefit of lessened shame and isolation is usually one of those you-can't-know-it-until-you-do-it experiences. Shame can have a powerful grip. Reflecting on the impact of disclosure within the therapeutic relationship may help, though some clients are inclined to say, "Well, that's different. You understand this stuff, but he probably won't." Disclosure is also a chance to practice interpersonal skills, offering both increased intimacy with others and the sense of presence and entitlement that comes with self-expression.

Of course, the therapist pushing the client to disclose probably is not useful even if her hunch is correct that disclosure would likely benefit the client. The act of telling someone needs to fit the client's sense of timing. Ideally, the client will feel more comfortable and empowered if he is in control of the timing. The issue may get pushed by current life circumstances, such as an upcoming doctor's visit where recent scars will be seen, or other precipitating event like swimming. The idea of the client talking to others may also occur to the therapist if the client reports feeling isolated and alone, making comments that he feels like no one really knows him, or no one could like him if they knew what he did to his body.

When these kinds of moments present themselves, one possible response from the clinician is to ask what it might be like to tell X (naming a person in the client's life), or simply, "to tell someone about yourself in this way." This may open the door, even if the client decides that now is not the time to tell someone. Such interventions may appear to be basic, simple counseling approaches, and, at one level, are just that. However, for some people who self-injure, these opportunities carry significance and can represent the beginning of a larger move toward healing.

Sometimes the idea of disclosure comes from the client when she reaches a certain level of intimacy with a friend or dating partner, or as the seasons change. One woman describes her fears about, and the value of, disclosure.

> Whenever I make a new friend, I have a tremendous amount of anxiety as summer approaches—can I wear short sleeves around this person? How will this person react? Will he or she think I am crazy? Will they decide not to be friends any more—will they see these scars as a sign that I am too fucked up? It's one of the many things that make me feel different and separate from other people. Most people I know do not have a legacy of white scar tissue coursing their arms.
>
> Every time I face this "interpersonal hurdle" I want to give up on the friendship. I want to decide that it's too hard to talk about. Too hard to reveal that part

of myself. But, somehow, there are parts of me with enough courage—and a desire for friendship and con- nectedness—that I do tell them, and explain how the scars happened. And, to my surprise, I have always been met with a very accepting response from others. People still want to be friends with me, even after knowing this information.

It also seems that experiencing some acceptance from others helps me grow a tiny bit more in my abil- ity to accept myself. I have noticed that in talking about my struggle, this often opens up the door for the other person to share more deeply about them- selves and their own struggles. In this way, having this conversation can be an opportunity, although it is al- ways difficult. I hope that with time and acceptance, both from others and from within, these scars will cease to be such a big interpersonal hurdle. Maybe instead, they'll be a sidebar.

Preparing for disclosure in a therapy session may be useful for some clients, while others will negotiate the pro- cess on their own. For clients who are working on increas- ing their interpersonal skills and have significant fears about intimacy, spending session time focusing in concrete, preparatory ways for disclosure is generally helpful. Role playing, generating possible scenarios, writing down actual words and sentences the client might use, and imagining various outcomes can all be good tools. Making plans for support after the disclosure is also a good idea, in case the person he tells is not supportive. Such preparation teaches the client, in a more global sense, how to pace and care for himself when taking on a difficult or emotionally de- manding task, regardless of the content.

One intervention that can be useful regarding disclosure of self-injury is the potential value of a therapist self-disclosing self-injury or other self-harming behavior.

> Laura, who self-injured in several different ways for many years, describes how powerfully she was impacted by a therapist's disclosure of her own self-injury. Laura had mentioned in her women's therapy group, with much difficulty, that she injured herself and that she felt horribly ashamed and different from others. No one in the group acknowledged that she too struggled with self-injury. The topic shifted and the session ended. As the women were leaving, the therapist took Laura aside and shared the fact that she herself had a history of self-injury. Laura says, "When she told me she self-injured, I felt like I joined the human race. I didn't know anyone else who did that; I thought I was the only one who injured their body. It was very helpful. I feel that there is less judgment when support comes from someone who has been there. And a therapist disclosing overeating isn't the same, because eating is socially acceptable. When you have this behavior that everybody judges as weird and you find someone else who also hurts themselves, it makes such a difference."

As with any self-disclosure by a clinician, the timing and context need to be assessed and the content of the disclosure carefully chosen. Too much personal detail or a disclosure at the wrong time is probably motivated more by the therapist's need for affiliation or connection than by what she perceives the client needs. However, if well considered, such an intervention can help reduce shame and isolation. (See the section in Chapter 6 on therapist self-disclosure for a discussion of the issues involved.)

The Use of Contracts

As mentioned in Chapter 6, employing contracts to cope with self-injurious behavior should be done only with great caution. There are clients and therapists who have found contracting to be useful in managing self-injury (Burstow 1992, Conterio and Lader 1998). These clients are often people for whom contracts are effective in other arenas. For others, a contract, especially one that focuses on stopping the behavior, can be problematic. The probability of a recurrence of the self-injury is often very high until there has been some fundamental resolution of core issues. A contract, therefore, can be a setup for failure, additional shame, and reinforcement about how out of control the client is.

The meaning of a contract needs to be explored. Is a contract desired by the therapist or the client? For whose comfort is the contract? If it is the client's idea, is it because he is feeling so tired of injuring that he wants some external structure, or is it because he thinks the therapist is getting fed up and he better do something to make things better? Is it that a contract represents a concrete and written commitment to change that would facilitate a larger process of change? Does the contract give the client a sense of taking action, and any action toward positive change feels necessary or helpful? The meaning of any contract is important and provides information about its usefulness as an intervention strategy.

The complexity of the dynamics involved in the contract are also relevant. The client and the therapist need to discuss what failure to comply with the contract means. What will happen if the client can't actually do what she is contracting to do? How might she deal with this eventuality? Will there be consequences? If so, what are they and who implements them? Is an element of punishment involved in using a contract, from the client's perspective? Possible outcome scenarios need to be explored to determine if there is an inherent setup or negative script for the client that a contract can help to enact.

Clarity about the power dynamics is another important aspect of how contracts are employed, as discussed in Chapter 6. Contracts regarding the client's behavior are, fundamentally, not contracts between the therapist and client. Rather, they represent a person's agreement with herself, with the therapist as a witness to the agreement. If used, they should detail the client's behavior, not the therapist's behavior. This frame helps keep responsibility issues clear, that is, the client is responsible and accountable to herself to keep the contract, rather than inadvertently placing the therapist in the role of enforcer. This underscores the fact that the client's desire to make the change is hers, not something externally imposed by the therapist.

When contracts are used, they need to embody a middle ground, rather than an all-or-nothing position such as "I will never self-injure again." A middle-ground position might be "I will use all of the following alternatives when I feel the impulse to self-injure," or "I will try to draw on other skills and resources when I want to self-injure. Ten of these alternatives are listed below" or "The next time I feel I need to self-injure, I will wait ten minutes first." These statements do not preclude the use of self-injury, but make a clear statement about the intent to utilize other methods of coping, or to intervene in some way. This avenue may be the most helpful and least harmful variant of contracting about self-injury when a client feels a contract would be useful. Other terms of a beneficial contract might address the client's desire to increase her awareness about the process of self-injury. An example might read something like this: "The next time I self-injure, I will sit down and write about my experience. I will try to include what I felt before and after I injured, and what was going on while I was injuring." For clients who need to clearly spell out action steps, or feel they are making inroads on what seems like an intractable problem, contracting to increase awareness may help.

Again, however, the internal pressure to stop self-injuring combined with an equally strong internal pressure to keep self-injuring may make the entire contract process one that is ultimately less than helpful for the client. It can serve rather as a distraction from addressing the underlying issues, or provide a forum within which the client and therapist get embroiled in a contest over power and control. Attending to these potentially complicating factors is a key responsibility of the therapist as he explores the use of contracts with his client.

Using a Twelve-Step/Addiction Recovery Model with Self-Injury

As noted earlier, the process of self-injuring can feel addictive to some people, and skills for coping with compulsions and obsessions can add to someone's bank of resources. Some clients in recovery from drugs or alcohol who are involved in twelve-step programs like Alcoholics Anonymous (AA) find they draw on this approach in dealing with their self-injury (Hyman 1999). Since this model is based on abstinence regarding the addictive substance (or behavior), this means that someone choosing a twelve-step model to interrupt her self-injury is deciding to eliminate self-injury from her repertoire of coping skills. This might be a fruitful choice for some people. For others who are not ready or desiring to make this choice, they may still find that some of the skills they have learned in AA or Narcotics Anonymous (NA), or in drug and alcohol rehabilitation programs, as well as the spiritual framework offered by a twelve-step program benefit them in their struggle with self-injury.

Concepts or slogans from The Program (AA or NA or Al-Anon)—such as "one day at a time" or "fake it till you make it"—offer quick and simple reminders when under stress (Alcoholics Anonymous World Services 1975). "One day at a time" prompts one to focus on the present and get through the immediate moment of distress, to avoid the often-demoralizing pull to look at changing one's whole life. "Fake it till you make it" stresses the need to practice new attitudes in order to actually adopt them, based on the idea that behavior change sometimes precedes a shift of belief. These values, and others from the program, can be helpful to someone working on injuring less or not at all. Finding a support group of people committed to making changes in their lives regarding addiction and addictive behavior can also augment the resources someone has. Ideas from others about how they manage obsessions or compulsions can help. The relationship with a higher power as encouraged by the program can also be beneficial. As always, it is essential that this approach fits a client's world-view and that any suggestion to explore a twelve-step model be thoughtfully considered.

Keeping Perspective: Helping the Client Intervene

Discovering more about the client's self-injuring behavior is generally very useful for the clinician. It provides a wealth of data that inform the clinician's understanding of the client's world. However, this is not the primary value of talking in some detail about the client's self-injury. Fundamentally, such conversations need to be useful to the client. The client is the one who is responsible for determining when and to what extent she will utilize self-injury. She is the only one who can stop self-injuring, if that is her goal. She is the only one who can reduce the degree of harm, or substitute less-damaging behaviors, or find workable alternatives and develop new skills. Clarity about this responsibility preserves and supports the therapeutic relationship by avoiding unnecessary power struggles and providing space for the underlying issues to emerge. When client and therapist can work together in this way, healing the core issues can occur with the greater promise of lasting change.

8

Repairing and Completing the Self-Boundary

When clients move to intervene in their self-injuring process, they find that there is rarely one solution. Rather, they find they increase their information base, develop alternatives, learn about and work on underlying issues, acquire new skills, and shore up their sense of self. The process is one of intersecting paths that lead them through the thicket of pain and confusion into an easier place. Wending their way through the thicket often involves repairing and completing the self-boundary.

A number of approaches can be useful for people with inadequate self-boundaries. Some frameworks address the resulting effects without specifically working directly with the self-boundary as it is conceptualized in this book. Cognitive-behavioral therapies, solution-focused approaches, and skill-based methods that teach practical ways to foster development in areas such as affect regulation, self-soothing, interpersonal communication, and distress tolerance offer valuable tools for managing daily living more effectively (Dolan 1991, Linehan 1993, Napier 1993). Constructivist self-development theory provides another framework for exploring and changing trauma-based cognitive schemas, with resultant changes in behavior, perception, affect, and interpersonal interaction (McCann and Pearlman 1992, Saakvitne et al. 2000), as do cognitive rescripting methods (Arntz and Weertman 1999, Chard et al. 1997, Smucker et al. 1995). Gestalt therapy invites and focuses on increasing awareness of the contact boundary, the point at which self meets other, impacting one's ability to embody self, and regulate sensation and contact (Clemmens 1997, Kepner 1995).

Some orientations lend themselves more obviously to the dilemma of an inadequate self-boundary. Transactional analysis presents both a conceptual frame and a method for reworking the self-boundary (James 1981). Some psychoanalytic and psychodynamic approaches hone in on internal representations of self and other, a pointedly relevant way of working on the self-boundary (Davies and Frawley 1994, Ehrenberg 1992, Hamilton 1992, Scharff 1992). Yet other orientations offer selective focusing, in particular areas that can be useful in helping people with an inadequate self-boundary cope or heal. In addition, the integration of past traumas, through various modalities, also facilitates the development of a more cohesive, engaged, and boundaried sense of self. Various paths lead to resolution and reparation.

Many clients and therapists who utilize these and other modalities do indeed focus to a greater or lesser extent on the incomplete attachment; some modalities actually help clients reach resolution, that is, complete the individuation process, either by design or inadvertence. For many, however, resolution remains elusive. People may feel better, function better, feel less out of control and more grounded in their bodies, and maintain healthier relationships, but still not feel whole or complete enough. Working specifically on completing the attachment-separation-individuation process can facilitate a greater sense of wholeness.

Reaching some degree of individuation by repairing the self-boundary does not mean that development stops, or the person is without flaws, defenses, or unresolved issues. It does not mean that she has arrived, or is done with healing or therapy. The process of individuation continues throughout one's lifetime, sometimes with increasing complexity and more specific focus, and in unexpected ways. Attachment needs remain relevant across the life span (Holmes 1998, Pistole 1999). And once a self-boundary is more solid, other issues may emerge more fiercely, clamoring for resolution, as there is greater ego strength and more capacity to address difficult feelings or concerns.

However, establishing or completing the self-boundary does provide a measure of relief. It creates a ground to stand on, decreasing chronic anxiety and the use of distressing coping strategies. It allows for healthy interdependence with others. It can mean that a man stops living his life with a belief that someone else can make him happy and okay, or that a woman finds her feelings no longer prompt her to fly apart at any moment. It can mean that a man no longer has to stay disconnected from others to maintain a sense of self, or that a woman can spend time alone and still feel grounded. It also often means that self-injury is less likely to be utilized as a regulator of intense affect or external stimuli.

This chapter outlines some steps that can be useful in the process of completing the self-boundary in adulthood. This process generally occurs within the context of a larger healing or therapy process, and can be integrated into different theoretical orientations and therapeutic styles. While the approach is clearly relationship based and utilizes object relations language to some extent, I believe it is an eclectic mix that can be useful to clinicians of many persuasions. The descriptions that follow are intended to highlight a particular and often central element in people's movement toward wholeness, rather than provide a comprehensive approach to all the sequelae of disrupted attachment. Skill development regarding coping strategies and life management skills are usually part of the process, and are addressed to some extent. The reenactment of early childhood needs regarding attachment in the therapeutic relationship is also discussed.

Again, it is important to emphasize that some (perhaps many) clients will effect the completion or partial completion of the self-boundary without emphasizing this work as it is described in this chapter. I am not suggesting that overt attention must be given to the self-boundary in order to reach a more individuated state. Rather, I offer this frame of reference and these concrete ideas as a way to augment and enrich the therapy process for those clients struggling with incomplete self-boundaries, particularly when a spotlight on these issues helps make sense of someone's struggles when nothing else has quite worked.

The Broad Framework:
How to Approach This Work

Helping clients to complete or strengthen an inadequate self-boundary involves teaching new ideas within the context of highly engaged interpersonal interactions. Perhaps all therapy, at some level, is about teaching within an interpersonal context. I believe my role as a therapist consists of three fundamental aspects: I serve as a teacher of new information and skills, I serve as a witness to the unresolved events of the past, and I serve as a co-creator of the container within which the mysterious process of healing can occur. Different parts of the therapeutic process lend themselves more or less to each aspect. Working on completing the self-boundary, in particular, demands that I draw on all three aspects as teacher, witness, and co-creator.

This means several things. First, it means that when my clients bring intense feelings or complicated beliefs, I am able to stay grounded, present, and engaged. It means that I bring my energy to the creation of the "envelope" of therapy (Scharff 1992) to help contain and organize their experiences (my role as co-creator). Second, it also means I sit with someone, for example, as she works through her recollection of being left to her own devices as a toddler, and processes the terror and pain of abandonment in the presence of a caring and engaged other (my role as witness).

Third, it means that I teach the concepts and new beliefs that are relevant to a more complete self-boundary in a variety of ways (my role as teacher). Sometimes this means I verbally share information like some of the ideas in this chapter. Other times, my teaching occurs through modeling, or a suggestion that the client practice new behaviors or try an exercise, or the recommendation of literature or other teachers (such as an assertiveness or meditation teacher). Like any intervention or approach, the timing must fit. The new information can only be received when the client is ready and it is offered in an accessible way for that person.

This work as teacher, witness, and co-creator involves four elements:

1. Communicating basic concepts about attachment, separation, and individuation, in everyday, understandable language.
2. Teaching three strategies that facilitate a shift in perspective—validating the needs of the child self, supporting the adult self to be responsible and care for the child self, and resolving old needs.

3. Helping the client develop self-management skills in areas such as coping with feelings, self-soothing techniques, distraction and self-talk, identifying and managing triggers, problem solving, and assertiveness.

4. Supporting the client to identify his "stuck" place in the attachment process and complete his self-boundary by embracing the child self and grieving the associated losses.

Written as it is here in stepwise form, the process sounds much more linear and didactic than it is in real life. In regular interactions, these tasks occur fluidly and sometimes with considerable overlap. For the most part, they emerge in response to an issue a client brings in. Keeping these concepts in my frame of reference helps me utilize them as I try to help a client make sense of her experience. My goal is to share this information or suggest a particular strategy or intervention in a way I think she can hear at a given point in time.

Diana, 36, comes to a session distraught about the loss of Bob, an old friend and neighbor. He and his wife have moved more than 2,000 miles away after being neighbors for the past twelve years. She misses his wife also, but is not upset in the same way about losing her. She doesn't understand why she continues to miss him so acutely. She plans to visit them next summer, but she still feels a low-level yet constant distress and finds herself thinking about him all the time. I ask her what he means to her. She is confused at first by my question, but then says she somehow felt safer with him next door. We continue to talk about her feelings for Bob and she says, "You know, I feel like a kid when I think about him now, even though I never did when we spent time together when they lived here." Even though he is only about ten years older than she, she realizes that he represented the good father to her—kind, generous, helpful with house maintenance, encouraging of her abilities. His presence afforded her a sense of groundedness.

This interaction opens the door for more explorations about Diana's self-boundary and her individuation process. I might, at this point, talk about how important Bob is to her and that I have a hunch it might be connected to unfinished business from childhood. I might say I notice that she glows when she talks about him, and that he sounds different from what she said about her father, who raised her and her older brother after her mother died when Diana was 2. I might talk a little about how children count on adults for their sense of well-being, and that I imagine she counted on her father even if he wasn't very approachable or overtly supportive after her mother died.

Up until this point in our relationship, Diana has insisted that she never really knew her mother who was ill all of Diana's life or felt close to her, and that her father, while not very available, was an okay dad. She has said she doesn't have sadness about her childhood, even though she experiences chronic low-grade depression. She also avoids most intimate relationships and has never had a long-term partner. Her brother "messed around with me sexually for a few years until Dad found out and beat him"; she has mixed feelings about her brother. As a teen, she pinched and bruised her breasts when aroused. This pinching and bruising has recurred on several occasions when she has gotten involved in short-term sexual relationships as an adult.

I might also say to Diana that I am sorry she has lost Bob as a neighbor and that I think this might be an opportunity to understand more about how she feels inside. That her feelings about Bob seem to be opening up something more than the loss of him in her present life. That I'm wondering about her early experiences because of how strong her feelings are. How much I say will depend on what Diana can tolerate in the moment. I probably wouldn't mention that I thought she might have sadness or other unresolved feelings about her parents. That would probably be too much at this point. This session might provide just the slightest opening, but it is the beginning of a conversation about unmet child-based needs, holes in her sense of self and how Diana can care for herself now. This education and sorting through of the past, as well as experiments with self-care now, will occur over a period of months, perhaps years. Some of it will occur without me as a part of the process. But we start with something Diana brings, so the past—as Diana now carries it—can begin to change.

Communicating Basic Concepts About the Individuation Process

Teaching about individuation can occur in a number of ways. Some clients find books helpful while others learn better through discussion. (I generally suggest Kaplan's *Oneness to Separateness: From Infant to Individual* [1978] and Goldbart and Wallin's *Mapping the Terrain of the Heart* [1996] for people who want to read about attachment and individuation.) Some understand general concepts about individuation, but need help making the connections between the ideas and what they feel or the events in their lives. Sometimes I draw pictures to show how I think about attachment and separation, and the development of a sense of self, similar to Figures 4–1 and 4–2 in Chapter 4. In situations like the scenario described above with Diana, a recent loss or especially strong feelings about someone in the present is often the opening that invites some basic teaching about attachment, separation, and individuation. For some clients, it is their relationships with their children that provide the impetus and context for the discussion. Other times it is the client asking, "Why do I always end up back in this same place with people in my life?" Somehow these concepts have to make sense inside the client's current worldview and priorities.

Teaching these concepts creates a shared language and perspective that anchors future discussion and exploration between therapist and client. Some clients will follow up spontaneously by asking questions about attachment and separation, requesting literature suggestions, or making their own connections with their histories. For others, I keep this frame of reference in my head, and try to check out how well it fits as a theory to explain and understand what the client describes. I may share my wonderings with the client in moments when I think the ideas will make sense to her. Finding ways to concretize and ground my theory about a client's incomplete self-boundary or disrupted attachment process in the current issues she brings to our work together is crucial.

Teaching Key Strategies that Facilitate Healing

As noted above, there are three strategies that I find fundamental to helping clients work through unresolved pain from childhood and take responsibility for their lives now. These strategies serve to effect a shift in perspective that both allows resolution of past experiences and supports self-control and accountability in the present. This "both/ and" approach is invaluable. (My colleagues and I used to call this the "Both Sides Now" approach to healing, borrowing the title from the 1960s Joni Mitchell song. It is not unlike Linehan's [1993] ideas about dialectics.) Many self-help and therapeutic efforts exhort people to move on by putting the past behind them and to act from a place of power and strength now. Other methods focus on examining past traumas to the exclusion of any practical attention to, or encouragement to focus on, the present. The former tends to simplistically discount or dismiss people's internal reality, and the latter often serves to keep people stuck and operating from a disempowered place. I believe a balanced view that incorporates the value of both approaches coupled with concrete support for managing the past in the context of the present makes the most sense, and is most helpful to adult survivors of childhood trauma.

Three interconnected beliefs or values (articulated here as action strategies) serve to concretize this concept of respecting and learning from one's past while taking charge of one's present. Two of these strategies need to go hand in hand to maintain this balance. The first is the importance of validating the needs stemming from the child-self. Unmet child-self needs may be expressed as longings to be valued as a person by one's therapist, to be respected by one's boss, to be loved unconditionally by someone, to be reassured and comforted, to have an attachment figure available as needed, and to be physically held in order to regain a sense of grounding and safety. Compassionate, positive acknowledgment of such longings affirms the child-self's need for such care and attention.

In order for this to be balanced and grounded in the present reality, however, the second belief or value also needs to be articulated (not quite in the same breath, but in some proximity to the first). This belief is that the adult-self needs to take responsibility for actually caring for the child self and managing daily life. Maybe the best way to illustrate this is to describe a conversation I once had with a client during her first hospitalization after we had been working together for several months. In that conversation, I made a comment to her about self-responsibility without quite realizing all of its significance at the time.

Samantha had asked me to hang in there with her when I visited her on the inpatient unit. (At the time I had only a glimmer of the fact that she was highly dissociative with an extensive trauma history, so I didn't really know what that meant.) She knew she had a lot going on, was upset about the dangerous situations in which she found herself at times, and sought reassurance that I would continue to work with her in spite of that. I said that I would, but that I needed her to always take respon sibility for herself. I told her I could weather a lot of difficult times with her, but I couldn't feel responsible for her well-being, safety, and daily functioning. That she had to be responsible, and I could then do my part. I said this because I knew I needed this kind of clarity in order to be able to make a commitment to her. I knew I couldn't hang in there if I somehow began feeling responsible for helping her get through each day. I was speaking from a place of truth for me, with some awareness that I was asking her to do something therapeutically useful. Some years later she told me how important my request/statement was and how powerfully it framed our work together. She said that it demanded that she always work as hard or harder than I worked, and that she did her best to take care of herself no matter what. She and I have lived through many complicated attachment issues and struggled to understand and resolve her needs in this arena, but always she has maintained a fierce sense of self-responsibility.

Some clients may not be ready to accept this framework. For people who have operated for many years with the belief that someone external to them needs to care for the child inside in order to heal, letting go of the idea of a rescuing external other can be difficult. Consistent, gentle education about the new concept of the adult self caring for the child self may be required over a period of time. Sometimes this education process must be coupled with mindful but direct attention and caregiving to the child-self by the therapist. For some clients, therapist modeling of nurturing behavior may be necessary. It can also be important to provide some level of fulfillment before the client can do it for himself; this is addressed later in this chapter in the section on reenactments in the therapeutic relationship.

Inevitably, if the first two values or strategies as stated above become part of the operating beliefs shared by client and therapist, the push to resolve old, unmet childhood needs will inevitably emerge. The third strategy involves articulating and understanding that there are three options for resolving old needs more directly. I often find it helpful to directly verbalize these options to clients when this issue comes up. Old, lingering needs from childhood are settled through either need-meeting by others in the present, need-meeting by self (as in the adult self caring for the child self), or grieving the needs that can't be met. The advantage of this perspective (that some needs can be met and some can't, that some can be met by others and some can't) is that it offers actual possibilities within realistic limits. It invites action, rather than inaction or stuckness regarding old needs. It also allows for a complex experience, rather than suggesting the oversimplified "just let go of the past"—something most people would indeed do if they knew how.

Articulating the concept that some needs can be met by others and some must be met by one's self can be useful to the client. More focused work on listing old needs, identifying who might be able to meet the need in an age-appropriate way now, and striving to develop ways to ask to get the need met can also be helpful. This is precisely the work we are doing when we help clients assertively express their needs and desires. Grounding these assertiveness skills in the larger context of unmet childhood needs helps people distinguish (to the extent that any of us can do so) these needs from adult-based needs of the present. It effectively shifts the unconscious or semiconscious child-based needs into greater awareness, where they may become clearer, less affectively charged adult-based needs.

An example of this might be the unmet child-based need to have a best friend. Unsorted and out of awareness, this need prompts Marianna to disclose too much to new friends, which in turn prompts them to withdraw. She then feels alone and isolated, as she did much of her childhood. This triggers a depressed mood and sense of hopelessness. Identifying the child-based need and addressing it directly can allow her greater awareness and the subsequent chance to make different choices about how she interacts with a new friend in the present.

> The first step for Marianna may involve accepting the truth that she is never going to have the delicious experience of being 8 or 9 and spending hour after hour hanging out with a best friend. Recognizing this might bring tears, or another emotional expression of loss,

including anger and disappointment. Once processed, however, she is then freed up to consider how she might get some of this need met in a way that fits for her now in her life. This might entail reviewing acquaintances with an eye to identifying one or two with whom Marianna thinks she might be able to be more intimate. She then can think through what exactly it would mean now to have a best-friend kind of friend. Perhaps it is someone with whom she could spend Saturday afternoon, running errands in easy camaraderie. Perhaps, to Marianna, it means having someone in whom she can confide. Maybe she wants a friend with whom she can go to plays and movies on the spur of the moment. Maybe it is having all of those qualities wrapped up in one person. Yet, once the child-yearning is somewhat removed or modified by accepting what cannot be, Marianna may realize that, at 41, she probably won't realistically find a friend who can be all those things to her. She may instead shift her goal to finding several different friends who can be significant in different ways. She may also find that she likes spending time alone more, now that she doesn't feel the constant nagging desire for a best friend when, for example, she goes to a movie by herself. Thus, grieving and clarifying the need can allow her to move on and get more of what she wants in the present and future.

This sorting-out process tends to expose the needs that cannot be met, usually now or ever. These poignant moments can be quite powerful and transformative. One very painful example of a need that cannot be met and must be grieved is the desire to be loved unconditionally, passionately, and delightedly by one's mother—to feel like the most important and most wonderful person in the whole world, basking in the glow of mother-love. Grieving and releasing this common child-self longing often overlaps with the work described in the section on completing the self-boundary. It is also one of the areas that can be quite fraught with reenactment between therapist and client, as the client tries to get this need met by the therapist.

Developing New and Enhancing Existing Skills in Self-Management

Great variations exist across self-injuring clients with regard to the need for developing skills that help people manage both their internal states and their external life experiences. Pearlman and her colleagues refer to these skills as self capacities (Deiter and Pearlman 1998, Saakvitne et al. 2000). Clients may benefit from enhancing or learning self-awareness and management skills as part of their efforts to solidify their self-boundary. They may learn these skills within the therapy process and in other contexts; different skills will be most salient for different clients.

Linehan (1993) offers a useful outline of key psychosocial skills in her model of dialectical behavior therapy for people who have been diagnosed with borderline personality disorder. Her four primary modules for skills training are

- mindfulness,
- interpersonal effectiveness,
- emotion regulation, and
- distress tolerance.

Other areas of specific skill development may be useful to people who self-injure. Many of these overlap with or are incorporated in Linehan's conceptualization and description of skills, but are delineated separately here to descriptively underscore skills needs:

- capacity to attend to the present moment
- identification of sensations and feelings
- sufficient language for feelings
- assertiveness training
- management of triggers and flashbacks
- grounding and orienting techniques
- relaxation and biofeedback training
- information management (regulation and access) across dissociative states
- systematic approaches to problem solving
- internal communication between ego states or alters
- distraction techniques
- self-coaching

Clearly, clients learn or enhance these capacities in a variety of ways. I find some clients actively pursue skill development on their own, seeking out classes, workshops, or books. Some clients look to me as a teacher of skills, and want to practice or try basic relaxation techniques (see Benson 1997), for example, in a therapy session. Clients sometimes see me as a consultant to their healing process, and ask for recommendations regarding a specific skill area. Participation in a dialectical behavior therapy or other skill-based group may be useful.

Three books written for survivors of trauma that offer useful information on skill building are Dolan's *Resolving Sexual Abuse* (1991), Finney's *Reach for the Rainbow* (1992), and Napier's *Getting Through the Day* (1993). All provide concrete, specific tips on grounding, flashback and trigger management, self-soothing, meditation and mindfulness, relaxation and other body-based approaches, increased control over dissociative processes and other self-care skills, as well as theoretical and contextual information about abuse and trauma.

Solidifying the Self-Boundary: Common Steps

The fourth element in repairing or completing the self-boundary is an actual reworking of the disrupted individuation process. This section lists ten steps as a way to summarize the work often involved in moving toward resolution of an incomplete individuation process. As noted earlier, these steps sound much more linear, discrete, and tidy than they are in actuality. They are summarized here as steps for conceptual clarity. For many clients, outlining the process in a stepwise fashion is probably not helpful; others may find they can take the framework as just that, and mold it to suit their own needs. This is not a formula, and the variations across clients are not just individual differences. Clients' various styles and approaches to an incomplete self-boundary are the very stuff of their healing work and are much more important than the steps outlined below.

1. Identify the approximate age of the disruption in the attachment-separation-individuation process. If more than one key disruption occurred, each may need to be identified and worked through separately. Look at the meaning the disruption holds for the client and what it might signify in terms of developmental theory. What is going on for a child at that point in a child's life? Many clients will describe or sense some disruption around and before 4 years of age. Some may also describe subsequent disruptions. Their recollections probably cannot be defini-

tive, detailed memories, as memory is so complicated, particularly in a child's early years. However, some felt-sense
of what was true at a certain age, combined with family
stories, known facts, and personal narratives, can often pin-
point one or more significant periods of disruption in individuation. (Certain developmental tasks as well as nodal
moments in the attachment-separation process can be fro-
zen in a person's internal sense of himself and his world,
even though development progresses in spite of unfinished
tasks. A good grounding in developmental, attachment, and
object relations theories can be extremely useful in helping clients to identify pertinent unresolved developmental
tasks.)

2. Describe the picture or image associated with the
disruption. What image emerges spontaneously when the
client is distressed? What image comes when the client or
therapist asks about the stuck place? It might be a memory-
like image (such as being left as an infant in a crib) or it
might be something more symbolic (such as seeing a little
rabbit adrift in a boat on the sea with no mother in sight).
How old is the child at the time? If it is a memory-like
image, what is the child wearing? Where is she sitting or
standing or lying? Are there any sounds? Any odors? What
does the child see when she looks around? If it is symbolic,
what is happening for the little rabbit, for example? What
sensations is she experiencing? Get enough information for
the recollection to be vivid. This will facilitate the subsequent steps.

3. Identify feelings at the time of the disruption and
express feelings that still remain if they are accessible. Put
simple words on the feelings, such as *scared, sad, lonely, hurt,
mad.* The feelings that remain often function as the cement
holding the building blocks of belief in place. Releasing the
feelings can allow the beliefs to begin to shift or be rear-

ranged. For some people, the feelings may not be accessible, and will emerge more slowly, or later in the process (see step 10).

4. Identify resulting beliefs that are still operative and probably entrenched. Articulating (and even writing down) the beliefs that emerged from the disrupted or traumatic experience and the child-self feelings is important. These beliefs are the building blocks upon which the client has constructed her worldview. She may be able to offer elaborate, adult-based rationales for these beliefs, but at their core they are simple child beliefs with great power. These beliefs tend to operate beneath conscious awareness yet strongly influence the client's sense of self and his approach to relationships, in particular. Some examples of operating beliefs are "I can never trust anyone again to be there for me," "I am all alone," "There is something unlikable/unlovable about me," "If I am just good enough, then she'll like me," "When I am older, I'll find someone who really cares about me," and "I have to rely on myself at all times." (See McCann and Pearlman [1992] for some ideas about beliefs or schemas in specific domains that are frequently affected by trauma, such as trust and intimacy.)

5. Imagine or conceptualize where/how the child self continues to hold open a space for the returning or fantasied caregiver (the hole or gap) in order to reattach and continue the separation process. This might literally feel like a hole residing in a certain part of the body, or feel like a bricked-up, closed-in space in the body. It may also be imagined as an extended hand that is waiting for the caregiver's hand, or a sustaining belief that the mother or caregiver is just away right now and will return in a moment. A concretized, body-based image is probably more facilitating as it connects more vividly to child-self, sensate-

organized experience. However, each client's perception will be different and a variety of images or concepts can be workable. The important element here is to find something specific to represent the sense of waiting for the perfect caregiver to come or to return.

6. Clarify beliefs that are accurate about the present, including "I am not a child any longer," "I am an adult and I can care for myself—even the 'me' who still feels so young and needy," "My child self never has to be alone or abandoned again; I am here," "I have adult skills and abilities to manage most things I have to cope with in my life; if I need help, I can safely seek it." It may take some time for these beliefs to feel real. The child self's protest may be long and loud, demanding that someone outside the self provide what feels like necessary care or support. This longing is quite compelling and, from the child's frame of reference, it does not seem possible that she, herself, could possibly meet her own needs. The therapist's task is to consistently, compassionately, and "gently challenge" (McCann and Pearlman 1992, p. 201) these child-self beliefs, and allow for the incorporation of a new set of beliefs based on the present.

7. Make a commitment to stop waiting for the caregiver to come or return. This commitment, like the incorporation of the new beliefs, takes time. Sometimes it occurs as a specific event, sometimes it is a more gradual process. Sometimes it can occur only after some developmental tasks are more fully resolved or achieved (see the next step). The crux of this step, though, is a shift in belief, a letting go of the longing and desire for the return of the caregiver. Framing this as a conscious choice or decision can be helpful to some clients, and can concretize what may feel like an amorphous grief process.

The acuteness of the pain involved in letting go of the fantasied or returning caregiver cannot be underestimated.

The sustaining fantasy that "someday my prince/mother/love will come" can be quite powerful. Often, this fantasy had to be powerful enough to sustain the child through abuse and loss that felt nearly unbearable. Letting go of the fantasy or belief is a loss in and of itself in the present, as well as triggering the release of pent-up losses from childhood.

8. Achieve some resolution of unfinished developmental tasks. Sometimes clients need to actively work to resolve the tasks they left behind when they had to move on. For example, a client who is stuck, in part, at a pre-differentiation phase of the attachment-separation process may need to spend some time differentiating. Differentiation begins to occur in the latter part of the first year of life, as an infant starts in a rudimentary way to sort out what is baby and what is mother (Mahler 1975). This represents the early movement from a position of fused connection, a being-one-with-mother (or other primary caregiver). A client who experienced significant disruption in her attachment to her caregiver at this stage might need to create the experience of differentiating now. This might mean distinguishing how she is different from and similar to her mother, or her therapist, or her partner (depending on how directly she can access the feelings about her mother, or who is starring in her reenactment). She might need to differentiate from all three. This can take the form of simple acknowledgment, as reflected in statements like "I really am different from my mother because she never liked having animals in the house," or "That's one way I am different from you [the therapist]," or "Rosa and I are very different in our approaches to household problems like that plumbing crisis we had." The need to differentiate can also take the form of changing how one dresses or wears her hair, shifting careers, or taking up a new interest or hobby.

9. Close the opening, gap, or hole that the client has kept for the returning caregiver in whatever way makes sense in the light of the client's image or metaphor. This may involve working through and integrating traumatic material related to the occurrence of the hole. It may involve creating a healing image, a way for the hole to grow shut. It may involve withdrawing the extended hand, or imaging new skin. It may involve visualizing bands of energy that encircle the client. It may involve a verbal statement made aloud that the client wants the hole to close, perhaps as part of a verbal commitment to not wait any longer for mom to return.

10. Hold and comfort the child self. Allow whatever expression of feelings that are still embodied or carried by the child self. This release of old affect can seem repetitive ("I just keep crying about the same thing") and sometimes is, if the other steps of shifting beliefs and letting go aren't part of the process. Simply releasing feelings about the past may not facilitate movement. Some clients find it useful to imagine their adult self holding their child self and actively providing comfort. Such an image concretizes the adult self caring for the child self. The child self can achieve the fulfillment of the need to be rescued, nurtured, and held. The adult self can remind the child self, "You're safe now. I'm here. You're okay." This may be combined with a visualization of actually retrieving the child self from an image of a past traumatic event or experience of isolation that still resonates for the client.

Individual Differences, Many Pathways

A client's personal style regarding change, her readiness for this work, and how much trauma is encountered in the recollecting will dictate how and at what pace a client does this work. Readiness involves how much other healing work has been done, the presence or absence of skills for dealing with feelings and stimuli, and the nature and amount of support the client has in his life. These and other factors such as external life demands contribute to how quickly the client moves through this process and what form and course it takes. The purpose of outlining this process as a series of steps is to offer an accessible model or framework to guide movement over time, rather than as a formulaic method.

For some people, the process described here may take a long time and be worked on in little pieces over a period of several years or more. They may work on some of these steps with one therapist, then pick up the process several years later with another therapist. Others will move through the steps fairly rapidly, in almost a concatenated or concentrated form. They may progress through the steps outlined above in several sessions. Some steps won't fit or make sense to some people. Some steps will be combined with others, or will happen quite quickly and automatically (such as moving from feelings to beliefs).

Not only must the pace be set by the client, but the actual course it takes will also vary considerably. Some parts of the process are likely to occur outside the session. A client may work quickly on the first few steps, identifying where she feels stuck in terms of individuation, and then stop. She may work on understanding beliefs and developing new schemas for a while. She may stop this work altogether for a time in order to deal with some current life issues or practice new skills, and then come back to the core issues of attachment and individuation.

Clients will also vary in how they work through these steps or tasks. Some might achieve these tasks through a series of guided-imagery sessions, with or without a therapist. Others may do it in the context of another methodology like the visual-kinesthetic dissociation technique described by Cameron-Bandler (1978), or by using energy processes like Thought Field Therapy or the Tapas Acupressure Technique (Gallo 1999). Some might work through the steps by writing or keeping a journal, or through their dreams. Others will do it relationally with a therapist over a period of time, using a more interpretative, working-through process. Some of the steps are akin to and can occur within a context of various cognitively based methods as well.

This completion of individuation can occur for a highly dissociative client in the context of working on internal communication and collaborative problem solving. Clients with dissociative identity structures often rework these issues in fairly literal ways, since their personality structure is one that is fragmented based on trauma and loss. Often, there are parts or alters who embody the child self's longings for the "good-enough" mother (Winnicott 1965). These parts tend to hold the sustaining fantasy of the returning or ideal caregiver and may be devastated as the reality of life breaks through. This grief may affect the entire system or be limited to certain child parts. Generally, there is some trickle-down (or across) effect to others in the internal system. Some of the longings for care and love may be provided by older parts to younger parts; often there is a concomitant reenactment with an external person like a therapist or partner.

The Role of Current Attachment Figures: Therapists, Partners, Friends, and Co-Workers

Attachment needs continue throughout the life span (Holmes 1998, Pistole 1999), and the reworking of disruptions in early individuation occur in various ways. Some clients work to repair and complete the self-boundary by using relationships with emotionally important people in their lives to concretize their feelings and needs. Grounding the work inside a relational model often helps to make the issues more real and accessible; reenactments of old issues are powerful communicators. The most common current attachment figures with whom clients reenact unfinished individuation are romantic partners or therapists (Davies and Frawley 1994, Dutton 1995, Goldbart and Wallin 1996). Sometimes these issues are activated by co-workers, especially supervisors, or friends. Occasionally an acquaintance on whom the client can project the longings for the perfect caregiver fills the role.

When a current relationship is being used as a vehicle for working through the unfinished individuation issues, part of the therapeutic focus involves sorting out and affirming early individuation needs against a backdrop of realism about the limitations of the real relationship. When the therapist is serving in this role, there is a particular affective charge, and care needs to be taken (as addressed in the next section). When the attachment issues are evoked by someone other than the therapist, the therapist may serve more as a coach to the client as she sorts out and reworks the issues in her present relationship.

Reenactment within the Therapeutic Relationship: A Relational Working-Through

For many clients, the way both they and we (as their therapists) will know they are attempting to work on completing their inadequate self-boundary is through their feelings about us. This means that the longings from the child self are often brought to the therapist in direct or indirect forms. Clients may make direct statements of attachment ("You have become so important to me" or "I have so many feelings about you"). Or their attachment can take a somewhat more indirect form, such as wanting the therapist to be available out of session for grounding or asking the therapist if she likes him (the client) or seeking approval and input for decisions the client is making.

Reenactments also mean that the client brings his confusion and pain about his sense of self and about others into the relationship. Expressions of negative self-esteem may be voiced, seeking both refutation by the therapist (e.g., "I don't think you are a bad person"), and further exploration as to origins. Sometimes clients also seek validation of their bad self-images and work to provoke such confirmation from us in an attempt to resolve the early, unfinished issues with their primary caregiver. This can take the form of provoking a feared response from the therapist, such as "Yes, you are crazy (or manipulative) (or too demanding) (or unlikable)." (Underlying these efforts is the secret and cautious hope that the therapist will disconfirm the negative self-image.) The need to discount the importance of the caregiver/therapist and to assert independence may also be brought up, sometimes expressed by clients' ambivalence about therapy or reluctance to address certain issues.

As noted in various places throughout this text, the therapist is often challenged to maintain her sense of balance and perspective when reenactments are particularly potent, violent, or evocative (Davies and Frawley 1994, Maroda 1998, Pearlman and Saakvitne 1995). The pull to respond to what the client is requesting, such as reassurance about being a good person, can be quite strong. (The pull to offer negative confirmation may be equally strong, but we usually have some awareness that acting on the pull is probably not helpful.) To respond to the client's request for positive reassurance might be precisely what is most helpful to the client. This is particularly true when fundamental beliefs about self are involved. Not that the simple statement by the therapist will change the belief; the change process is more complicated and involved, occurring over a period of time. However, the client may need to hear the therapist state the counterbelief ("I think you are a good person") in order to feel enough support to move into doing the work required to actually change the belief.

Finding the right balance is more difficult when it comes to old, unmet longings for love, comfort, and care. The line between what can be a corrective emotional experience with another that supports the healing of old injuries and moving toward completion of the self-boundary, and an overreaching effort to meet a client's old needs can be difficult to discern at times. As stated, grieving the early losses related to disrupted individuation is key to resolution. If the therapist attempts to fill up the space—the hole left by the departed caregiver—with too much care and concern, the client is then protected from her feelings of loss. The grieving can be avoided, and the hole remains open and in place, despite need-meeting by the therapist. At the same time, sometimes the dearth of care and comfort can be so great that the client feels locked into a deprivation mode. Some measure of responsivity by the therapist may be very helpful in shifting the movement into useful grieving and appropriate need-meeting.

Davies and Frawley (1994), writing from a psychoanalytic perspective, note that it is unhelpful to take a hard-and-fast stance about not responding to any of the child longings that clients bring.

Certainly, work with adult survivors requires certain gratifications within the transference. Experiences of nurturing, holding, containing, protecting are intrinsic to work with both child and the adult persona. The analysis simply would not proceed without emotional availability on the part of the therapist. . . . Any approach that clings to notions of abstinence and total nongratification serve merely to intensify such [counterdependent] defenses, as well as the shame and humiliation that accompany any experience of need in the therapeutic relationship. [p. 228]

They continue in the next paragraph, on the other hand, to address the inadvisability of attempting to meet all of the client's unmet needs from childhood.

From the therapist's perspective, it can feel cruel to withhold the gratification of needs, especially when what the client is asking for feels reasonable and possible. An example of this might be the client's longing to have his hand held or be reassured that he matters to me as a person. But again, the line can be a very hard one to discern. The pull into rescuing behavior can be sharp, and the capacity to sit with the client's grief, especially when it is couched in anger at us for not meeting the need as stated, may be hard to access if we are feeling anything less than strong and focused. It helps to have previously provided information and education about attachment and separation, so the client has some knowledge base in which to ground such frustration and sadness. Compassionate sharing on the therapist's part about how hard it is to not respond, as well as clear statements about the therapist's own limitations or desires, also facilitates the learning process for clients. Rarely is it painless for either client or therapist.

The following story illustrates with poignancy the struggle one client and I have had in trying to find the middle ground between genuine care and need-meeting by the therapist, and the importance of grieving what can never be.

Sarah and I have worked together for nearly four years. During this time, we have worked on attachment issues, severely traumatic memories, self-care, and current life concerns as they have arisen. She still self-injures on occasion, though her heaviest intervals of cutting and burning herself were during high school and college. Throughout our work together, the salience of our relationship has been a central feature. She has consistently sought reassurance that I like her, won't hurt her, am not mad at her, still want to work with her, and so on. Her need to check out how I feel about her, and why I feel as I do, has at times been quite strong and has become the focus of the work in those moments. We have spent considerable time sorting out our interactions with each other, especially when Sarah has felt that I misunderstood what she was saying, or responded in a way that did not feel supportive or on target. She is very alert to nuance, and, as a trained therapist herself, she is gifted with considerable insight about human relationships.

Her gradual attachment to me as a safe haven and grounding element in her life has deepened over the years. From a child place inside, she has said that she wishes I could be her mother, that we could live together and she could just feel safe and warm. She has asked me if I would have protected her if I had been her mother. We have talked about attachment, her longing for a good mother, the process of individuation, the basic human need to feel safe and loved, the fact that I can't be her mother. We have acknowledged that we feel loving toward one another. We have talked through what that means and doesn't mean. We have weathered some painful miscommunications. And there have been several occasions when the acute pain that comes with knowing that she will never have the mother she wants has broken through. One such occasion cast her loss and grief into sharp relief. Although extremely painful, this event and the ensuing reactions have allowed Sarah to begin to let go of her fantasy that someday she would have the mother she always wished for.

On this occasion, Sarah brought me a card she had made from a child place inside, showing in colorful detail and tender words how much she loved me. She said she felt celebratory and expansive. I thanked her and said it was very sweet. This was toward the end of the session, and we looked at it together for several minutes. She then asked me what I was going to do with it. I wanted to be honest, though I knew that what I would say was likely to be painful. Perhaps I could have couched my response more carefully; I felt some press for time as it was the end of the session, and felt that I couldn't lie to her about what I would do with her card. I said that I would put it in a file to keep it. That I appreciated her feelings and the fact that she made me the card.

Sarah was devastated. Her longing or fantasy had been that I would be as touched by the card as she was happy to make it and give it to me. That her love for me would be as important to me as it was to her. That I would keep the card out and look at it. She knew, from a realistic adult place, that I probably wouldn't keep it on display. She understood in her head how her feelings for me wouldn't be as important to me as they were to her. Nonetheless, she felt devastated. She felt she had fallen into a hole and couldn't get out. She had come upon the truth that she would never have the mother she wanted, and she was grief-stricken.

She left my office. She cried on and off for several days. She kept hearing in her head that she would never know mother-love, and to live without ever knowing that kind of love was intolerable and impossible. That she would have to die. Sarah could not imagine living through the pain she was feeling. She and I spoke on the phone the next day and again in the subsequent session about how my love for her can't take the place of the love she didn't get as a child. About how I can't say that I love her as if she were my child (which she wanted me to say), even though what I feel for her is similar to mother-love. I tried to walk this fine line of two truths: that I can love and care about her in a way that is not unlike what a mother feels for a child, but that I cannot love her in that complete, unconditional way that she longs for so desperately. That the fact remains that I am not her mother and can never fill in the gaps of her childhood. That my responsibility as her therapist is to help her tolerate and live through the devastation she was now experiencing.

Gradually, in the sessions following this event, Sarah and I processed what was happening for her and what had transpired between us. She stayed connected to her longing and continued to ask me why I couldn't "just love her like that," reminding me that she knows I believe love heals, and challenging me to explain why it was wrong for her to want what she wanted. I stuck with what I believed to be true, and as much as I wanted to give her what she felt she needed, said that I had to stand strong in what I felt my role to be. We talked about how hard it was for both of us to hold to our positions. I told her I wished I could give her what she wanted. I continued to say I believed she could live through this, even as she refuted the idea with anger and sarcasm.

Since then, Sarah has been able to incorporate her
adult understanding of the issues into her strong feelings
about this loss. She has some distance from the all-con-
suming pit of those feelings, but still actively feels the
loss in moments. She has said that she still doesn't know
if she can go on, knowing that she will never have an
experience she feels is so crucial to being alive. She realizes how fiercely she has held on to the fantasy of a
loving, protective mother, and how letting go of it means
growing up in some way. And that she isn't sure what
that will mean. I know we will revisit this issue in the
future, as Sarah continues to grieve and let go.

In a recent session, we were focused on her profound
sense of aloneness, stemming from childhood memories
she was processing. Toward the end of the session I
asked her what might help with the aloneness. She said
she didn't think much would help. We talked about a
few options. Then Sarah said that she had something she
wanted to ask from a child place inside, but that she
knew that asking would mean I would have to struggle
to find a kind way to say no to her. I suggested that she
not ask for what she wanted, but that she state it as a
longing. Therefore, she could give voice to her desire,
but wouldn't put herself in a position of being rejected
and hurt. This felt especially important since it was the
end of the session. (We both recalled the experience of
the card.)

She thought about it for a moment and then said,
with some embarrassment, that she wished she had a
shirt or sweater of mine, so she could wear it when she
was at home. That having something of mine like that
would feel helpful. I said I understood her wish, it made
sense to me that she wanted some concrete experience
of me to wrap around her, keep her warm. She recalled

a time when she had once borrowed a small blanket from my office for six months, how that had helped back then. I remembered with her, gently teasing that I thought it might have been more than six months. Although she felt sad and still wished for a piece of my clothing, she stayed grounded. She was able to state her desire and not experience great distress at not having her need met. Even though Sarah's self-boundary and attachment work is still in process, there is movement. And we will keep moving through it together, as best we can.

Working with the Original Attachment Figure in the Present

Some clients will find that they are interested in working on their current relationship(s) with their mother or father, or other original attachment figure as part of this process. While working on individuation issues—on their own, with a therapist, or through their partner/spouse relationship— some clients find that the most important aspect of the work is to alter the working model inside their head or psyche and achieve a greater sense of wholeness. For others, while this internal work is important, they need some kind of direct contact with the person to whom they were originally attached. Some clients have close relationships with these attachment figures in the present, some have little or no contact, and others have varying degrees of contact along the continuum.

Part of the work involved in completing or repairing the self-boundary can involve making changes in the quality, quantity, and frequency of contact with the original attachment figure. There is no definitive right amount of contact, type of contact, and so forth. Each person must discern what fits or doesn't fit as she works through this process. Sometimes clients need enough contact so they can gather realistic information about who that person is now, and perhaps extrapolate to who she or he was when they were children. Other times clients need to change the type of interactions they have, shift some boundaries in the present, or change the frequency of phone calls and visits. For example, some clients serving in emotional caregiving roles with parents find this role ceases to be as functional for them as they make changes in their internal experience. Others may find they don't need to keep as much distance as they develop a more solid self-boundary, and choose to provide more caregiving than they had previously. Still others may find they simply need to set limits and make choices that affirm their increased separateness. There are many variations in what behavior supports a particular client's process of completing his self-boundary.

For the therapist, the focus needs to be on helping the client assess whether there is work to do in changing the current relationship, and, if there is, support the client to effect the changes. Again, this may take the form of coaching, by using role-play techniques to practice new limit setting, or risk taking to share feelings. Working on these present relationships can also serve to open or dislodge old grief, and release stored affects from the child self.

Healing the Self: Is It Reparenting or Not?

Much of the work involved with repairing or completing the self-boundary on the part of therapist mirrors the task of good parents: finding a balance between, on the one hand, being present and available with unconditional positive regard, and, on the other hand, being clear about the limits of the relationship and realistic about the constraints of everyday life. Such a balance requires continual attention and care. Is it fair or accurate to compare good therapy with good parenting? While the comparison has some validity, it is also dangerous. Certainly one of the damaging errors of mental health practitioners has been to see clients or consumers as childlike and dependent. While some imbalance of power is inherent in helping relationships, and the need to reenact unfinished business seems relentlessly human, the fact remains that adult clients are adults. Juggling this dual frame—that clients are adults and at the same time they require the sort of gentle and thoughtful care from us as would our children—is akin to the multiple frame a therapist must bring to her understanding of someone who is "multiple." A client with a dissociative identity structure is indeed one person (and we do well to always remember this), even though the felt experience for both the multiple-personality client and the therapist who is interacting with her is that she consists of a collection of different people. Both are simultaneously true.

Perhaps the most useful way to answer the question "Is therapy reparenting?" is to understand it as a process wherein the client is reparenting herself, what James (1981) called self-reparenting. We function as consultants and mirrors, to coach, teach, model, and sometimes stand in until the client can take on the leading roles of both parent and child. With some clients, we may need to take an active part in reflecting back their internal images with as little distortion as we can muster. With others, we stand in the background and simply hold the frame steady while our clients work to reach a new level of individuation. Regardless of the nature of our engagement in their reworking process, fundamentally we stand alongside them as they develop a more whole, more solidly bounded sense of self.

From a slightly different perspective, I sometimes wonder if our task in helping clients with attachment-separation-individuation is to serve as a channel to universal love and hold open the door to possibilities. I think that good mothers—or fathers or grandmothers—are attuned by and to love, providing an energetic field of certain frequency that the infant recognizes and intuitively understands, and subsequently works to tune into for himself in the future. And the subsequent tuning in to this frequency provides a sense of groundedness, wholeness, a sense of self. Disruptions and trauma vibrate at another frequency, or scatter existing signals, thus interfering with the frequency of lovingness.

Perhaps it is our ability as adults to tune in effectively, to re-create within ourselves a sense of completeness in our connection to universal love, that we perceive as a solid self-boundary. In this way, the experience of a boundary is actually the lack of boundary (with the feeling of connectedness evoking a perception of a boundary), or is, in other words, a boundary that serves as a pathway or channel to that which is beyond us. This reminds me of Jordan's (1991) description of boundaries as pathways or channels that allow connection rather than fences or barriers that separate and contain. Maybe what we do as therapists or healers is to function as a receiver or channel to locate the frequency of universal love amidst the myriad frequencies floating around until our clients can recognize it and tune in on their own. Real or metaphoric, I do believe the energy field we create with our clients—wherein change is possible and love is a given—facilitates healing and wholeness.

9

Working with Core Issues and Other Interventions

Self-injury sometimes stops once clients understand the function served by the self-injury and they get the underlying needs met in other ways. For example, simply getting attention that is focused, supportive, and nonblaming may contribute to the reduction or cessation in self-injuring behavior by meeting an underlying need for attention for the original trauma and the resulting pain from supportive others (professionals, family members, or friends). Developing alternative coping skills and working on the incomplete self-boundary may also help clients stop or reduce their use of self-injury.

However, for many people, trauma-based emotional conflicts, skill and information gaps, and belief systems continue to fuel the need for self-injury. The frequency and intensity of self-injuring behaviors can recede and even disappear if the underlying issues are addressed (Alderman 1997, Briere 1992, Conterio and Lader 1998, Davies and Frawley 1994, Hyman 1999, Miller 1994). Processing and integrating traumatic material (Briere 1992, Chu 1998, Herman 1992, Matsakis 1994, van der Kolk and Kadish 1987, Young 1992), revising and replacing old cognitive schemas with new ones (Linehan 1993, Matsakis 1994, McCann and Perlman 1992, Young 1992), finding a sense of community within which to understand one's experience

(Herman 1992, Lew 1990), mourning the losses inherent in trauma (Courtois 1988, Davies and Frawley 1994, Herman 1992, Matsakis 1994), and the development of additional life management and emotion regulation skills (Linehan 1993, Saakvitne et al. 2000) are all fundamental to a more complete resolution. Clearly, this level of healing takes place over time, in and out of a therapy context.

Many therapeutic approaches benefit clients who self-injure. Since the self-injury itself is not the primary problem, focusing on the core issues ultimately proves most healing and beneficial. This chapter addresses some common ways to approach unresolved trauma and its aftereffects, and some not-so-common methods that might be useful. It also addresses a number of other issues that arise in the context of working with clients who self-injure: the use of medication, coexisting substance abuse, clients' concerns about scars, the needs of family members and friends, and the role of spirituality in healing.

Resolution of Old Traumas

There are many ways to resolve traumatic experiences. Effective resolution usually incorporates a range of perspectives, contexts, and resources. Trauma survivors find that they often draw on many different sources for healing, and that over the course of some years, they reach a sense of resolution. By "resolution," I mean that the traumatic event is not the overt or covert focus of the client's life, driving decisions in the present and interrupting her capacity to function in one or more areas of her life. Resolution of past trauma means that the event(s), or the more global invalidating environment (Linehan 1993), can be recalled without overwhelming stress, and that the event or experience has somehow been integrated into the person's sense of personal history. Trauma may always leave a mark, but it doesn't have to be a controlling factor in the present.

Different paths are useful at different points in time. To effect healing, trauma survivors may need to develop supportive relationships, situate themselves in a peer community where they feel they belong (this can be a support group or a work setting, to note just two examples), seek out individual or group counseling, make use of partial hospital programs, learn new skills through workshops or books, engage in creative processes, and draw on other personal resources. There is no one right way or one right theoretical approach. The process of healing is larger than any therapeutic process, and usually incorporates more than one clinician, modality, or program. The healing process exists as a facet of the survivor's life, as he moves through integrating the traumatic event into the fabric of his present life. It is a gradual, often slow process with great variations across survivors, even for different survivors of the same event.

Herman (1992), Chu (1998), van der Kolk and colleagues (1996a), and others describe a stage-wise approach to the resolution of past traumas, reiterating the basic themes of stabilization, integration of the trauma, and consolidation. They articulate these steps against the backdrop of a thoughtful therapeutic relationship and with an expectation that healing takes time. Herman describes three stages: the establishment of safety, remembrance and mourning, and the reconnection with ordinary life. These stages represent "a gradual shift from unpredictable danger to reliable safety, from dissociated trauma to acknowledged memory, and from stigmatized isolation to restored social connection" (p. 155). In this, Herman summarizes the core of healing from trauma. Of course, the lived experience is not quite as tidy, but as a guiding conceptualization, her frame is remarkably simple, accurate, and human. (I believe that Herman's book *Trauma and Recovery* remains the best integrated and most human-oriented text on the impact of trauma, the sociopolitical context in which it occurs, and the key elements of the healing process.)

Chu (1998) also notes three stages. He utilizes the acronym SAFER to describe the five primary tasks of the first stage: Self-care and symptom control; an acknowledgement of the role of trauma in the symptoms someone experiences; the capacity to function as normally as possible; the ability to express feelings in safe ways and with words; and the development of useful relationships, especially with a therapist. These tasks serve to focus and contain, not just in the early stages but throughout the healing process. Chu's second stage is characterized by the exploration and abreaction of memories—the actual processing of traumatic material. The third stage is composed of the consolidation of gains and a larger focus on the outer world, with the awareness that other traumatic material may subsequently emerge as the survivor gains mastery and improves functioning. These stages mirror the stages described by Putnam (1989) in working with clients diagnosed with multiple personality disorder and by others working with trauma survivors.

Van der Kolk and colleagues (1996a) describe similar steps, but in a slightly different framework. Their stages are:

1. Stabilization, including (a) education and (b) identification of feelings through verbalizing somatic states.
2. Deconditioning of traumatic memories and responses.
3. Restructuring of traumatic personal schemes.

4. Reestablishment of secure social connections and interpersonal efficacy.
5. Accumulation of restitutive emotional experiences. [p. 426]

Similarly to Herman, Chu, and others, the initial goal here is stabilization, with the tasks of reworking and changing traumatic reactions, schemas, beliefs, and relational patterns occurring over a period of time. These steps are interwoven to some extent and primarily provide a conceptual framework to ground the clinician. Van der Kolk and colleagues, like Herman and Chu, emphasize the importance of a relational context in healing the effects of trauma.

Reworking beliefs, patterns, and reactions starts with the beginning of a therapeutic relationship, even as our focus with clients is on helping them feel more stable and less out of control in their lives. Stabilization does not occur in a vacuum; in fact, the development of a solid therapeutic alliance (with the concomitant shifting of beliefs to accommodate a relationship that is built on trust and respect) is a central feature of the process of establishing safety and the movement out of crisis. The task of stabilization, too, is a recurring one. Throughout the course of working through past traumas, clients find they need to return to the task of maintaining balance and safety as painful or difficult issues arise. This effort, however, often requires a decreasing amount of energy overall, thus freeing up energy for actually processing and integrating the events from the past.

The operating goal of functionality (i.e., being able to work, care for children, go to school, buy groceries and clean house—whatever the client's life requires) is at the crux of good trauma work. This perspective dictates that unfinished business from the past be addressed at a manageable pace over time, so the client can incorporate into her life that which has been or felt unmanageable in the past. Moving too quickly to process or uncover memories is not helpful, in spite of the client's sense of urgency to "just get this over with." Recollections and feelings emerge as the client has enough supports and ego strength to allow this process to unfold.

When the client is flooded and overwhelmed, he and the therapist need to work together to slow down and find a stable ground. Sometimes this means developing new skills. Sometimes it means identifying underlying anxiety or addictive-like processes that spin out of control. Generally, slowing down entails putting the actual processing of trauma memories on hold. It often means focusing on anxiety reduction or other basic management skills, or involves the beginning of recovery from addiction (see section later in this chapter on issues related to addiction). It may mean talking about very practical details of life management and finding new, creative solutions.

Two Metaphors that Frame the Process of Healing

I have found two metaphors that can be particularly useful in framing the overall healing process of past trauma.

Cleaning Out the Closet

The metaphor of cleaning out a closet speaks to the purpose and timing of the healing process. Working through the past is painful and complicated for most people. One does such work with ambivalence, alternating between feeling "I *must* do this work" and "I *cannot* do this work." At times, it's as if the process of healing is the only thing that makes sense, and at other times, it doesn't seem to make any sense at all, feeling like a drain of time, energy, and money. The metaphor of cleaning out a closet can be a way to describe the goals and parameters of working on past traumas, providing a middle ground that attends to the wide swings of ambivalence and helps frame the process as a more manageable one.

Often, when we suffer painful things, we throw them into a closet so we don't have to look at or deal with them. We may figure that we don't have the time or energy to cope in the moment and so we put them away. We may just be too overwhelmed. These experiences tend to be jammed into the closet somewhat chaotically. We may even forget what's in the closet. It is usually not easy to walk into such a closet and find anything. Eventually, we may stop even trying to open the door, for fear of things falling out on our heads.

We may reach a point in our lives, however, when we decide, either consciously or unconsciously, that it is time to peek into the closet. Maybe it is because we are moving out (or moving on), or maybe we feel we have lost something and think it might be in the closet, or maybe it just seems like the right time. Maybe we tried to stick something else in the closet and things fell out. Regardless of the reason, when we decide to clean it out, it is best to do it carefully. It probably isn't wise to simply throw open the door and yank everything out. Instead, it might be more helpful to take things out slowly, in pieces. That may be difficult at first, if things tend to fall out of the closet abruptly. But finding a way to open the door a crack and gradually look or remove things is better. It doesn't help to clutter up the living room or kitchen or bedroom with everything from the closet—that makes everyday life too unmanageable. It's hard to walk around stacks of boxes and unsorted stuff. The closet-cleaning task may take a while, so it is good to have a plan for the interim, as one might when remodeling a kitchen.

This plan might entail taking one box or item out of the closet at a time, or neatly stacking things in a new location for now. It might involve building a set of shelves for temporary storage. The next step is often to go through these items, in greater or lesser detail. Sometimes we can open a box and know immediately that we don't need to go through the whole thing; we know what's in there and we can just throw it out. Other times, we may have to spend some time sorting the contents in greater detail. Sometimes we have to figure out what an item *is*. Once sorted, we then can decide what to keep and what to throw away. Some of the things we find, we throw out, because we realize we don't need them any more—such as certain attitudes, beliefs, or coping strategies. Other things we may also throw out, because they originally belonged to someone else and we somehow ended up storing them—such as shame and guilt.

We also find treasures in the boxes, things that accidentally got put away with the old junk, things like a love of piano music, good memories of making pies with a favorite aunt, a sense of humor, or the ability to draw and paint. We then have a choice about putting these treasures back into the closet or placing them around the house or reincorporating them into our everyday lives. Some of what we find in the boxes are things we decide we must keep, like old documents or photographs, because they help us know our history. But we can now more efficiently pack them into one or two boxes and seal them up. These boxes now go back into the closet where we can find them if we need them, but where they won't be in the way. There is more room for other items and we can organize the closet. We have more space. And things don't fall out on our heads anymore.

The Jigsaw Puzzle

Another metaphor I find helpful is that of a jigsaw puzzle as a way to understand the process of piecing together a sense of one's past. Maureen Burke (a nurse consultant from the United Kingdom who has developed the first comprehensive mental health training program for working with clients who self-injure) has discovered and utilized this same metaphor; she refers to it as "the shattered jigsaw," a phrase initially used by one of her patients (Burke 2000). Burke's patient described her life as a picture that was shattered like a jigsaw, with the pieces scattered about her. She saw the healing process as a gradual piecing back together of her life.

Similarly, I have often referred to the retrieval of memories as the process of being given a jigsaw puzzle without the cover picture and trying to put it together. Fragments of experience are in bits and pieces. Sometimes the pieces look like they fit together, but it later turns out that they don't really fit. Some pieces actually belong to another puzzle altogether. The mess of puzzle pieces (recurring images, flashbacks, feelings and sensations, vague narrative memories) may turn out to be several different puzzles or memories with similar shapes or colors. We may think we know what the puzzle looks like, but it may turn out differently from what we expect. Some of the puzzles may have missing pieces, while others may actually belong to another scene not traumatic in origin. The process of sorting over time can feel tedious and confusing, but is usually the only way for the person to make sense of the

jumble of experiences often related to previously unresolved traumas.

Managing Intrusive Imagery and Affect

One of the recurring difficulties for trauma survivors, and
a factor contributing to self-injury, is the unexpected, sudden intrusion of traumatic images, feelings, and sensations.
As noted in Chapter 3, the images and sensations related
to trauma often are not processed through or grounded in
language, context, or historical personal narrative. This
means that feelings that don't seem to make sense, or to
be warranted by anything occurring in the present, may
suddenly wash over a person. A benign movement or gesture by another evokes fear, complete with startle response,
increased heart rate, and sense of panic. This offers concrete evidence that trauma is grounded in the body, or,
rather, the body-mind.

Distinguishing between the body and the mind is increasingly difficult these days, as we see more evidence that
the body and mind as we have dichotomized them actually
interact in elegant and complex ways, influencing each
other to the extent that it is hard to discern biology from
belief. We are able to change our biology by altering what
we believe (as evidenced by the relaxation response; see
Benson [1997]). Similarly, our biology continually impacts
what we think, believe, and feel (look at the power of hormonal differences [Love and Robinson 1994] or the role
of neuropeptides in creating emotions [Pert 1999]). Certainly, this body-mind is the conceptual belief underlying
cognitive therapy: we can manage our feelings (as they are
expressed through our bodies via sensation) by changing
our beliefs and schemas. This interaction between trauma-

based mental schemas and physiologically-based trauma reenactments (i.e., flashbacks and stress responses) serves to keep alive old traumas in the present.

One early, and periodically recurring, focus of therapy with trauma survivors is on interrupting and reinterpreting physiologic reactions to the past trauma. This may involve exploration and education about the client's current experiences of flashbacks and stress responses. It may involve active work on deconditioning those responses using cognitive-behavioral techniques or approaches developed from hypnotherapy. Dolan (1991) offers a number of useful techniques for grounding and increasing control over these seemingly automatic responses in *Resolving Sexual Abuse*, as does Linehan (1993) from a different perspective. Benson's (1997) tips on eliciting the relaxation response are also quite helpful, providing guidelines for meditation that are designed around a client's particular belief system or faith. Evoking the relaxation response allows the autonomic nervous system to readjust, thus interrupting the reliving of old trauma.

Working with Dissociative Process

Essentially, these activities and techniques offer methods for working with the client's dissociation, which is a coping mechanism. The use of dissociation is not inherently problematic; it is a creative and often useful skill. It involves basically the same process of altering consciousness that comes with learning hypnosis in order to manage pain (Chaves 1993, Eimer and Freeman 1998). What is problematic about dissociation in response to trauma is the lack of control or choice. Thus, techniques that help clients increase their ability to manage their dissociation can be valuable.

This work generally involves addressing the two major ways dissociation feels disruptive: disorientation in relation to time and inconsistent information management. With dissociation, the control of information is imperfect; information is either unavailable when needed (as with state-dependent memory) or intrudes unbidden (as with flashbacks). The example of making lists as noted in Chapter 7 is a technique for improving access, by providing an overlay of a new information management system. Other techniques include keeping a journal and using flashcards with affirmations. An excellent article published in *Many Voices*, a newsletter for people who are highly dissociative, details many strategies for managing information and organizing one's life when living with alter personalities ("The Shadows" 1997).

Viewing dissociation as a problem of time disorientation means that the past and present get confused because dissociated experiences tend to be experienced as something occurring in the present, regardless of when they actually occurred. So, during a flashback or memory, it feels as if the trauma is occurring in the present. Time disorientation operates on a continuum, whereas in a complete abreaction there is only the traumatic past experienced as the present, while at the other end of the continuum, the dissociated past is completely unavailable and only the present exists. Most people experience some mixture of past and present, both in their conscious awareness and in their bodies. For example, a difficult experience at work may trigger an old experience of being criticized and then feeling panicky. While the person may be able to remain in the present enough to be cognitively oriented, she may still feel scared and upset in a way that is mostly about the past. She is both reliving the past and remaining in the present. Working on grounding herself in the present may help decrease her sense of fear and panic, pulling her awareness further into the here and now.

One common and valuable technique is to use an object as a reminder of the present. A rock, seashell, or other small object that definitively represents the present time can be kept in a pocket or a desk drawer, helping someone reground when he feels distressed. A transitional object—something that serves as a reminder of an important attachment (Winnicott 1965) to a therapist, partner, or other significant person—can serve this purpose, sometimes more powerfully because it represents a human connection in the present. Again, small, simple objects work best, such as a stone or other object collected from nature, a photograph, a miniature toy or figure, or a drawing.

Another technique that can help with shifting a client's internal experience of past and present and permit access to other information involves the creation of an internal safe place. This technique allows someone to feel protected from memories and the physiological arousal states related to trauma. Creating a safe place is most often done using imagery; drawing or painting can also be used to concretize the image. The client creates the perfect environment in her imagination in which she feels safe. It can be indoors or outdoors, any type of room or space, it can have as much or as little light as feels safe, and it can be just the right temperature. Comfort items such as quilts or rocking chairs, favorite foods and beverages, toys and activities, and anything else that would be helpful can be placed in this environment. Developing it in as much sensate detail as possible is useful in making it real; it may also help to be very clear about doorways or entries, as well as a method for accessing the space quickly when needed. Some people place a shield or wall or energy field around their safe place, so they know they will be protected

there. People with child-parts or -selves sometimes find that
it helps to ask child parts go to the playroom (or whatever
they call this safe place) while they are at work, during sex,
or when dealing with a difficult adult situation. This can
allow for increased grounding in the present and greater
access to adult problem-solving skills.

Working with a client's experience of dissociation may
also involve a more detailed exploration of her dissociative
process. Dissociative personality structures may necessitate an
emphasis on how a client uses dissociation; clients who are
highly dissociative to the point of having periods of amne-
sia (or "losing time") need to address their dissociation at a
systemic level. This means learning more about their internal experience of fragmentation or compartmentalization,
and working toward increased internal communication and
collaboration. It may mean using other specialized approaches (see the references cited in Chapter 4 on working
with highly dissociative clients), but I agree with Rivera
(1996) that this work is more similar to work with less dissociative clients than it is unique or different. It is just *more*—
more intense, more complex, more painful, more amazing.
The particular relevance of working with highly dissociative
clients with regard to self-injury is in understanding the functions. Because self-injury is often a mechanism for controlling dissociative process, sifting through and sorting out how
clients' dissociation works is informative and useful, and
ultimately impacts their use of self-injury.

Processing and Integrating Traumatic Events

Many different elements contribute to the processing and
integration of traumatic events. The various methods described in this and the several preceding chapters all con-

tribute to the resolution of prior trauma. In general, the integration of past traumas involves the capacity to articulate a word-based narrative of one's history that includes the traumatic events without evoking overwhelming affect; such integration reflects some modification of the psychobiological remnants of trauma described in Chapter 3. Some of the approaches aimed at integrating traumatic material are, in particular, geared toward understanding and transforming the actual recollections of traumatic events. As usual, different methods suit different people. Some of these methods are noted later in a subsequent section on energy-based approaches. I only mention a few here.

Simple verbal descriptions—telling what happened—can be beneficial and relieve the tension of unexpressed feelings (Pennebaker 1997). Some people find they can use a modified hypnotic technique in which they play a video or a movie of the event in their mind and describe what they are seeing (Cameron-Bandler 1978). Other methods include the use of a sand tray, expressive arts, and writing. The sand tray, wherein a tray with sand and a number of miniature life figures are used to depict traumatic events, allows the survivor to be both observer and participant (Khan 1994, Mitchell and Friedman 1994). This approach, along with the use of expressive arts techniques such as drawing, painting, and collage-making, promotes expression of feelings and events while allowing the client to maintain some degree of distance from the intensity of the experience. For people who were told not to tell about what happened to them, such nonverbal methods can be facilitative. Writing also offers a measure of distance and the additional benefit of word-based narration, shifting, to some degree, the sensory-affective base common to many traumatic events. Writing also tends to circumvent the

"Don't tell" injunction, even though it is a process involving words.

Adjuncts and Alternatives to Talk Therapy: Body–Mind Approaches

Body-related approaches are often beneficial for trauma survivors because of the powerful body–mind connections. Physical activity and various forms of bodywork often facilitate awareness and relearning in ways that verbal methods cannot. Increased physicality can contribute to a sense of greater control and strength. Many survivors find they are better able to ground into their bodies when they are physically active. Dance, exercise, playing sports, and walking or hiking can all be useful, especially for victims of physical and sexual abuse (Kepner 1995). The term *bodywork* includes many forms of direct touch by a professional; some examples are full or partial massage (of which there are numerous methods), physical un-learning and relearning such as Alexander or Feldenkrais work (Feldenkrais 1993), and chiropractic adjustments. Other physical methods often described as bodywork are actually grounded in theories about energy or vibrational fields, such as Reiki, therapeutic touch, and hands-on healing, as are some forms of chiropractic work (Gallo 1999, Krieger 1993, Stein 1997, Walker 1992).

Newer Methods of Uncertain Mechanisms

A number of techniques have been developed over the last fifteen years in an effort to reduce or eliminate the intrusive elements of unresolved trauma. Some have been studied with varying degrees of documented effectiveness, and others have not. Some of the newer methods are based on concepts related to the energy system of the body; a brief description of some of these methods follows shortly. Other methods utilize different mechanisms about which little is understood. The most frequently studied of these new methods at this point is that developed by Francine Shapiro (1995, 1999) known as Eye Movement Desensitization and Reprocessing (EMDR). This approach, as one tool to be used in the context of a viable and grounded therapeutic relationship, is based on a series of steps that include specific eye movements and/or other gestures while thinking about an upsetting event.

Shapiro acknowledges that the naming of this method is unfortunate, because most researchers agree that the eye movement part of the protocol is probably not essential and is misleading (Cahill et al. 1999, Shapiro 1999). A number of clinicians and some researchers claim that EMDR is efficient in reducing the distress associated with recalling traumatic events through an unidentified but unique mechanism. Others believe that EMDR's effectiveness is primarily a function of repeated exposure to the visual imagery related to the trauma (Cahill et al. 1999, Cusack and Spates 1999). (See Acierno and Cahill [1999] for a journal issue devoted to research on the mechanisms and efficacy of EMDR; they report mixed results.)

EMDR was one of four alternative methods studied by Figley and Carbonell in an effort to better understand what helps trauma survivors (Carbonell and Figley 1995, Gallo 1999, Wylie 1996). These four were selected from many alternative modalities. The other methods in this study were Traumatic Incident Reduction, Visual-Kinesthetic Dissociation, and Thought Field Therapy. Knowing more about if, when, and how these and other modalities work would be helpful, and researchers and practitioners are pursuing these goals. The different methods draw on different theoretical constructs. Visual kinesthetic dissociation, for example, utilizes intentional dissociation in order to help someone gain mastery over the traumatic event (Cameron-Bandler 1978). Other approaches include Grove's (1989) work, Ochberg's (1996) counting method, various flooding/exposure procedures, and other cognitive-behavioral techniques (Rothbaum and Foa 1996).

Energy-Based Approaches

Another set of methods for resolving trauma that bear further exploration and systematic research are ones that have recently been grouped under the rubric of energy psychology (Gallo 1999). This work is based on the concept of an energetic force as the common denominator or fundamental level of experience. The roots of energy medicine and psychology go back more than 3,500 years, when Chinese physicians began articulating a set of principles based on the concept of "qi" or life energy (Cohen 1997). Other indigenous traditions in India, the Far East, and the Americas also describe life energy by various names and concepts (Gerber 1996), all based on the same framework of energy as the primary ground for experience and reality.

"According to Chinese medicine, qi is the animating power that flows through all living things" (Cohen 1997, p. 1). In this framework, trauma causes emotional and physical distress because it is an impediment to the flow of qi (sometimes spelled 'chi' because it reflects the English pronunciation). When energy flow is unimpeded and coherent, health is maintained (Gerber 1996, Hunt 1996, McArthur 1998). Acupuncture is one of the qi or energy-based techniques developed thousands of years ago that has been scientifically proven effective for pain reduction and in other areas of improved health (Ceniceros and Brown 1998, Gerber 1996). The intent of acupuncture is to re-open blocked energy channels (although Western medicine has postulated several different explanations of the mechanism, including the activation of beta blockers, and nerve-stimulation theories) (Ceniceros and Brown 1998). As noted earlier, various forms of healing touch are based on the concept of qi.

More recently, this concept of energy has been applied to healing psychological trauma. Gallo's *Energy Psychology* (1999) offers the most current overview of energy-based methodologies. He summarizes various energetic approaches to physical health as a backdrop to the newer psychological applications, placing all in historical context. Gallo includes information about the methods developed by chiropractors and others to assess energy or vibrational fields (called applied kinesiology and other similar terms), and specific chiropractic approaches to healing trauma such as neuro emotional technique (NET) (Walker 1992). He describes several methods in detail, providing what is essentially a manual for doing Thought Field Therapy (TFT).

TFT, developed by psychologist Roger Callahan, is theorized to work in ways similar to other energy approaches. Unresolved trauma is held in an energetic thought field and, when activated, evokes anxiety or other distress. In using TFT, the client taps on specific points on her own body that correspond with key points on the meridian lines (meridians are the Chinese medicine name for the pathways in and around the body which serve as channels for qi). The tapping is thought to open the blocked channel (similar to the use of needles in acupuncture), allowing the traumatic thought field to be released. Energy can then flow freely, with a concomitant reduction in anxiety or distress.

While TFT and many other energy-based approaches have not been studied systematically, they are characterized by both clinicians and clients as useful tools for reducing anxiety and other intrusive traumatic effects. Informal reports suggest that TFT, the emotional freedom technique (a variation of TFT developed by Gary Craig), NET, and Tapas Acupressure Technique (developed by acupuncturist Tapas Fleming) can provide additional support to traditional therapeutic methods with self-injuring clients.

Another energy-based option involves the use of flower essence remedies. Flower essences are considered herbal remedies (Kaminsky and Katz 1996), cousins of a sort to homeopathic remedies. Homeopathy is based on the concept that very small amounts of plant substances can be healing; this approach was developed to address physical illness (Gerber 1996). Although flower essences, homeopathic remedies, and other herbal preparations are all derived from plant material, they differ from each other. Flower essences do not impact our biochemistry (as do many herbal preparations) nor are they based theoretically or empirically on the tenets of homeopathy. (See Kaminsky and Katz [1996] for a more in-depth discussion of what flower essences are and aren't, and Wright [1998] for a theoretical explanation of how flower essences stabilize the electrical system of the body.) Flower essences are believed to contain the energy patterning of flower blossoms, and to work primarily in affecting attitudes and emotions. Flower essences are said to decrease stress and anxiety, and to increase the ability to integrate traumatic experiences. Drops of a diluted solution of the essence are taken orally, and are either self-administered or provided by a trained health care practitioner.

It seems, based on informal reports from both clients and practitioners, that energy approaches do not immediately transform and integrate a trauma but clear the blocked channels at an energetic level. This opening of channels allows for the gradual processing and integration of an event, rather than keeping an experience locked in no matter how much effort is put into talking, feeling, or otherwise working through an event. These approaches are not magic wands, and need to be taught or utilized by trained practitioners. There are some advantages for clients to draw on practitioners other than their therapists in using adjunct approaches. Having more than one person in the role of healer broadens the client's professional support network and counters a tendency to see the therapist as the only one who can be helpful.

Overall, clients may find various alternatives useful. The lack of negative side effects enhances some people's willingness to explore these options in spite of the lack of research in many cases. No one method works with surety, and it is not clear why certain methods work even some of the time. Some people question if these methods have any efficacy beyond exposure or the relief provided by a discussion of the trauma in a relational context; some believe we are simply seeing a powerful placebo effect. Benson (1997), a cardiologist, suggests that we look more carefully at what we dismissively call the placebo effect and reframe it as "remembered wellness"—an opportunity to utilize our inherent ability to heal. Even if the underlying mechanism for some of these methods *is* remembered wellness, they may offer relief and help while we await more definitive data on mechanisms and efficacy from researchers.

Medication and Self-Injury

Along more traditional lines, medication may also be an adjunct for some survivors who self-injure, particularly when they describe strongly compulsive or obsessive qualities to their self-injury. Increased data about the psychobiology of trauma suggest possible pharmacological interventions for the relief of anxiety, depression, and unstable mood, and in the opioid system. Overall, researchers and clinicians report mixed success in pharmocological approaches to posttraumatic stress (Davidson and van der Kolk 1996, Dominiak 1992, Saporta and Case 1993) and for self-injury in particular. Informally, some clients have reported less compulsivity with their self-injury with the use of selective serotonin reuptake inhibitors such as fluoxetine.

Only a few studies actually document the ability of medication to decrease self-injury, and they involve small samples or are case study reports. Markowitz and colleagues (1991) reported a decrease in self-injury with fluoxetine, as did Primeau and Fontaine (1987). Several others, however, noted that fluoxetine was not effective (Bystritsky and Strausser 1996, McGee 1997). Chengappa and colleagues' (1999) chart review of patients with severe self-injuring behavior showed a decrease in self-injury with clozapine, an antipsychotic. Roth and colleagues (1996) and Sonne and colleagues (1996) reported on the effects of naltrexone, a long-acting opiate receptor antagonist that has been found to be helpful in reducing relapse in alcohol addiction; both groups reported decreases in self-injurious thoughts and actions. McGee (1997) and Bystritsky and Strausser (1996) also noted success with naltrexone in individual case reports. With trichotillomania specifically, pharmacotherapy studies have shown mixed results, with a minority of patients experiencing some relief with medication (O'Sullivan et al. 1999).

However, there is also some indication (Cowdry and Gardner 1988, Gardner and Cowdry 1985, Lebegue 1992, Little and Taghavi 1991, Soloff et al. 1986) that a range of medications may increase how out of control clients feel and actually *contribute* to self-injurious behavior. Further, a pharmacological approach is by nature directed at reducing behavior, which, as stated previously, is generally not the most useful overall goal for therapy with self-injuring clients. Focusing on finding the right medication can actually divert attention from the underlying issues and impede the healing process. The factor of iatrogenic harm (damage caused by treatment) is also relevant to the decision to approach self-injury pharmacologically. Medication studies do not adequately address the impact of negative side effects of the drugs, or the short- and long-term impact of medication on clients' abilities to process prior traumas, understand their dissociation, or make connections about their self-injury (Mazelis 1998).

In short, while pharmacological aid in regulating intense arousal states linked to self-injury may be helpful for some people, it should be undertaken with great care. Only one medication should be prescribed at a time, in order to assess its effectiveness and the side effects. The knowledge base on the efficacy of medication is limited at this point (Dominiak 1992, Saporta and Case 1993, Winchel and Stanley 1991), and in spite of recent advances, the potential for harmful—or at least confounding—effects is quite high. Too often the draw to pharmacotherapy stems from impatience or frustration felt by both clients and professionals or the demands of managed care, rather than the known usefulness of prescribed drugs, so the decision needs to be well considered.

The Presence of a Substance Addiction

A number of clients who self-injure also have an addiction
to drugs and/or alcohol (Alderman 1997, Hyman 1999).
Some may be in recovery for the addiction at the time of
our work with them, while others may still be using. Some
addicted clients experience their self-injury as another addiction, while others do not, even if they perceive both
their substance addiction and their self-injury as forms of
self-harm. Other self-injuring clients may not be addicted
but use substances as a coping strategy at times. The extent of the substance use or abuse needs to be assessed with
the client and appropriate referrals made for rehabilitation
as required.

Issues of balance and timing often arise with recovering addicts and alcoholics as they begin to address self-
injury and related traumas. Maintaining sobriety or abstinence from alcohol or drugs always needs to be the first
priority, because without sobriety the client cannot resolve
other issues. Some clinicians working with women have
rightfully questioned this abstinence-first model (Burstow
1992, Root 1989). It is true that some women (and men) are
able to gradually decrease their use of substances over time,
rather than achieving and maintaining complete abstinence.
I do think, however, that working toward a goal of sobriety
is crucial for anyone with a full-blown addiction. My experience is that clients in an active addiction are not able to
process much information and cannot approach psychotherapeutic work with much long-term success. I also believe
we must recognize that relapse occurs as a part of the work
with newly recovering clients, and we must avoid a harsh,
punitive stance about the temporary loss of sobriety.

What it takes to maintain sobriety will vary across clients. For some, this means they need to avoid working on

previous traumas until they have a solidly established recovery program, with good supports and new coping skills to deal with difficult feelings. Having at least two years of sobriety before opening up the work on previous traumas is probably ideal whenever possible. This suggestion is consistent with the general framework noted earlier about the importance of helping clients reach some degree of stability and garner adequate supports prior to processing traumatic events from the past.

However, there are some clients for whom staying sober will not be possible without addressing some of the traumatic material (Simmons et al. 1996). Some people find that as they reach three to six months of being clean and sober, they begin having nightmares or flashbacks in the forms of intrusive imagery, intense affect, and body memories (Bollerud 1992, Root 1989, Simmons et al. 1996, Young 1990). The client may experience more-or-less-detailed fragments of sensation or imagery that feel out of context or like bits of information that make no sense. Some people may begin to self-injure as these fragments emerge (Wise 1989) (this can be true for nonaddicted clients as well).

Mindful of the overall guideline of stabilization, clients often need help in framing what is going on. This may involve the therapist's assisting the client to acknowledge that it seems that something from the past is emerging, even though it is not clear what it is or what the client will need to know or do about it. Clients often need reassurance that they aren't crazy and the perspective that, in time, they will figure out what the fragments mean. They also need help managing the intense feelings that often accompany the images and sensations. This focus—learning about and naming feelings, and finding new ways to cope without using substances—is a large part of the process of early recovery regardless of trauma history (Clemmens 1997, Gorski and Miller 1986, Young 1990). The significant difference is simply the additional need to acknowledge that something traumatic from the past is emerging; such an acknowledgment is fundamental to healing and stabilization (Chu 1998). The key is to add this element of acknowledgment without opening up too much too early (Young 1990). It is, again, an issue of timing and balance.

Throughout the course of therapeutic work with self-injuring clients in recovery, a challenge to their sobriety can emerge under increased stress. This risk of relapse needs to be considered and safeguards kept or put in place. This might simply mean checking in with a client periodically about her attendance at twelve-step meetings, or the degree of contact with her sponsor or others from the program (AA or NA). It might mean helping her revise her current efforts to maintain sobriety so she has more support during a period of intense therapeutic work. The therapist and client need to be alert to signs of relapse prior to the actual use of substances (Gorski and Miller 1986, Simmons et al. 1996).

Clients' Concerns about Scars

Issues related to scars from previous or current self-injury have been mentioned several times in this book, but merit some specific focus here. People who self-injure generally have some embarrassment about the resulting marks and scars on their body (Hyman 1999, Mazelis 1992). However, they may have other feelings about their scars as well, such as pride for having survived all they have survived, respect for their strength and determination, sadness about having had so much pain, and relief that their self-injury has changed somewhat. As one woman says, "I need my scars. I need to have physical, visible proof of my pain. I need to see that wounds can heal and hurt less with time. I need to wear them as a badge of courage."

The shame some people feel about the presence of scars can interfere with interpersonal relationships, getting needed medical care, physical activities such as swimming, and wearing short sleeves or shorts in warm weather. Clients sometimes find that they want to spend time working with their feelings of shame and discomfort so they feel freer to pursue activities they want to pursue (see the section Helping Clients Talk to Others in Chapter 7). At first, they are likely to still feel some shame or embarrassment, particularly if they have hidden their scars in the past. In time, however, many clients reach a level of comfort with their bodies and their scars. Some people discover that the shame they experience about their scars is partially related to underlying issues of past abuse and body-image distortions, and they find they feel less discomfort about their scars as they feel more confident being themselves, in their bodies, and as they resolve the underlying concerns.

Some people continue to feel uncomfortable with their scars and decide to have them removed or treated surgically. For some, this act signifies movement in their healing process, rather than the need to hide or cover up their histories. Tanya (1997) writes about her decision to have surgery in *The Cutting Edge: A Newsletter for Women Living with Self-Inflicted Violence*: "I have had cosmetic surgery on some of my scars as they hadn't healed very well and were very noticeable. I didn't do it because I feel shame from my self-injury or to try to forget, because I'm not ashamed to have survived and will never forget SIV [self-inflicted violence] and why I did it. I did it as a loving gift to myself and as a symbol of moving away from the need to self-injure" (p. 5).

As always, our task is to support the client to determine what is right for her regarding her scars, how to live with them, and what it might mean to live without them (or to reduce their presence). As with any decision to undergo a surgery that is not immediately necessary, a thorough exploration of the client's options and the ramifications of each choice is probably a good idea. What might feel compelling to someone at one point in time may shift in six months. It is useful to take some time to explore the client's feelings about and desires for surgery. Encouraging the client to interview several plastic surgeons, talk with or read the writings of other people who have lived with scars, and learn about the potential outcomes and dangers of the surgery can also help.

Addressing the Needs of Family Members and Support People

As with all distressing behavior, self-injury impacts not only the person doing it but his family and friends as well. Because a number of people self-injure in private, friends and family members may not know about the self-inflicted violence. However, family members and support people who *are* aware of someone's self-injury often need information and assistance. Not only can direct support to family and friends be helpful in and of itself (by meeting their needs), it can also serve to increase the self-injuring person's network by allowing family members and friends to function as allies.

The needs of family members and friends vary a great deal. Fundamentally, most need accurate and useful information. Until recently very little helpful information about self-injury has been available, so support people have tended to operate somewhat in the dark, as have professionals and the public at large. One common result of this has been less-than-supportive interactions with the person who is self-injuring, such as, "Why don't you grow up and quit that?" or "What's wrong with you?" stated in a way that doesn't really invite conversation. With written or verbal information, at least some family members and friends are able to become more supportive and feel less distressed themselves. Some family members and friends may also need some therapeutic aid in sorting out their reactions to the person who is injuring and all that it evokes for them.

Issues of responsibility and control often come up for family members. Those who are in regular contact with someone who self-injures, particularly those living in the same household (most often partners, parents, or roommates), need to discern for themselves the fact that they are not responsible for stopping the self-injury. The pull to intervene can be very strong for close family members. Often, there is a history of confused responsibility-taking for each other (in either direction, i.e., taking responsibility for things for which we aren't responsible, or avoiding appropriate responsibility-taking), and the sense of overresponsibility for the self-injury is part of an old dance between the person injuring and the support person. Teasing out these issues is key for both, and allows for a more clearly supportive and open relationship, as well as healing the larger issues. Again, external help such as therapy or a support group can be useful. Family members who are involved in Al-Anon or other twelve-step programs may find that these resources are especially helpful in clarifying responsibility issues.

In partner relationships, self-injury can be a significant stressor, not only with regard to responsibility issues (though that can become a common arena of struggle for some couples). Since people who self-injure generally have an unresolved trauma in their pasts, issues related to trust and intimacy are likely to coexist with the self-injury. This makes sexual relationships more complicated, particularly if the (or one of the) traumatic event(s) was childhood sexual abuse, or rape in adolescence or adulthood. The self-injury may be intricately related to sexual arousal or sexual contact, or it may be triggered by any intimate connection with another person. The inadequate self-boundary may prompt feelings of invasion by an intimate partner, contributing to the use of self-injury. A partner may find that his own issues of loss and trauma are evoked, or that he feels out of control when his partner injures and he has a reaction of his own. A session or two with the self-injuring client's therapist, or a referral to a couples' therapist, may help sort out some of these complications.

One particular difficulty that can arise for members of a client's family of origin as they become educated about self-injury is their feelings about the role of previous trauma. If they acknowledge that someone they love self-injures and they seek more information, this tends to lead to an awareness of what underlies the self-injury, namely some form of trauma—abuse, loss, or other difficult experience. Having this knowledge may feel conflictual to family members for a number of reasons: they played a role in the trauma itself, they were responsible for protecting this person at the time of the trauma and they failed to do so, they did not seek help or act supportively when it occurred, or they didn't know that the event had occurred. For some, it is simply that they love this person and feel heart-broken that their loved one experienced a difficult event. These complicated feelings may confound the family members' abilities to be clear and supportive allies to the person self-injuring, and may necessitate outside support such as family therapy, or individual therapy for the family member. Their own denial about the past or current distress may also contribute to the struggle with imbalanced responsibility-taking. Some people may feel overly responsible now in order to compensate for *not* having been responsible (or for having been responsible) for past distress.

Other people in the self-injuring person's network may also be potential allies and in need of information and support, such as those in the workplace. Supervisors and co-workers may have some awareness of current or past self-injury, due to visible scars or wounds, and feel uncertain about whether or not to broach the issue. Alternately, a woman who self-injures may need to be able to take sick time for therapy appointments, or use flextime to schedule creatively to better manage life stresses. Different people who self-injure have different needs for privacy, not just about self-injury but about various issues in their lives. The extent to which it feels appropriate to have any discussion with others in the workplace varies with each client. Nonetheless, some accommodation for clients with self-injury may be appropriate and facilitative. To this end, Hyman (1999) outlines a number of recommendations for the workplace that can offer support to people who self-injure. She includes positive work environment behavior such as teaming with colleagues and good supervision, timely breaks to help manage tension, the ability to use sick or leave time in relation to the self-injury, and a responsive employee assistance worker.

What About Spirituality?

The interface between psychological and spiritual concerns has become quite textured over the last twenty years. Some clinicians and some theologians have long been interested in this interplay, noting that the *psych-* prefix stems from the Latin *psyche*, meaning "soul." The recent upsurge of interest in both spiritual needs and psychological matters likely has many common roots that will not be explored here. However, both trauma survivors and clinicians working in the trauma field for any period of time find they come face to face with spiritual questions with some regularity. As Wilson (1995) has pointed out, the word for trauma in many Native American cultures actually means "dispirited" or "loss of spirit." Indigenous beliefs often describe the event of trauma as one in which the spirit (or part of the spirit) of the person is removed (Ingerman 1991). Certainly, this is the felt experience of many traumatized people.

Spiritual or philosophical beliefs provide us with a backdrop for the universe. They organize ideas about all that is beyond our five-senses experience of being human, about the unknowable and unexplainable, about "the big place," as one of my clients says. Spiritual beliefs can help us feel comforted and a part of things, rather than alone or crazy. They may bring us a sense of community, of belonging. They can ground our anxiety about living and dying, and give us a framework within which to make meaning of our existence. They help us discern or create a sense of purpose for our lives. Spiritual beliefs can offer hope.

For trauma survivors, whose experiences have been shaped by challenges to meaning, belonging, and sanity, finding a spiritual frame of reference may be even more salient. The longing to understand and make sense, to find hope and community can be strong. Clients who have experienced systematic, sadistic abuse in which religious rituals were used may have a special struggle as well as a high need to find some way to organize their spiritual beliefs (Young 1992). A similarly complicated struggle can exist for people who were victimized by clergy, or whose abusers were or claimed to be highly religious in spite of their abusive behavior.

The need for a spiritual framework that is compatible with a client's worldview can emerge during the course of therapy. People who have never felt much interest in spiritual matters sometimes find themselves looking for a system of meaning as they move out of crisis mode and begin to integrate past traumas. Others bring a set of beliefs that stand them in good stead throughout the healing process. Still others carry a belief system, but find they need to revise it as they revise other beliefs about themselves and the world. Not all trauma survivors find they need to address spiritual issues or develop a system of meaning. However, most feel their worldview is changed in some way as a result of coping with and weathering trauma.

Similarly, therapists working with trauma survivors often discover the need to examine philosophical and spiritual beliefs. We too struggle to make sense of a world in which children are terrorized or ignored or misused in horrible ways. The pain of acknowledging that people are hurt, sometimes unintentionally but too often by the conscious choices of people they know and love, can be difficult to assimilate. We can refuse to believe some things are possible ("That can't be true"), or deny the impact ("It wasn't that bad"), or try to avoid the truth ("There must be a simple biological reason for her distress"). To accept the wide range of human behavior, from all of the glory and magic to all of the horror and cruelty, demands that we expand our perceptions of the world. This often challenges the systems of meaning we have brought with us into this work, and evokes powerful feelings of loss, disorientation, anger, and grief. And, often, we too must revise what we believe.

For our clients and for ourselves, this means that we may need to spend some time exploring the difficult questions of "Why does this happen?" and "What does it mean?" For some, this process involves questions like "Where was God?" or "How could God allow this to happen?" It requires that we sit with the ambiguity of not knowing the answers to these and other questions, realizing that they have both psychological and spiritual meaning. Addressing these concerns might also involve exploring traditional and nontraditional religious beliefs in order to discern a personal belief system that fits.

A return to a childhood faith works for some people. Finding a new church or temple or mosque works for others. Joining or developing a community of like-minded individuals with shared beliefs but not of a traditional religion suits others best. Some people find kinship and comfort with various faiths but do not feel inclined to join any group. The process of discernment may take time. At the core, though, when searching for meaning and the presence of spirit, the task is to find a way to feel connected. For some people, the desired connection is with an experience of the sacred. This can mean being able to see the sacred in everyday life. Or it can mean finding a sacred space (be it a temple, a church, a shrine, a forest, a home altar) and creating a time and place to honor spirit. It might mean regular prayer or meditation, to petition for help, to feel at one with the universe and all living things, to join with others in ceremony and ritual, to be thankful. It might mean simply finding a quiet place and stillness.

As helping professionals, our job is to attend to our own spiritual needs and invite our clients to do the same. Therapy is not religion (one hopes!), but ideally there is room for spiritual questions and searching in a clinical context. Some clients will seek help from spiritual leaders such as priests, rabbis, teachers, and ministers, and from other sources. Regardless of the outside supports, many clients need to know they can bring these questions to the space we create together, for a more integrated experience. And, as is so often the case, our main task is to simply be able to sit with what they bring.

Conclusion

There are many ways clients heal; our task is to help them discern which pathways can help at a particular moment in time, and to offer what we know and feel and see as companions along the way. To do this, we must take care of ourselves, so what we offer is the best we can offer. With this in mind, the next part, *Managing Our Own Responses to Self-Injury*, addresses common feelings and needs of clinicians, focuses the task of finding the right action in response to self-injury, and touches on how we can better care for ourselves.

III

Managing Our Own Responses to Self-Injury

10

What Happens
to Good Clinicians?

As a psychiatric nurse once said, "It's seeing the blood that makes us all lose perspective." Few clinical concerns so consistently pose a challenge to a therapist's equilibrium as does self-injury. The greatest impediments to useful and effective response to self-injury are the feelings and reactions of helping professionals. Many professionals feel a sense of urgency when self-injury is disclosed or identified, and abandon the more thoughtful, empathic, and empowering stance they might commonly employ. Self-injury evokes potent and primitive countertransferential reactions in many of us (Briere 1992, Brown 1995, Burstow 1992, Davies and Frawley 1994, Miller 1994).

A client's action to harm herself touches on many issues for therapists. A common response is, "I don't understand why she'd hurt herself, especially after she's been hurt by so many others." Or our clients' behavior may remind us of our own impulses or actions to harm ourselves in some way. It may tap into our fundamental desire to be helpful and stop others' misery, or trigger echoes of our futile childhood efforts to manage our parents' feelings. Self-injury often cues us into our own reservoirs of pain, shame, guilt, or rage; it almost always elicits a sense of helplessness and may cause us to question our competence. It may evoke fears of internal chaos and disintegration, or worries about liability. It is both the wide range of issues touched and the depth of the touch that makes self-injury such a charged element in a helping relationship. As a result, clinical responses to clients who self-injure often become extreme or reactive, rather than supportive and useful.

Many professionals respond, with or without awareness, to the evoked reaction inside themselves, rather than recognizing and channeling this reaction into useful action with the client. Criticism, blame, demands for change, and efforts to either control the client's behavior or avoid the issue are common responses. Such responses often mirror our clients' childhood experiences (Brown 1995, Herman 1992, Linehan 1993, Pearlman and Saakvitne 1995, Shur 1994). Unfortunately, we sometimes go so far as to create environments that exacerbate clients' issues by participating in a mutual reenactment of their core conflicts and beliefs, such as the controlling and blaming culture evident in many mental health institutions and programs (Shur 1994).

The cost to both therapists and clients can be great, ultimately resulting in harm to the client. Untangling and addressing the countertransferential issues can offer an alternative path that affirms the needs of both clinicians and clients, and can release creative energy that can be invigorating and useful in the therapeutic process (Ehrenberg 1992, Maroda 1998). This chapter describes the dynamics and elements often active for therapists when they work with self-injuring clients.

"I Just Don't Understand"

This common response by family, friends, and helping professionals associated with someone who self-injures is the starting point for the more complex reactions to self-injury as a clinical concern. (Even people actively struggling with self-inflicted violence can move in and out of not understanding their own behavior.) Some people feel horrified or shocked; others have greater familiarity with self-inflicted violence and simply feel perplexed. Even experienced health and mental health providers often describe a gut reaction of discomfort or confusion regarding clients who self-injure. Arnold (1995) reports that "many women felt that professionals with whom they came into contact had very little knowledge about self-injury, and even less understanding, often resorting to very crude models of causation (typically that the injury was either a failed suicide attempt, manipulation or 'attention-seeking') and treatment" (p. 18). For some, fear underscores this lack of understanding—fear about what will happen to the client, what the injury means, what will happen next. Sometimes the fear has no specific focus, and is often out of the professional's awareness.

A Threat to Professional Competence

Most clinicians experience some anxiety when a client discloses self injury. Worry about how the client is coping, how intense his feelings and needs are at the present time (increasing the likelihood of self-injury occurring), or what might happen if the client's internal experience spirals out of control tends to evoke a sense of concern, at minimum, and panic, in the extreme. This concern may manifest itself as simple anxiety, as a sense of incompetence, or as a feeling that the therapy process is out of control. The fundamental response boils down to feeling inadequate as a helper.

The majority of helping professionals enter the field because we want to help. We want to make a difference in people's lives in a positive way. We want to ease pain or anxiety, or help people see new options and create happier lives. This desire sometimes gets obscured by the varied stresses of working in health or mental health settings, by overloaded schedules, or by other external constraints that interfere with being able to provide needed care. Nonetheless, underneath many reactions to a client's behavior is the therapist's concern that she is not able to make a difference. Similar to reactions to a client in addiction recovery reporting use of alcohol or drugs, the disclosure of self-injury usually triggers a sense of failure in the therapist (even when we know better!).

One woman stated, "[Self-injuring] has nothing to do with how much you listen to your therapist or how good your therapist is. Sometimes the only way to release the 'crap' is by hurting yourself and therapists should not feel bad or feel they can't help or are a failure." The client's use of self-injury may mean, in fact, that the therapy process is working effectively. Work is occurring, even if the client's coping resources are being taxed. Just as the client who uses drugs or alcohol when overstressed, the self-injuring client is doing what is familiar and what may feel most useful at the moment to manage an overwhelming or confusing experience. Therefore, it is the therapist's task to hold onto the larger reality and remind herself that the client's behavior is not a sign of her incompetence. (This does not mean that the therapist has no responsibility to assess the pace of the work, inquire of the client about his current capacity for coping, explore useful next steps, or support the client in using other coping skills if the client wants help to do so.)

The current focus in health care on controlled, short-term approaches to mental health problems can augment the therapist's frustration and sense of inadequacy. The operative belief is that distressing client behavior can and should be managed or redirected, and this can be accomplished in a limited number of sessions. The therapist who works responsively with a client who self-injures is not likely to fit well into this model, and may feel she is not only incompetent but also unethical and irresponsible. This lack of confidence can undermine her clinical work in a more general way as well as in relation to the self-injury. Novice therapists may be particularly vulnerable to such beliefs.

Liability Concerns

Sometimes the focus of the threat to professional competence shines on the therapist's concerns about legal and ethical liability. A fuller discussion of liability concerns follows in Chapter 11; the salience here is how the therapist is impacted by these fears. Some clinicians express worry that if the client self-injures they will be held liable, either in a court of law or by a licensing or ethics board. This fear can color all of the therapist's interactions with a client who self-injures, making it difficult to focus on the underlying issues, or help the client develop alternative coping skills, or address other issues that the client brings to the therapy process. Depending on the clinician's experience base, personal history, strengths, and vulnerabilities, the centrality of liability concerns will vary.

Certainly, the recent climate surrounding health care in general, and mental health care in particular (especially when dealing with trauma), has become more litigious, and some attention to legal concerns is valid. Ethical considerations always merit attention. However, like all fears, the therapist has a responsibility to accurately assess the potential danger to the client and to oneself, develop a proactive plan to address the danger, and then responsibly manage the fear reactions so the therapy can progress in a useful way. Frequently, the actual threat to legal or ethical duty posed by a client's self-injury is minimal, and the task becomes one of managing feelings. A therapist who is overly concerned with liability issues in general probably should not work with clients who self-injure.

Compassion Fatigue, Vicarious Traumatization, and Empathic Strain

Pearlman and Saakvitne (1995), Wilson and Lindy (1994b), Figley (1995), and others have written in detail about the effects on therapists of ongoing work with trauma survivors. Pearlman and Saakvitne in particular have described the lasting impact of vicarious traumatization on professionals as a result of working with clients who are trauma survivors. Some of the effects can be deleterious, such as stress reactions, cynicism, and personal or professional crisis. Other changes can involve a shift in worldview, values, and sense of self that may be both positive and negative. The negative effects have also been described as secondary posttraumatic stress by various writers and researchers.

Figley (1995) has coined the term *compassion fatigue* as a way to denote the specific failure to sustain a capacity to respond usefully to trauma survivors. While all of the previously mentioned concerns are elements in the occurrence of compassion fatigue or secondary posttraumatic stress, framing the distress we can experience as professionals as compassion fatigue provides insight into the crux of the dilemma for many therapists.

Our ability to work with survivors of trauma from a compassionate stance is predicated on our ability to be empathic. Empathy is a necessary prerequisite for effective work with trauma survivors (Freyd 1996, Herman 1992, Pearlman and Saakvitne 1995). The presence of empathy permits the disclosure and processing of the traumatic event and contributes to the rebuilding of connections severed by the trauma. Therefore, sustaining empathy is central to healing work with survivors. As stated previously, our capacity to be empathic with self-injurers is key to their willingness to talk with us about their self-injury.

The capacity to sustain empathy is dependent on a range of factors, including the degree of exposure to traumatic material and/or people who have been traumatized, the professional's own history of traumatic events, the professional's internal and external resources, and various contextual or systemic factors in the helping environment (Figley 1995, Pearlman and Saakvitne 1995, Wilson and Lindy 1994a). Ironically, the capacity for empathy is also one of the factors contributing to compassion fatigue. It is only when we can empathically connect with clients and coexperience the trauma with them that we open ourselves to the impact of vicarious traumatization.

Resiliency is not unidimensionally determined (e.g., more trauma survivors in a caseload means less capacity for empathy), but rather is a complex of interactive factors with individual variations. However, with repeated and ongoing exposure, professionals often experience compassion stress. Our ability to be empathic wanes, thus diminishing our ability to respond effectively to clients. When we reach a place of burnout, compassion fatigue sets in and we are unable to be effective workers. Professionals experiencing compassion fatigue are unable to manage daily stress effectively, and generally feel out of control in both their personal and professional lives.

The Therapist as a Person: Threats to the Self

Another aspect of reactivity involves how the therapist as a person is impacted by his work with clients who self-injure. The fact of self-injury may resonate strongly for the therapist for whom self-injury (or other forms of self-harm) has been or is currently a personal issue. Like all characteristics therapists may have in common with clients, identification with clients' use of self-injury as a coping mechanism can elicit a range of strong feelings. Some of these feelings may facilitate understanding and empathy on the part of the therapist; others, such as shame or anxiety, may be alienating or confounding.

While direct identification with the self-injury may not be present for some clinicians, most therapists working with clients who self-injure are likely to identify with some of the underlying issues linked to the self-injury. Clinicians' own experiences of loss, prior traumas, or unresolved childhood issues are likely to be tapped by work with self-injuring clients. The intensity of clients' affect and their fierce struggle to manage complex internal experiences increase the likelihood that therapists will manifest strong reactions of some sort. As Pearlman and Saakvitne (1995) describe in detail, working with trauma survivors is challenging to therapists because the work is so evocative at various levels.

For therapists with an inadequate self-boundary, working with clients who self-injure can be threatening and disorganizing. The client's efforts to maintain a sense of self in the face of overwhelming affect can resonate strongly for the therapist with a sometimes shaky sense of self. Watching and experiencing a client who is struggling to maintain the self-boundary echoes loudly for the therapist who has an inadequate self-boundary, triggering unease and anxiety. How this unease and anxiety move into awareness or convert into action varies, depending on the personal style of the therapist. Some therapists tend toward controlling or angry behavior, others express fearfulness about the client's safety, others move toward blame or shame. The underlying shift, however, from personal discomfort to action directed to the client, has the same net result of impeding therapeutic progress.

Countertransference Responses to Reenactments in the Therapy Process

As described in Chapters 4 and 8, clients struggling with self-injury generally bring a need to sort out and rework relationships with parents and primary caregivers in order to more completely develop their own sense of self. In this process, some will reenact the complicated and unsatisfying relationships they experienced in childhood within the context of the therapeutic relationship. This means that therapists are placed in the position of various roles with which the client is familiar in order to better understand and transform their earlier experiences. These reenactments often focus not only on the need for nurture but on issues of power and control. In this vein, Davies and Frawley (1994) state:

It goes without saying that episodes of violent or self-abusive behavior will call forth powerful countertransferential reactions, involving the therapist in often-times dramatic therapeutic reenactments of the relational paradigms with which the adult survivor organizes her internal object world and her external interpersonal relationships. Inherent in such enactments are the seeds of a power struggle for control of the patient's body and mind. This struggle, once lost by the abused child, may be fought to the death or near death by the adult survivor who is convinced that control of her own person is more important than any other single motive in her life. [p. 145]

For example, a client whose mother was dogmatically religious, highly controlling, and arbitrary in her decisions often perceives the therapist as one who can (and should) determine what will happen in the therapy process. In the client's eyes, the therapist is the queen who issues commands. The client then is alternately upset if the therapist refuses the role (e.g., supports the client to decide what occurs in the session), and angry if the therapist accommodates to the client's wish (e.g., tells the client what to do in the session). This dilemma, if not well understood or if it occurs repeatedly, can elicit a range of feelings in the therapist, such as anger, frustration, confusion, hurt, and disappointment, depending on the therapist's own history and issues.

Another example can arise within the context of separation and abandonment issues. Some clients manage anticipated feelings of loss or rejection at the impending departure of a therapist for vacation by self-injuring. The longing for a rescuing parent, one who sees and knows all of the child's distress, who is willing to do anything to help her child, may get enacted just prior to the therapist leaving for vacation. Self-injury (or the threat of self-harm) may escalate during this time. With awareness of what is being reenacted, the therapist and client can utilize these elements in enlightening and helpful ways. However, even with awareness, the therapist can feel frustration and strain at having to address these concerns at this juncture. Without awareness, the likelihood is that irritation and anger will be evoked in the therapist, often followed by a power struggle with the client.

Such interactions and dynamics in the therapeutic relationship challenge therapists to maintain a high level of self-awareness and reflection. They exaggerate or highlight preexisting boundary problems in the relationship. The more impacted the therapist becomes by the client's trauma history, the more intense the countertransference reactions can be. "As a therapist experiences increasing levels of vicarious traumatization, her countertransference responses can become stronger and/or less available to conscious awareness. This interaction creates a spiral with potentially disastrous results for the treatment, often resulting in a therapeutic impasse" (Pearlman and Saakvitne 1995, p. 34).

Feeling Helpless or Out of Control: The Beginning of the Slippery Slope

When the therapist doesn't understand, is unable to regulate her own feelings of incompetence, and is experiencing compassion fatigue, her feelings of helplessness escalate. The client's self-injury can provoke a perception that nothing helps, eliciting helplessness and hopelessness. The therapist may feel out of control in that she feels unable to respond in a way that can make an immediate difference for the client, or impact the client's behavior. Further, she may resonate with the client's own despair, helplessness, and out-of-control feelings, adding to her own feelings of powerlessness.

In describing this sense of powerlessness, helplessness, inadequacy, or being out of control, it should be noted that many therapists who are experiencing such feelings do not pause to identify them as such. Often, clinicians don't have awareness that they are feeling helpless. Instead, the feelings get converted into action, usually in the form of words telling the client what he must do (such as sign a contract to stop injuring, go to the hospital, or disclose the self-injury to a significant other). This action serves as an antidote to the therapist's sense of helplessness. Unfortunately, clients sometimes respond to this eagerly, as they too are tired of feeling out of control and helpless and long for the answer. (In the long run, this is not useful to the client.)

Other clients perceive what is going on for the therapist and resent having to manage the therapist's feelings and reactions along with their own. In *Women Living with Self-Injury* (Hyman 1999), one client spoke to many clients' desire for therapists to claim and address their own feelings: "I have had too many professionals who take it [her self-injury] as an insult: 'This is something you are doing *to me*' rather than 'This is something you are doing and it bothers me and I need to deal with my feelings'" (p. 153).

The Results of Unsorted Feelings on the Part of the Therapist

One of the most common responses to the strong feelings and reactions of therapists is to use power in unfair ways to gain relief from our own distress. This fundamental shift, endeavoring to move from a powerless position to one of power, moves the therapist into a decidedly unhelpful stance vis-à-vis the client. The therapist is now engaged in the classic dynamic that motivates or drives perpetrators of abuse. Unable to tolerate feeling powerless or out of control, the therapist takes an action at the expense of the client that serves to reestablish a feeling of control on the part of the therapist. It helps the therapist regain an internal self-image of competence and temporarily dispels the feelings of inadequacy, helplessness, and attendant shame. What the client really needs ceases to be the focus, in spite of the projections onto the client about causing or provoking the therapist's behavior.

Mary, a client, is preparing to leave for vacation. She has planned this vacation so it will coincide with her therapist's vacation, in order to minimize her experience of loss. Mary and her therapist have worked together for some time and focus intermittently on the intense feelings Mary has about her therapist. Both feel Mary is making progress overall. The night before their last session prior to vacation, Mary is flooded with feelings, triggered in part by the impending break, but also by stress at work as she prepares to leave town for two weeks. The final straw occurs when Mary's mother calls and asks her to come help her out with a project. Mary says she cannot, as she is packing for her trip. Their interaction is somewhat strained and Mary is upset because she knows her mother is aware that she (Mary) is leaving town soon and is busy. Even though she doesn't go over to her mother's house, Mary feels guilty, and, late in the evening, burns her upper thigh. She has not burned herself for more than a year, and she is upset that she felt she had to resort to self-injury again.

In the session the next morning, Mary is tearful and irritable. She talks somewhat disjointedly about the phone call with her mother, feeling stressed about work, her fears about being away for two weeks, asking twice when the therapist is coming back to work. Her therapist had been anticipating a relatively easy session, since she and Mary have worked on issues about separation for several years, and the last few times the therapist has gone away Mary has been fairly calm and contained. Also, they have talked in the last two sessions about how Mary was going to manage her anxiety on her trip, and Mary's concerns about missing the therapist, and established a plan for backup should Mary need to touch base with someone while her therapist was away. In this session, the therapist feels thrown by the intensity and somewhat disorganized style of Mary's distress. She (the therapist) was already feeling somewhat stressed herself as well, as she prepared to take time off. She also feels disappointed and concerned that Mary is having such a hard time, and that the attachment-separation issues seem to be flaring up again.

Toward the end of the session, after Mary and the therapist struggle somewhat futilely to figure out what Mary needs to feel more grounded, Mary tearfully and angrily says, "It feels like you don't even care that I burned myself last night." The therapist had no idea that Mary had burned herself, and now, ten minutes before the end of the session, feels overwhelmed by this statement and all that it implied. Mary feels truly beside herself and had simply blurted out something to try to effect a shift in their interaction, to let the therapist know how distressed she feels. The therapist, who normally would perceive what Mary was needing, snaps back quickly with, "What are you talking about? Why in the world didn't you tell me that earlier? What is going on with you?" Mary recoils, because this remark was unlike her therapist's typical response, and says sharply, "Nothing. It doesn't matter. I know we don't have much time.

Never mind. Just go on your trip and I will do the same. I'll see you in a few weeks," and got up to leave. The therapist, exasperated, replies, "I don't think this is a good way to leave things. Maybe we need to talk about your being safe. Are you sure you can go away and be safe? I think we should have a different backup plan, in case you need to go to the hospital or something."

In this example, the therapist moved into a more blaming and controlling position than was the norm for her. She acted out her frustration, anxiety, and stress, rather than using her awareness of her feelings as clues to discern a better path. This experience of failed empathy, with its concomitant shift in misusing power, can loom very large for clients. For some, the damage done by this brief interaction would take some months to repair. For a few, it might even mean a permanent rupture in the relationship (Elkind 1992). Others can bounce back more quickly, putting it into some perspective about the fallibility and humanness of therapists. These clients are able to draw on the shared experiences between themselves and their therapists. The potential for harm, though, in moving into a blaming, punitive "power-over" stance can be significant.

Other Unfair Uses of Power to Manage Feelings

Not all therapists impacted by their own unsorted reactions respond punitively; some also move into a "power-over" stance and re-create abusive dynamics but with a different tenor. The nonpunitive response is a form of rescuing with overtones of "good-mother bossiness." This response may actually feel nurturing and caring to clients at first. This is not to suggest that caring, human responses are inappro-

priate or abusive, but rather that therapists need to be
aware of their motivation to nurture and how they choose
to act this out with clients. Over time, the rescuing 'power-
over' stance deteriorates, because it is based on an imbalance of power and is serving the unconscious needs of the
therapist (as well as being a reenactment for the client).

Alternately, therapists who do not engage in overt
power acts to manage their own unsorted feelings tend to
become distant and removed (a covert power act). They
may ignore the client's reference to the self-injury, minimize its importance or significance to the client, avoid the
underlying issues, or simply be perceived by the client as
uninterested. All of these variations represent a shift away
from appropriate responsibility-taking as described in Chapter 6, with the ensuing complications that attend a power-
over stance.

At a systems level, the amplified reactivity of helping
professionals to clients who self-injure becomes institutionalized and codified. In some systems, any evidence of self-
injury is cause for immediate hospitalization, regardless of
what the client says about what is happening for her. (This
stance is probably somewhat mitigated by the profit motive
for managed care companies in recent years—a right action
for the wrong reasons.) The need to control patients' behavior becomes marked in inpatient settings, and there is
often a very quick, protocol-driven response to any self-
harming behavior. Efforts to understand and support the
client to understand his self-injury occur only because an
individual worker expresses interest, not because the system
values such pursuits. The misuse of power to ensure protection for the system or agency (in the name of protecting the client) is generally taken for granted and seen as
acceptable, in spite of the harm it causes. Further, this attitude invites reenactments of old relational paradigms

based on abusive power dynamics, particularly for patients who have spent significant time in mental health systems. (See Shur [1994] for a comprehensive elaboration of this idea.)

I believe this systemic attitude contributes to the use of self-injury for young women whose adolescence is peppered with hospital stays and placement in residential treatment programs. Some, originally hospitalized because of self-injury, describe their self-injury worsening over time and not really knowing why. I believe that without adequate or useful attention to the underlying issues, these young women "learn" to become patients (Rieker and Carmen 1986); facilities become "home base," and residential treatment providers become significant attachment figures. To be out on their own is frightening since many developmental issues are unresolved, and self-injury is too often a guaranteed ticket back "home."

Our Challenge Is to Maintain Integrity

Judith Herman (1992) writes:

Integrity is the capacity to affirm the value of life in the face of death, to be reconciled with the finite limits of one's own life and the tragic limitations of the human condition, and to accept these realities without despair. Integrity is the foundation upon which trust in relationships is originally formed, and upon which shattered trust may be restored. The interlocking of integrity and trust in caretaking relationships completes the cycle of generations and regenerates the sense of human community which trauma destroys. [p. 154]

Our struggles with our clients—with all that our clients evoke in us, with all we bring to our work—are essentially about how to find a decent, honest way to manage and transform our responses so we can be helpful. This is both the bane and the gift of trauma work. The potential for transformation—for our clients, ourselves, and society—is great, as is the potential for further harm. It is up to us to discern and take the right action, and to sustain and nourish ourselves. The next two chapters address the options we have and we create as we work with people who self-injure.

11

Finding the Right Action

Making deliberate choices, about how we respond, both in the moment with a client and in the larger world of systems and policies, allows us to stay grounded in our work with self-injuring clients. If we can find the right action, as best as we can discern it at any given time, we feel more confident and accepting of our errors or lack of certainty. Such actions interrupt our sense of helplessness and bring us back from the edge of unsorted countertransference and the chasm of unconscious reactivity. While comments on managing our reactions and acting from a place of thoughtfulness are scattered throughout this text, this chapter offers some specific focus on this topic.

Suggestions about how to respond to clients when self-injury occurs or seems imminent are included here rather than in Part Two because such interventions with clients are based on effective management of our own responses. Extemporaneous or immediate postsession reactions can be potent expressions of unsorted countertransference, and clients bear the brunt of unhelpful or harsh interactions if we don't anticipate our needs. In addition to staying connected to what we feel and think, and creating good opportunities for processing our reactions, our task is to develop personal operating policies that enable us to stay rooted and clear when clients begin or appear ready to self-injure in our presence.

This chapter also addresses the importance—for ourselves and our clients—of advocating for appropriate policies about self-injury in the larger systems within which we work. Issues of liability need to be balanced with a concern for justice. By staying mindful of the power inherent in our role as professionals, we may be better able to minimize the harm of common practices and policies.

Managing Our Feelings and Using the Information We Glean

The first step is managing our own feelings. This requires that we have enough self-awareness to know we are having a reaction, and that we contain this reaction until we have time to think about or process it. As is often the case with strong countertransference, the clinician's reaction may hold relevant information about the client's experience that, when used with thought and care, can build greater empathy and connection within the therapeutic relationship (Davies and Frawley 1994, Ehrenberg 1992, Elkind 1992, Maroda 1998). Our capacity to reflect on and identify our reactions to our clients' self-injury increases our knowledge base. We may be able to discern certain aspects of our experiences with them that we can convey directly in empathic terms. Many clients find such communications potent trust-builders. The rest of our reactions we need to explore in supervision, consultation, or our own healing work.

For example, the degree of helplessness and despair we feel when a client tells she has self-injured after a period of growth and consolidation can be informative. It may communicate her internal experience to us more powerfully than any words she could use. If we were aware of our reaction, we can formulate some ideas about what might be going on with the client and check them out. Rather than just reacting by expressing frustration or anger, we can stay present and emotionally connected with the client. We might ask, "How are you feeling about this?" and then follow up with an empathic comment or remark based on our own gut reaction, such as, "I wonder if you are feeling hopeless about this whole process." It may or may not be accurate, but it often opens the conversation more effectively than simply acting out of our own sense of helplessness and being critical or withdrawn. In some cases, a client may need us to actually feel what she feels so she can know that we really know how hard things are. This process, while demanding for the therapist and sometimes confusing for both client and therapist, can be an effective way for the client to communicate until she learns other methods and develops a more cohesive self-boundary. It also meets the client's need to feel understood—a powerful need for someone who was emotionally abandoned as a child. (See Maroda [1998] and Strean [1999] for more information about when and how to share countertransferential reactions.)

To effectively manage our feelings, we may need to do one or more things. We may need to teach ourselves some of the skills outlined by Linehan (1993) and others for regulating affect and staying grounded. We may need to work on increasing our self awareness by seeing an individual therapist, joining a therapy group, meditating regularly to increase mindfulness, or doing bodywork with a practitioner. We may seek out a supervisor with whom we can look at our affective responses to clients. We may need more training about trauma, or on working in depth with clients, or in child development theory. These and other forms of self-care are discussed in Chapter 12. The important point is that we attend to our feelings, and make choices about our responses.

When Self-Injury Occurs in Front of Us

One of the difficult moments in work with self-injuring clients is when they begin to hurt themselves in our presence. This raises complex issues and demands a response of some sort, even if we choose to do nothing. The immediacy of the conflicts about power and responsibility may come into sharp focus. If a client begins to cut or head-bang in front of us, we may decide we need to intervene directly, using our power and taking responsibility for stopping the client's behavior. The decision to stop someone from doing serious bodily harm to herself in our presence requires thought and caring. The degree of harm, what the therapist can tolerate, the context within which the self-injury is occurring in the session, and pertinent therapeutic relationship issues are some factors to consider.

Sakheim and Devine (1992) eloquently discuss such a decision within the frame of the power and safety issues in the therapeutic relationship and against the backdrop of the complex dynamics of childhood trauma. They describe some of the thinking that might go into such a decision. To *not* act, to choose to watch the client get hurt while we do nothing to help, can place us as an unconscious participant in a reenactment of the client's childhood experience. Intervening gently, such as putting a hand over the client's hand holding the sharp object or between the client's head and the wall, can be very important. Such an action can communicate caring (when done gently), a nonjudgmental refusal to allow the client to be hurt (i.e., extending protection), and an openness to meeting the client where she or he lives. Allowing significant harm to come to a client in our presence may contradict our human values as well as our professional training and duty; a genuine, human response of care, without blame, offers a valuable intervention.

On the other hand, therapists who can tolerate some self-injury in their presence may offer their clients a chance for healing that can be matched by few other experiences. The role of therapist as active witness can be quite powerful. One woman has described how, in a therapy session, a child part carefully cut her arm and acted out an earlier experience of abuse involving blood. This part had few words and very much wanted the therapist to know about this aspect of her history. The internal words accompanying the experience were "Now you know the worst." She felt that her therapist's willingness to sit with her while this occurred was a rare and healing opportunity, and allowed her to move on; issues related to that particular memory have not resurfaced since this event some years ago. Clearly, the context of the self-injury and the quality of relationship influence what action is right in any given moment.

If a client is repeatedly self-injuring in our presence (not a common occurrence in my experience), we need to look into the power dynamics in the therapeutic relationship as they intersect with the client's need for attachment and caring concern. Repetitive experiences of self-harm during interactions with a therapist convey a strong message about needs not being met, overwhelming affect at some level (conscious or unconscious), and a reenactment between the client and therapist about power and control. Assessing these issues with a supervisor or colleague may be the most useful approach for the therapist at this point. Changes in the interactional style with the client and efforts to better meet the client's need can be discovered in such a context.

When We Think Self-Injury May Occur Momentarily

More confounding are situations where we anticipate self-injury in the upcoming moment—because of a client's direct verbal communication, or by observing body language and action—but it has not yet occurred. The dynamics of power and responsibility, as well as safety in the therapeutic relationship, become activated, and sorting out how to respond in a few short moments can be a challenge.

Maggie had discussed her history of self-injury in several previous sessions, noting that she tended to self-injure when flooded with feelings. In this session, she became upset while discussing her relationship with her father. Her eyes filled with tears, her fists clenched, her face got red, her breathing shifted, and she abruptly stopped talking. She looked away and then back at me. She said, "You know I want to hurt myself," and reached into her pocket. She left her hand in her pocket as I said, "Yes, I thought that might be happening." We looked at each other, Maggie's hand still in her pocket fingering something. I wasn't sure what she was holding or what she might do.

I tried to weigh the impact of various courses of action. Should I ask Maggie what was in her pocket? Should I ask how she would hurt herself if she did? Should I ask Maggie not to hurt herself? Should I suggest an alternative? What would it mean in terms of Maggie's ability to contain her feelings if I stepped in and endeavored to effect a particular outcome? Would it be an opportunity to model using an alternative, or would it reinforce a belief that someone from the outside had to control Maggie's behavior? Would it set up a power struggle between us? How could I remain an ally and best support Maggie in this moment?

All of this occurred quickly. As I sat with the alternatives, Maggie suddenly stood up and said she had to use the bathroom. She asked if that was okay. I paused briefly and said, "Sure." I didn't know if she was going into the bathroom to cut or otherwise hurt herself, or to use the toilet, or to simply get a break from the intensity of the moment. Maggie went into the bathroom while I continued to ponder my options. Still uncertain, I felt inclined to let Maggie's process unfold and intervene later if I needed to, though I had some discomfort with this plan. She emerged from the bathroom and looked a little less upset. I asked her how she was doing. She said she felt somewhat better, that she had needed to use the bathroom since arriving because of the amount of coffee she had drunk that morning. I didn't know what else might be true, but I accepted her explanation. I didn't have a sense she had hurt herself in the bathroom (she was gone only a few minutes and she showed no injuries).

She sat back down and asked me if I thought she had been going to hurt herself in the bathroom. I told her I didn't know, that I had been unsure. I said I assumed she had not (which she confirmed) and that I was glad. She asked what I would have done if she had; I said that I didn't know but that we would have dealt with it however we needed to. I asked how she was feeling now, and she said she felt somewhat better. We continued to talk about her feelings about her father and Maggie was able to stay grounded, though she did experience some strong affect.

I felt intuitively that Maggie was both struggling with the impulse to hurt herself and also checking out how I would manage a challenge. I think she wanted to know how easily I might get scared, and what I would do when I was scared. I felt very uncertain about what the right choice was, but leaned into my general policy and stance of not eliciting a power struggle. I knew power issues in various forms were potent for Maggie, and I felt that I needed to err on the side of stepping back, rather than stepping in. It seemed, then and in subsequent sessions, I made the right decision. (At a much later date, Maggie confirmed my surmises and affirmed the choices I had made.)

Sorting Complicated Situations with Clients

Fundamentally, I think that our primary responsibility is to being willing to sort out complicated situations on a case-by-case basis. My general policy is to assume that clients will do their best to manage their behavior and that my job is to make my support and belief in them available, along with care and information. Therefore, I generally don't intervene unless someone is hurting himself right in front of me (and not always even then). The example above illustrates this position. This means that I take risks that might not be comfortable for others. Had Maggie injured herself in the bathroom, I might have felt I made the wrong decision. On the other hand, I believe I would have tried to use the situation as an opportunity to talk about the dynamics operating between us. This would mean I would need to raise the issue of not knowing what was the right thing to do, and wonder aloud what Maggie was hoping I would do. I would need to tell her I did not want to be in the position of being in charge of her behavior, that

I also felt uncomfortable being present while she hurt herself, and wondered what we could do the next time something like this occurred. That I wanted us to work together to formulate a plan for managing such a situation in the future. This approach keeps us as collaborators, especially in light of the power dynamics. It also clarifies the client's issues about power and control in a way that allows for eventual resolution rather than pushing her into a continuing reenactment.

In the Context of Hospital or Residential Settings

There is an added complexity to the process of respecting clients' rights and their ability to be in charge of themselves in residential and hospital settings. Concerns about contagion and the need for control by the setting due to the legal responsibility complicate the decision-making process. The decision about what action we take is also impacted by how people other than the self-injuring client will be affected. Further, I believe there can be increased shame for the client who injures herself in a somewhat public setting, regardless of the external bravado some patients may exhibit. The potential for large-scale reenactments are great, not only for the client who self-injures, but for the other patients and the staff (Shur 1994).

In these environments, the sorting process becomes much more complex, and the need for clear, responsible policies and adequate staff training about self-injury is high. In such settings, Burstow (1992) recommends increasing the awareness of workers about the underlying needs, assigning more staff to evening/night shifts when women in shelter may feel more vulnerable or needy, and acknowledging the level of neediness and the inability of staff to meet all the needs. She also suggests not having a rule in shelters and residential programs stating that residents cannot self-injure, or acting in punitive ways when someone does self-injure (e.g., telling someone she must clean up the resulting mess alone). Attention to staff needs is crucial to developing and implementing responsive, respectful institutional policies about self-injury. The more the staff members feel supported, the more they will be able to respond helpfully to clients who engage in self-injury.

Developing a Personal Policy

Determining a general guiding policy for our behavior in response to clients' self-injury helps with the inherent difficulties present in these situations. Each of us needs to develop a personal plan of action. Prior planning and thoughtfulness about the implications of our behavior can minimize harm and create a safer environment for clients, and reduce anxiety for us to some degree. To develop a personal policy about how we will respond to self-injury if it occurs in front of us, or if a client reports recent or intended self-injury, we need to know what larger policies guide us by profession, setting, or legality. These might include the code of ethics from a professional organization such as the American Counseling Association, American Psychological Association, American Psychiatric Association, or the National Association of Social Workers. It might also involve the ethics guidelines from the state licensing board or other certifying body. Agency or hospital policies and procedures provide necessary information as well. Further, any relevant statutes or case law decisions need to be considered.

Legal liability for mental health professionals with regard to the broad area of self-harm tends to focus on potential dangerousness and preventing foreseeable harm. In this context, harm generally denotes either violence toward another person and the duty to warn that person (as articulated in the Tarasoff decision [VandeCreek and Knapp 1993]), or situations wherein the client or patient may endanger his own life. This latter situation incorporates the criteria relevant to involuntary commitment to a psychiatric facility. Liability with regard to self-injury is largely unspecified, except as a potential indicator of the intent or capacity to commit suicide. Weiner and Wettstein (1993) state, "Prior attempts at suicide or other intentionally self-destructive behavior such as self-mutilation may suggest commitment under this criterion" (p. 51), while also noting that the degree of lethality of self-harming behavior is relevant. Agency or program policies recommending involuntary commitment for self-injury tend to be grounded in this framework. (See Weiner and Wettstein for a full discussion of the issues involved with legal liability.)

Determining "clear and imminent danger" (a phrase commonly used in ethics codes) can be difficult with regard to self-injury—even if we assume that the danger does apply to the self-injury itself and not only to self-injury as an indicator of suicidality. What is danger? Can it be as broad as any harm to oneself (including getting drunk, for example) or is it limited to serious, life-threatening harm? How do we determine "clear and imminent"? If a client has self-injured recently, how likely is she to engage in the same behavior in the near future? With what degree of accuracy can we predict a client's self-injury?

My experience is that a number of factors contribute to the actual occurrence of self-injury, and even though a client may state, "I feel like I need to injure myself when I leave your office," I cannot predict the likelihood that she will indeed harm himself. Sometimes it is simply a statement of feeling, and not a statement of intent. Sometimes she may think she is going to cut when she gets home, but she unexpectedly runs into a friend and her mood changes, obviating the need to cut. Sometimes she "guts it out" and weathers the feelings, and is able to refrain from cutting. Many different outcomes can occur, making it hard to know what is a clear and imminent danger.

Overall, using existing policies and ethics codes as guides, the challenge is to articulate a more concrete, focused personal policy. By this, I mean making an effort to define what I will and won't do in light of a client self-injuring in front of me. The first step of this process is to determine my own values and beliefs about self-injury, clients, and healing. Our values direct us, along with legal and ethical constraints, and provide a more solid base than a personal policy that is designed according to external policies. Once we know what we believe and what our duties are, then our task is to loosely outline our intended future behavior. A policy might be as simple as "I accept that self-injury is an attempt to communicate and cope, and that using self-injury is within a client's right to self-determination. I also cannot tolerate watching someone hurt her/himself in front of me. So, the goal for my behavior is to be accepting of a client's self-injury except when the harm occurs in front of me. I will then gently intervene. I will not involuntarily hospitalize clients because of self-injury, nor will I advocate for their hospitalization because of self-injury."

A personal policy may also be more complex, outlining differing therapist behavior dependent on varying client behavior. It might, for example, include a phrase or paragraph about degrees of lethality, and the action I will take if I feel the client is at risk for losing her life. Determining such a policy is essentially an extension of our own personal code of ethics about boundaries. As noted in

Chapter 6, we each must determine some basic boundaries that define our interactions with clients. We may choose to act outside those lines, but they give us a framework within which to work and guide our deviations. The important thing is that we are informed (with regard to legal and ethical duties, our own values, and the level of risk we can tolerate) and we are clear with ourselves. Clarity may be enhanced by writing out what we determine as a personal policy.

Negotiating the Interface of Conflicts between Policies

Sometimes we determine a policy for our own behavior that conflicts with the operational policy of our work setting. This happens with some frequency in hospital or residential settings, and in some outpatient programs. Self-injuring behavior may be cause for filing an incident report or taking action to restrain or restrict the activities of a client. It may necessitate an evaluation for hospitalization or notification of a supervisor. As a worker, we may disagree with a policy even as we must enforce it. Being as humane as possible in our interactions with the client as we do so (rather than expressing our frustration and sense of conflict by being testy or sharp with the client) can help maintain a sense of connection with the client, and minimize the harm of such a policy. Sometimes it works to say, "I really am sorry and this doesn't feel right to me, but you know what the rules are—I can't let you off the unit for dinner because of your cutting. Let's talk later about what is going on for you—I want to know what's happening. I think you are having a hard time and I want to help if I can."

Care needs to be taken when apologizing for a policy or action. Setting ourselves apart from the policies of the setting can be problematic, both for the client and for the program. It may get us into trouble with supervisors. What allows this to work in terms of clients and the program itself is the sense of clear responsibility for our actions that we communicate at the same time we apologize. In other words, we own that we are taking this action and have a duty to do so. Adherence to the policies and procedures of our employer is part of our contract as a worker. We are apologizing for the aspect of the policy that feels unfair or not right. We must delicately walk a line where we maintain an alliance with the client as we also remain allied with the setting or program. We cannot ally with the client against the program. It creates damaging dynamics for everyone.

There may be day-to-day operational guidelines that can be negotiated with a supervisor about particular clients or about self-injury in general for workers who are in conflict with an institutional policy. Any discussions of the decision to vary from such policies should be noted in the client's file (when appropriate) or in a memo to the supervisor, both for liability and malpractice protection and to provide guidance in case management should the decision feel confusing in the future. Other conflicts with institutional policies may need to be addressed at the policy-making level, with workers and supervisors advocating for changes in the problematic policy.

The Implicit and Explicit Power of Our Profession

The power to impact someone's life by the use of operational policies is great. This impact extends to diagnostic labels and the psychiatric framing of an issue in a more general way as well, since labels and pathologizing tend to accompany unhelpful policies about self-injury. Sometimes we forget the impact we can have, even long after the client or patient has stopped working with us. Mental health professionals need to be scrupulously careful, as Garbarino (1999b) writes,

> since it is they who are charged with the responsibility for deciding who falls inside the circle of normality and who does not. This determination has many important ramifications. It affects personal liberty and self-esteem. It has financial and political implications. It shapes family functioning. It influences who receives drugs or psychotherapy, and who is certified "normal."
>
> One of the biggest dangers faced by mental health professional as they take up this responsibility to judge and assess is that they will see human behavior through a biased lens and thus be drawn into making false or distorted analyses. Sometimes, these biased analyses are based on political or economic interests. The use of psychiatric diagnosis to serve political purposes in the former Soviet Union is one example of this danger. Other times, the source of the bias reflects deep religious and intrapsychic issues. The historical classification of homosexuality as psychopathology in the United States is a case in point. Often, the bias has its origins in gender politics. The medicalization of female sexuality as a vehicle for the subjugation of girls and women throughout the world exemplifies this tendency. [p. 14]

Similar biases have driven much of the policy development and treatment planning regarding self-injury at the institutional level. The need to control patients' behavior because it defies cultural, personal, or political norms gets covered over by rhetoric regarding fears about liability and professional responsibility. Recall the story from Chapter 1 about the woman who had the right to smoke, even though it endangered her health and most likely her life, without the fear of being involuntarily committed to a psychiatric hospital or put in five-point restraints. We may have legitimate worries about clients' self-injury, and we need to communicate these openly to clients in nonblaming ways. We need to attend to clients' behavior and endeavor to help them stay safe. But we also need to take responsibility for not institutionalizing our fears into policies in order to avoid the tough, time-consuming conversations or interventions.

Not an Easy Struggle

Part of the difficulty in sorting out these issues reflects the inherent dilemma of most hard ethical questions: it is not a matter of right versus wrong, but rather a matter of right versus right (Kidder 1995). Situations that involve a decision between right and wrong are clear; this choice is much easier, even if we feel pulled by fear or shame to make what we might perceive as the wrong choice. Situations involving a decision between two rights are much more complicated. Kidder notes that there are three common right-versus-right dilemmas: individual need vs. collective or community need; justice versus mercy, and loyalty versus truth. In each of these, we are faced with having to carefully balance valid, competing needs, the essence of any genuine conflict.

Regarding self-injury, this right-versus-right dilemma might be framed in several ways. One can be described as the therapist's need for comfort versus the client's need to be self-determining. It is reasonable that as therapists we need to feel some measure of comfort in our work. If we are continually afraid or distressed, we cannot be effective helpers. I know I don't work well if I am anxious and worried. So our comfort is a valid ground (as one factor) for decision-making, just as is the client's right to self-determination regarding the use of her body.

Another right versus right regarding self-injury is the client's need for control over her body/being versus the client's need for support and protection of her body/being. The inherent dilemma here is oftentimes at the crux of the client's struggle with self-injury. She wants and needs to be protected and safe, and at the same time, she has a powerful need to have control. It harkens back to the larger dilemmas about control discussed in Chapters 6 and 10. If we engage in the struggle for control, we end up reenacting the client's struggle with herself, with varying degrees of usefulness and complication. As Davies and Frawley state, "So here, as therapists, we dance on the head of a pin, caught maddeningly between the dangers of under- or over-reaction to the patient's violent behavior" (p. 145).

A third right versus right is the common one noted above: individual needs versus community needs. These can be seen most clearly in inpatient or residential settings, where workers and policy-makers are challenged to address the multiple needs of different clients or patients. What might be more useful for the community can be quite different from what is more useful to an individual client. Finding a balance without violating either individual or collective rights isn't easy.

Balancing Liability Concerns with Justice Issues

Our task is essentially one of conflict negotiation, of balance and respect, for our clients, our selves, our institutions, and our professions. Unfortunately, it is not a level playing field. The inherent power imbalance in helping relationships creates unevenness. The litigious climate of the late 1990s highlights the fears of many health professionals, and unsorted and unmanaged feelings often center around and find institutional support in the area of liability. This adds more bumps. And the mistreatment and labeling of clients who self-injure continue, with less immediately clear but still devastating consequences. Defining a place of equilibrium between the competing needs of therapist comfort and fears about liability, and the basic civil rights of clients is difficult. The more we can focus on respectful, human interactions that take into account the presence of a conflict of needs, the better able we are to both manage risk and provide clients with what they seek.

In highlighting the issues about justice and self-injury, Mazelis (1999) describes a fictitious scenario of a woman being hospitalized because she has asthma and smokes (similar to the story I told in Chapter 1):

> If people learned that someone lost her civil rights and was forcibly institutionalized because she had asthma and also smoked, there would be a tremendous outcry. The American Civil Liberties Union would be swamped with various communications and demands for action. People in government on all levels would be contacted, and quotes made from the Constitution decrying what happened to this woman. There might possibly be a swarm of demonstrators outside of the hospital protesting her incarceration. Whatever might happen, I am sure there would be a strong reaction amongst most people. It would surely get the interest of the talk shows and tabloids. People with hypertension would probably hide their salt shakers, and those with diabetes would be afraid to enter donut shops where policemen eat.

After all, if this could happen to someone with asthma, it could happen to them. And yet this does happen, not infrequently, to women living with SIV [self-inflicted violence], whose self-injury often has fewer health consequences than smoking or unhealthy eating. Women living with SIV are in constant danger of losing their rights. [p. 3]

The loss of basic civil rights is not the only justice issue related to self-injury. As noted by Garbarino (1999b) in the earlier quote, psychiatric labels are potent identifiers of normal and not normal, okay and not okay. Too often, the labels we give carry the power of a self-fulfilling prophecy, even if that power comes only in the eyes of the beholders. In education, this consequence is referred to as the Pygmalion effect, wherein teachers' expectations of students actually impact the students' performance and behavior (Tauber 1997). If someone is repeatedly viewed as borderline or manipulative, she may indeed take on those characteristics; even more likely is that the label will stick and future therapists or workers will greet this client with preconceived ideas about who she is. The interactive effect—what comes from the client and what comes from the therapist—might be hard to determine, but the role of labels is significant and impacts future care delivery in many cases. We have a duty, therefore, to be exceedingly careful in our judgments and use of diagnostic and clinical labels.

Working for Change as Advocates within Systems

As a group, self-injuring clients have less clout and financing than those in positions of power inside institutions and care networks, and the task of advocating may fall, in part, upon us. Advocacy is something that mental health professionals with integrity have done for many years. This duty includes speaking on someone's behalf when he is not at the table or is unable to do so, and working to help him speak on his own behalf whenever possible. The mental health consumer movement emphasizes the need for clients' voices at all levels within service delivery systems. I believe that we have a responsibility to speak up as well, lending our voices and support when we can.

This may mean we do individual advocacy or education within mental and physical health care delivery systems for particular clients. It may also mean we need to advocate for this group of clients within these systems of care and among our colleagues for a more informed, humane understanding and treatment of self-injury. This may mean we challenge practice guidelines or hospital rules that restrict our capacity to stay clear about power and responsibility in the presence of self-injury. Working with public policy committees within our professional associations, writing letters, questioning a colleague's blaming attitude, or speaking up in a case conference can all be avenues for advocacy and education. Ultimately we may be able to clarify and revise ethical guidelines within our professional associations and our agencies or programs, or clarify or change statutes, thereby reducing the ethical and legal conflicts we might experience in this work.

The personal benefit of such advocacy work is that it provides a concrete and effective counterbalance to the powerlessness and helplessness sometimes engendered by working with self-injuring clients. Clients may feel powerless to change their self-injury at times, and we may feel helpless in trying to be of use to them. Both therapists and clients are likely to experience some degree of despair and a sense of being overwhelmed by all that self-injury brings.

By speaking up, by advocating for respect and kindness and understanding, we can shift the heaviness of despair and create a space for light and fresh air. In this space, a more informed, humane, and grounded understanding of self-injury can emerge.

12

Nourishing and Sustaining the Self of the Therapist

Working with clients who self-injure pushes us to our edges and to our cores. The intensity, the range, and the depth of the feelings connected to the impulse or inclination to hurt oneself stretches all who come close to it. Sitting with someone as she examines how her life has been shaped by trauma or walking the journey as she reworks childhood pain changes us. These experiences prompt us to examine our beliefs and values, what we treasure, how we have been hurt, what we long for and need, who matters to us, what we want in this life. Such work also necessitates that we take care of ourselves amidst this intensity.

Sometimes the simplest things are the hardest to do. We often know what is good (or bad) for us and yet we trip over ourselves again and again in our efforts to actually do good self-care. Many writers (Figley [1995], Pearlman and Saakvitne [1995], Wilson and Lindy [1994b] to name a few) have addressed the need for self-care at various levels, and have outlined some of what helps trauma workers cope with the inherent stresses. Laurie Pearlman and Karen Saakvitne, psychologists committed to work with trauma survivors, offer grounded and comprehensive information about the needs of therapists working with trauma survivors (see Pearlman and Saakvitne [1995] and Saakvitne and Pearlman [1996]).

Their workbook, *Transforming the Pain: A Workbook on Vicarious Traumatization* (1996), provides exercises and a framework to facilitate this process of self-care.

Saakvitne and Pearlman (1996) succinctly summarize the core elements of self-care as the "ABCs of addressing vicarious traumatization" (p. 76): awareness, balance, and connection. They encourage us to be aware of and attuned to our needs, limits, emotions, and resources; to strive toward balance in the areas of work, play, and rest; and to maintain connections with self, others, and something larger in the universe (loosely, some form of spiritual or philosophical connection). Using these concepts as a ground, they suggest that we assess the impact of our work with clients, identify areas of distress, and transform what we can in some way. Saakvitne and Pearlman's self-assessment tools may be of use; see the workbook as well as the training curriculum they co-authored with Sarah Gamble and Beth Tabor Lev (Saakvitne et al. 2000).

Drawing on this general perspective in this chapter, barriers to taking good care of ourselves are addressed, followed by some basic ideas for self-care. Attending to the self of the therapist—the person of the clinician—is essential. This attention is described here from five angles: support for our clinical work, physical and emotional self-care, a passionate engagement with life, creative process, and a spiritual ground. Some specific ideas are offered.

Barriers to Self-Care

Many different factors can interfere with our ability to take care of ourselves in the ways we wish or know are good for us. Perhaps it is simply part of the struggle of being human to continually wrestle with the tension between self-harm and self-care, to work to muster the energy to expend effort to be healthy and do the right thing. Nonetheless, there are sometimes specific barriers that hinder our self-care abilities. It can help to identify what gets in our way and work to remove these barriers so we can move toward greater self-nurturance and away from self-harm (see Arnold's continuum in Chapter 2).

Simply asking the question "Why don't we take our own advice about self-care?" can be a productive starting point. Not enough time, feeling too tired, and a lack of support are often at the top of the list for many people. Personal vulnerabilities and unresolved issues may keep us from acting in our own best interest. The demands of children, aging parents, or other people who are dependent on us for care may add to the burdens we are juggling and prompt us to place self-care lower on the list of priorities. Other external pressures such as lack of sufficient economic resources, the tasks of life maintenance (shopping, cooking, housecleaning, bill paying, laundry), a partner's schedule or career, and community commitments can all interfere with our willingness and capacity to place our needs closer to the top of the list. The "both/and" approach mentioned in an earlier chapter can be useful here, so we can place others' needs *and* our own needs in equal position and attempt to meet some of both.

The systems in which we work may also disrupt our efforts to take care of ourselves. Staying client-focused can be a challenge in some mental health delivery systems, especially ones that are large or profit-oriented. Some clinicians working with trauma survivors find it difficult to locate colleagues with a shared worldview—colleagues who appreciate the role of trauma in their clients' distress, take responsibility for their own issues and work on their countertransference, respect clients' needs, avoid blaming attitudes, and operate with an awareness of power dynamics in interpersonal relationships. Therapists may feel their efforts to support clients to do what they need to do to heal are undermined by co-workers or supervisors. Policy conflicts about how to respond to a client's self-injury may add to the sense of alienation or isolation a therapist feels in some work settings. The chronicity of these stresses can lead to a depletion and misdirection of energy, and interfere with adequate self-care strategies.

The cumulative effect of not being sure about what clients need or what we should do also deters us from good self-care. Being willing to stay present with clients and support their self-determination, to not assume that we know the answers, and to be flexible and responsive require that we have a tolerance for ambiguity. It means that we must be able to bear not knowing, not having answers. This stance is often in direct contradiction to our training, particularly those with a medical orientation. Not knowing can be anxiety-producing and cause us to question ourselves. In so doing, we may also question what we really need and not act in our own behalf at times.

Perhaps we can frame an overall focus to self-care as an attempt to stay present to our best intentions and accept that self-care is an ongoing, ever-changing process. We will come back time and again to the question, "What do I need?" We will never arrive, finding *the* way to best care for ourselves. We must remain open to new needs and new solutions. We need to always maintain awareness, as Saakvitne and Pearlman (1996) advise, so we can then develop pertinent self-care strategies that work for a particular moment.

Supporting Our Work as Clinicians

One of the self-care strategies that is probably universal is the need for support directly related to our clinical work. The form this support takes can vary a great deal from one clinician to the next, and for the same clinician at different points in her career. This support might entail a good relationship with a supervisor either in an agency setting or in private practice, or participation in a peer supervision group. It might mean having several close colleagues with whom we can talk openly and in depth, no matter the issue. It might mean adopting or developing a clear theoretical or philosophical framework on which to draw, particularly when confusing or unsettling events occur in our work with clients. For clinicians newer to trauma work, or those working intensely with clients who are processing traumatic material, having someone who can hear us out after a tough session can be invaluable. For some therapists, being able to simply recount what our clients have related—to debrief—helps us release the images and feelings that may be engendered by this kind of client work, thereby reducing vicarious traumatization.

Ongoing education and training, in various forms, are also crucial forms of support for our work as clinicians. Attending conferences and seminars, pursuing further higher education, or participating in postgraduate training programs offer varied formats for learning and growth. The act of learning tends to shift our perspective, sometimes subtly and sometimes more dramatically. This shift can give us wider views of our clients, ourselves, and our work. Avid readers are sustained by the private pursuit of knowledge; some clinicians combine this with the support they get from peers by forming a reading or study group. Others can take advantage of a journal club, grand rounds, or other staff development activity in their setting.

Other professional options that can support ongoing clinical work with clients include adding teaching or supervision to our professional responsibilities, conducting research projects, or becoming active in professional associations. Doing advocacy work in our geographic region within public care systems, or at a national or international level regarding policy, or serving on relevant task forces or other multidisciplinary endeavors, may also serve to diversify our work and provide some balance. Speaking up on behalf of clients as a group, as noted in Chapter 11, can be a strong antidote to the helplessness and powerlessness evoked by ongoing work with trauma survivors. Writing and training others often challenges us to integrate our knowledge base, augmenting our clinical work indirectly and providing support that grounds us more solidly. Seeking some diversity among our clients may also offer a sense of balance, as can adding group or couples work to our repertoire of services.

These options, overall, reflect an attitude that values growth and development as a life process. They speak to the need for balance (a continually shifting pattern) and connection with colleagues as key aspects of our professional lives. Although structural and interpersonal impediments to balance and connection do exist as noted, self-care entails that we make our professional needs a priority.

Physical and Emotional Self-Care

Just as we encourage our clients to discern what they need to physically and emotionally care for themselves amidst the stresses of everyday life and a therapeutic process, we need to do the same for ourselves. This includes everything from getting enough sleep to processing difficult feelings that emerge in response to our work with clients. Discovering what sustains and nourishes us takes time and effort. Although some aspects of self-care may seem obvious, what truly sustains and nourishes us may require more discernment. We may need to continually assess a best-practice guideline for our own self-care. And, our needs change over time. We may find we can determine some overall guidelines, knowing they will need to be modified during stressful times.

Physical self-care includes eating well at regular intervals, sleeping enough hours at a stretch, attending to our health care needs, maintaining a regular exercise regimen, planning our days effectively (number of hours and scheduled breaks), and avoiding an overuse of toxic substances such as alcohol, drugs, tobacco, and sugar. Other forms of physical self-care may include meditation or relaxation, bodywork such as massage or Feldenkrais, playing sports, focused breathing, learning a new skill, and effective time management. Simple things like doing stretching exercises between clients, going outside on a lunch break, or pacing our schedule so we have an additional ten minutes between clients may make a significant difference in how we physically carry or release stress.

As noted previously in this book, the line between the physical and the emotional is somewhat fuzzy. Many of the forms of physical self-care also have an emotional benefit. Meditation is a good example. Not only does meditation reset our brain waves and autonomic nervous system, it also provides us with a sense of calm and peace. Meditation can shift our mood, as can breathing exercises or a short walk outside. Some forms of emotional self-care focused more specifically on our emotional selves include:

Soothing and comforting behavior
- Listening to music
- Taking a bath
- Using relaxation techniques
- Going for a drive

Distraction techniques
- Watching a video
- Going to a movie
- Reading a novel or a magazine
- Doing busywork that needs to be done

Talking and sorting with others
- Friends
- A therapist
- Self-help group members
- Others in our social network

The use of positive self-talk
- Affirmations
- Cognitive reframes
- Reminders we need to hear about our work
- Prayer

Playful activities
- Romping with the dog in the park
- Being silly
- Blowing bubbles
- Taking children to the playground

Recreation
- Gardening
- Hobbies
- Crafts
- Sports
- Reading

The presence of beauty and order
- Keeping a tidy office
- Creating beauty by the simple placement of treasured objects
- Having flowers (cut or potted plants) in rooms where we spend time
- Maintaining a peaceful home environment
- Being organized in terms of objects and space

Identifying three key physical/emotional strategies that work consistently and don't require extraordinary effort or a lot of time can make self-care easier. Much as our clients may have trouble remembering and activating self-care strategies when stressed, so may we. Focusing in on three approaches that fit well with our personality or style can help us remember to care for ourselves in stressful moments. Cognitive reminders like flashcards or small signs on our desk can be useful.

Also in the realm of emotional self-care is the need for clinicians to attend to their own unresolved experiences of trauma and loss. These and other core issues are often evoked in our work with self-injuring clients. While we are all hampered by our unconscious issues, achieving some degree of resolution about the issues of which we *do* have awareness is a professional and personal responsibility. Just as is true for clients, how and where we do this will vary. Sometimes it means pursuing personal therapy, other times we may find that the various professional supports listed earlier can help us reach resolution and maintain self-awareness. It is likely that a variety of approaches will be most useful. Finding other colleagues, either as individuals or through a support group, who have experienced similar traumas can be instrumental in transforming the shame and sense of being an impostor that some survivor-clinicians feel.

Having Enough Life Unrelated to Our Work: A Passionate Engagement with Life

The therapeutic stance advocated in this book entails a high level of engagement with clients. This approach needs to be complemented with an equally high level of engagement with life outside of our relationships with clients. Although many therapists get some intimacy needs met through our contact with clients, we will end up in problematic situations if clients constitute our primary intimate connections. We need enough people and interests outside of our work to provide the needed balance and nourishment. We need to feel a part of the process of life, to be engaged in vibrant, alive energy patterns. To be passionately engaged in the world around us is one of the best antidotes to the stress and burnout associated with trauma work.

Passionate engagement with life is not to be confused with being busy. Having many activities outside of work may or may not be restorative. It may or may not indicate a high level of involvement with life forces. And what is nourishing to one person is completely draining or anxiety-producing to another. Regular get-togethers with a group of friends, for example, may be very rejuvenating to one person while it is exhausting to another. Personality type, family demands, and different stages of adult development all necessitate varying ways to be passionate about life. The importance of this element of self-care is to identify a few ways to feel alive and involved that work for us.

For some people, this sense of sustaining vitality comes from interaction with the natural world. This might include the replenishment that comes from a short walk in a city park on a break in the workday, or from camping on the weekend, or a leisurely drive through the countryside.

Some find that their gardens are oases amidst the demands of intense client work, a quiet "playroom" where they can commune with plant life and nature spirits. Others may canoe or hike, take long vacations at the beach or in remote national parks, or go to the woods to think. Others have denizens of houseplants, or a lovely collection of found objects from nature like rocks, shells, nests, fossils, and dried roots. For some, animals provide a powerful link to the natural world. Caring for pets, doing volunteer work with strays, or watching birds and animals in the wild can provide a grounding connection to the natural world and all that is alive.

Another expression of the passionate engagement with life is the presence of love. I have written earlier in this book about the power of love. I do believe that our capacity to be in love, that is, in a place of loving, counters much of what is debilitating about trauma work and the pain often associated with self-injury. We may experience love in relationship to certain people including our clients, in relation to animals, and in a more abstract way about being human or about the natural world. Fundamentally, I believe this capacity to be connected with the loving forces in the universe is about a willingness to open our hearts and let the life force flow through us with less resistance.

Creative Process: The Passion of Making It Anew

To create something is to bring to life that which did not previously exist. This element of transformation is inherent to creative process. Because of this quality, creative expression can be a powerful remedy to the strain of working with clients who self-injure. Many self-injuring clients have an intimate experience of brokenness. They often feel irreparably broken, even though many people also hold hope and other beliefs about the possibility of healing. As therapists, we often absorb the helplessness and despair that attend brokenness. Active involvement in creative process can be a potent and transformative contrast to this experience of being so broken.

There are several aspects of engaging in creative process that can nourish us. The satisfaction that comes with having something to show for our creative effort in very concrete terms can be gratifying, particularly if we primarily do long-term work with our clients. While long-term work is deeply fulfilling, there are stretches of time where the pain and struggle is much more present than the sense of accomplishment that accompanies change. Producing an object can satisfy our desire for concrete evidence of change. Constructing an object of beauty that we can continue to enjoy may also be a very pleasing aspect of creativity. Often, however, the result or product is not as significant or transformative as the ability to tap into our creative energy, to kindle the spark to make something new and different.

There are numerous ways we can be creative; many paths are restorative. What matters is that we give our natural curiosity and interest room enough to grow, that we listen to and act on the quiet longings inside ourselves. For some people, creativity is indeed rooted in the arts; many find painting, playing music, using a camera, writing, dancing, sculpting, composing songs, quilting, sketching, and singing highly rejuvenating. For others, creative juices flow when they garden, cook, build furniture, sew or design clothing, repair cars, set up housekeeping systems, fashion miniature worlds with railways or dollhouses, invent computer games, or teach music to children.

We might take a hand-built pottery class, or go off to adult camp for a week to learn jewelry making. We might take the piano lessons we always wanted as a child, or dust off the saxophone we have stashed in the basement, or join a choir. We might pursue our interest in Pacific Rim cooking, or build a table fountain, or take up story-telling as an art form. We might capture old photos on videotape with a narrative of our family history, or research the art forms associated with our ethnic heritage to invent a craft project. We might play the guitar or write poems, or lazily watercolor in the sun. We might build sandcastles at the beach. We might design a new herb garden. We might make rag dolls or paint eggs or study print-making. All these activities can evoke our creative abilities and nourish our souls.

A Spiritual Ground

Few clinicians who spend significant time with clients addressing core issues of profound pain and life-changing trauma operate without a spiritual perspective. As discussed in some detail in Chapter 9, trauma tends to evoke existential questioning (Herman 1992) and challenge our spiritual or philosophical beliefs. Our worldview is altered, and our worldview is often intimately connected to our spirituality. From a perspective of self-care, these challenges can mean utilizing, developing, or modifying our faith beliefs, especially with regard to life purpose, causality of harm, and the availability of grace or goodness.

Clinicians who do not bring a strong faith perspective to their work, or who have only a vague idea about what they believe with regard to divinity and the meaning of life, will find themselves spending time questioning these ideas and searching for a comfortable ground. Others who have a strong faith tradition may also question or doubt what they have been taught in light of the new information they receive by being proximate to trauma, and need to reframe some of their beliefs. Regardless of where we start, we are likely to stand in a somewhat different place (or places) as we work with issues related to trauma.

Finding a form of spiritual practice—be it meditating, attending services at a temple or mosque, gardening, participating in a prayer group, doing t'ai chi, keeping a kosher home, journeying, working a twelve-step program, studying the Koran or the Bible, casting a circle, saying the rosary, reading a daily affirmation, chanting, or walking the medicine wheel—can be useful as well. Regular (or even somewhat irregular) spiritual practice tenders us a gift larger than each individual action of meditation or prayer. The act of practicing, even more than the particular form, tends the soul in subtle ways and can offer an almost indefinable sense of support by its simple constancy. Such practice may be especially grounding and helpful during difficult or emotionally demanding times.

My colleague Anita Mallinger offers this reflection on the therapist's experience of personal change and spirituality as a result of working with trauma survivors:

> Doing this work has transformed my worldview. It's like another lens has been added to my camera, and I can see in sharper focus—in greater detail—the astonishing complexity of being human. For example, when I was doing abreactive work with a client whose father had cut her with glass, and in the abreaction I saw the cuts appear on her arm and bleed and then heal and disappear as we worked through the memory, I knew that to be human is just bigger than I ever imagined; and the connections between mind and body are far more intricate than we have even begun to understand. I'm not a theist—haven't been one for

a long time and probably won't ever be one; I just know now that we human beings are *so much*—have dimensions that haven't been explored—and that knowledge, along with grabbing up whatever joys I can find for myself in this life without hurting anyone else, is enough to sustain me spiritually.

Perhaps what is most helpful regarding spiritual needs as we work with self-injuring clients is our willingness to explore the meaning of life. Not that we will necessarily find definitive answers. But our capacity to tolerate this ambiguity, to ask questions, to wonder aloud, and to be open to possibilities will stand us in good stead, both with our clients as they struggle with self-inflicted violence and all that is underneath it, and in our own beings. And, perhaps, along the way, we will discover more joy and dimension in this adventure of life.

Living the Vision in All Its Imperfections: The Best We Can Do

Our ability to care for ourselves is directly related to our capacity to work with clients who self-injure. Self-injuring clients struggle overtly with self-care; their histories dictate against being able to care for themselves adequately. Not only do we model useful strategies for our clients when we care for ourselves, self-care actually dictates who we are and what we bring to our work. I offer my *self* to my clients. While I also bring knowledge, access to resources, some techniques, and other skills, fundamentally what I offer to my clients is my being, my values, and my faith in their ability to heal and grow. These are all enhanced when I stand strong in nurturing my self. As Marcia Hill (1990) writes, "The process we use to create change becomes the change we create" (p. 57). All of what we bring into the room with our clients, no matter the context or length of contact, exists as part of the change (or lack of change) that occurs in our work with them. Let us bring the best of ourselves, replete with inadequacies, to our work with clients. The wholeness of our presence, full of holes and vulnerabilities, is the most significant and honest offering we can make.

Appendix A

Sample Questions that Might Be Useful When Talking with Clients about Their Self-Injury

These questions and comments are sample ideas for therapists who want to express interest and invite responses from their clients regarding the clients' self-injury. There is no right way to inquire or show concern and interest. Each clinician must find a comfortable style in talking with each client that suits that particular client. These sample questions are intended to stimulate ideas and suggest possible avenues for exploration, to help create a ground for conversation. They are not intended as a protocol or a structured interview format, and should not be used in a way that feels like an interview or interrogation to the client. See Chapters 5, 6, and 7 for more information about talking with clients about self-injury and the importance of a relational context when exploring this issue.

Comments or Questions that Communicate Interest

1. I am glad you told me about what you do to your body. Are you feeling okay about having told me?
2. Thanks for telling me. I am glad to know.
3. Thanks for telling me. I am glad to know. How are you feeling right now, having told me about this?
4. I noticed the scars on your arm. I hope it's okay to say that. I am interested in knowing about them if you want to tell me.
5. I'm wondering if you have ever hurt yourself intentionally. I thought maybe that's what you meant when you said _____.
6. Can you tell me about the times when you hurt yourself?
7. Sometimes people cut or hit or bite themselves. I wonder if that's something you've done in the past or even more recently.
8. I am so glad you told me that. If you want to tell me more, or feel like saying more sometime in the future, I am interested in hearing about it.

Questions that Invite the Client to Decide If and to What Extent She Wants to Explore Her Self-Injury

1. Does it feel like it would be helpful to talk more about your cutting?
2. Would you like to talk more about this with me? I'm willing to hear, if you want to tell me more.
3. Do you think it would be useful to learn more about your self-injury? Sometimes people find it helps them sort things out when they talk about it.

4. We can explore some alternatives to your self-injury if you want to. Do you think that would be helpful?
5. Do you have a sense of how your self-injury works for you? Would it help to learn more about it?
6. Sometimes talking about how you hurt yourself can be useful. What do you think?
7. Would it help to have more information about self-injury in general?

Questions that Can Help Elicit Information about the Patterns Associated with Self-Injury

1. Do you know when you are most likely to injure yourself?
2. Do you know how often you hurt yourself?
3. Does it happen at any particular time of day?
4. Are there particular situations or events that trigger your self-injury?
5. Is it connected with certain feelings?
6. Do you know what feelings you have right before you burn yourself?
7. Do you know what you feel while you are hurting yourself?
8. Do you tend to self-injure at certain times of the year? (If yes:) Do you know what that is connected to?
9. Do you know what you feel after you self-injure?
10. Do you experience pain when you do that? Some people do and some people don't.
11. What do you notice about when and how you hurt yourself?
12. What do you use when you cut yourself?
13. Are there times when you want to self-injure but

somehow you don't? (If yes:) How does that happen? What makes those times different from the times you do hurt yourself?

Questions that Can Help Identify the Function of Self-Injury

1. How do you think your self-injury helps you?
2. Do you know why self-injuring is important to you?
3. I think most people hurt themselves because it helps in some way. Does that make sense? Do you know how it helps you?
4. Do you have any idea why or how self-injury helps you cope?
5. Does self-injury have a particular meaning for you?
6. Often, self-injury serves some function—or even more than one. Do you have any ideas about what functions it serves for you?
7. I think you did this because you needed some relief or some kind of help. Is that right? How did it help?
8. What changed or became different as a result of self-injuring?

Questions that Can Help Identify Alternatives and Other Resources

1. Would you like to talk about what else might work, kind of like the way self-injury works?
2. Do you think it would be useful to find some other ways to cope with feeling so mad and helpless, along with cutting?

3. You could add some other ways to cope, along with hurting yourself. Would that feel useful?
4. What else might work, do you think?
5. If hurting yourself relieves tensions and helps with the pain inside, what else do you think might be useful in those moments? What else could you do?
6. What could be an alternative to self-injuring?
7. What else can you do? Let's make a list of possibilities.
8. In the times when you want to self-injure but you don't, what helps in those moments?

Appendix B

Checklist for Identifying the Functions of Self-Injury

What is important to you about self-injuring?

_____ I need to feel pain.

_____ It helps me feel sensation.

_____ It helps me stop feeling.

_____ It's a channel for my rage.

_____ It lets me know I'm alive.

_____ It helps me stay alive.

_____ It helps me space out.

_____ It helps me feel grounded.

_____ I need to feel punished.

_____ It's how I ask for help.

_____ It helps me forget.

_____ It helps me remember.

_____ I don't know—I just have to.

_____ I get more focused when I self-injure.

_____ It just happens.

_____ It's a way for my tears to come out.

_____ I feel more in control then.

_____ I can't be angry any other way.

_____ It's mine and no one else's.

_____ It helps distract me from memories.

_____ It's a safe way to let myself feel.

_____ It's a way to express what's inside.

_____ It helps me cry.

_____ It's soothing and comforting.

_____ It releases tension.

_____ I know where I begin and end.

_____ It's the only way I can feel sexual.

_____ It makes everything more real.

_____ It makes everything less real.

_____ It's what I learned to do.

_____ It's a way to communicate.

_____ It's familiar.

_____ I need see the blood or the marks.

_____ It helps me "go away."

_____ I release my frustrations that way.

_____ I can't remember why it's important.

_____ I just feel like I'm supposed to.

_____ It helps me know my edges.

_____ It helps me not hurt anyone else.

_____ Other:_____

_____ Other:_____

_____ Other:_____

(Revised from Trautmann and Connors 1994, p. 30.)

Appendix C

The List of Lists

Ways to Identify and Access Resources

1. 20 Things that Help When I Feel Overwhelmed
2. 20 Things that Help When I Am Suicidal
3. 20 Things that Help When I Think I Might Self-Injure
4. 20 Things that Help When I Am Having A Hard Time Dealing with Memories
5. 20 Things that Help When I Am Anxious/Having Panic Attacks
6. 20 Ways I Can Comfort Myself
7. People Who Can Support Me (identify who, phone number, when to call, how each is helpful)
8. Things of the Present: How I Know What Year It Is
9. 20 Things I Really Like to Do
10. Places I Can Go When I Feel Miserable
11. 20 Useful Things to Do with My Anger
12. Things that Help Me Cry When I Need To

13. Things of Beauty and Pleasure in My Life Today
14. Nourishing Foods I Like (by category, if helpful)
15. The Things I Most Need to Remember about Myself (affirmations)
16. 20 Things that Help Me Get/Stay Grounded
17. My Favorite Things: A List of Treasures
18. Things that Are Different Now Compared to Five (Two, Ten) Years Ago
19. 20 Things that Help Me Feel My Body
20. 20 Other Things I Can Do When I Want to Drink/Use Drugs

References

Acierno, R. A., and Cahill, S. P., eds. (1999). Advances in conceptualization and research on the efficacy and mechanisms of EMDR (entire issue). *Journal of Anxiety Disorders* 13:1–223.

Ainsworth, M. (1982). Attachment: Retrospect and prospect. In *The Place of Attachment in Human Behavior*, ed. C. M. Parkes and J. Stevenson-Hinde, pp. 3–30. London: Tavistock.

Alcoholics Anonymous World Services (1975). *Alcoholics Anonymous*, 3rd ed. New York: Alcoholics Anonymous World Services.

Alderman, T. (1997). *The Scarred Soul: Understanding and Ending Self-inflicted Violence*. Oakland, CA: New Harbinger.

American Psychiatric Association (1994). *Diagnostic and Statistical Manual of Mental Disorders*, 4th ed. (*DSM-IV*). Washington, DC: American Psychiatric Association.

Anderson, G., Yasenik, L., and Ross, C.A. (1993). Dissociative experiences and disorders among women who identify themselves as sexual abuse survivors. *Child Abuse and Neglect* 17:677–686.

Anthony, E. J., and Cohler, B. J., eds. (1987). *The Invulnerable Child.* New York: Guilford.

Anzieu, D. (1989). *The Skin Ego.* New Haven, CT: Yale University Press.

Arnold, L. (1995). *Women and Self-Injury: A Survey of 76 Women.* Bristol, UK: Bristol Crisis Services for Women.

———. (1997) *Working with People Who Self-Injure: A Training Pack.* Bristol, UK: Bristol Crisis Services for Women.

Arntz, A., and Weertman, A. (1999). Treatment of childhood memories: theory and practice. *Behavior Research and Therapy* 37:714–740.

Barach, P. (1991). Multiple personality disorder as an attachment disorder. *Dissociation* 4:117–123.

Becker, R. O., and Selden, G. (1985). *The Body Electric.* New York: William Morrow.

Benson, H. (1997). *Timeless Healing: The Power and Biology of Belief.* New York: Fireside Books/Simon & Schuster.

Bick, E. (1968). The experience of the skin in early object relations. *International Journal of Psycho-Analysis* 49:484–486.

Blessing, S. (1990). *Self-inflicted violence: perspectives on women's self injury.* Paper presented at the Seventh International Conference on Multiple Personality/Dissociative States, Chicago, IL, November.

Blizard, R. A. (1997). The origins of dissociative identity disorder from an object relations and attachment theory perspective. *Dissociation* 10:223–229.

Blizard, R. A., and Bluhm, A. M. (1994). Attachment to the abuser: integrating object relations and trauma theories in the treatment of abuse survivors. *Psychotherapy* 31:383–390.

Bollerud, K. (1992). Long day's journey into night: the treatment of sexual abuse in substance-abusing women. In *Sexual Trauma and Psychopathology*, ed. S. Shapiro and G. Dominiak, pp. 143–159. New York: Lexington.

Bowlby, J. (1973). *Attachment and Loss, Vol. 2: Separation: Anxiety and Anger.* New York: Basic Books.

Bowman, M. L. (1999). Individual differences in posttraumatic distress: problems with the DSM-IV model. *Canadian Journal of Psychiatry* 44:21–33.

Briere, J. (1992). *Child Abuse Trauma: Theory and Treatment of the Lasting Effects.* Newbury Park, CA: Sage.

———. (1993). *Borderline personality disorder and the trauma model.* Paper presented at Fifth Eastern Regional Conference on Abuse and Multiple Personality Disorder, Alexandria, VA, June.

Briere, J., Elliot, D. M., Harris, K., and Cotman, A. (1995). Trauma symptom inventory: psychometrics and association with childhood and adult trauma in clinical samples. *Journal of Interpersonal Violence* 10:387–401.

Briere, J., and Gil, E. (1998). Self-mutilation in clinical and general population samples: prevalence, correlates and functions. *American Journal of Orthopsychiatry* 68:609–620.

Briere, J., and Zaidi, L. (1989). Sexual abuse histories and sequelae in female psychiatric emergency room patients. *American Journal of Psychiatry* 146:1602–1606.

Brodsky, B.S., Cloitre, M., and Dulit, R.A. (1995). Relationship of dissociation to self-mutilation and childhood abuse in borderline personality disorder. *American Journal of Psychiatry* 152:1788–1792.

Brown, R. (1995). Columbo therapy. *Family Therapy Networker* May/June:42–44.

Bryer, J., Nelson, B., Miller, J., and Krol, P. (1987). Childhood sexual and physical abuse as factors in adult psychiatric illness. *American Journal of Psychiatry* 144:1426–1430.

Burke, M. (2000). The shattered jigsaw. In *Forensic Mental Health Care: A Case Study Approach,* ed. D. Mercer, N. McKeown, and G. McCann, pp. 111–117. Edinburgh: Churchill Livingstone.

Burstow, B. (1992). *Radical Feminist Therapy: Working in the Context of Violence.* Newbury Park, CA: Sage.

Bystritsky, A., and Strausser, B. M. (1996). Treatment of obsessive-compulsive cutting behavior with naltrexone. *Journal of Clinical Psychiatry* 57:423–424.

Cahill, S. P., Carrigan, M. H., and Frueh, B. C. (1999). Does EMDR work? and if so, why?: a critical review of controlled outcome and dismantling research. *Journal of Anxiety Disorders* 13:5–33.

Calof, D. L. (1995). Chronic self-injury in adult survivors of childhood abuse. *Treating Abuse Today* 5(4/5):31–36.

Cameron-Bandler, L. (1978). *They Lived Happily Ever After.* Cupertino, CA: Meta.

Carbonell, J., and Figley, C. R. (1995). *The active ingredient project: preliminary findings.* Paper presented at the Annual Conference of the American Psychological Association, New York, August.

Carmen, E. H., Rieker, P. R., and Mills, T. (1984). Victims of violence and psychiatric illness. *American Journal of Psychiatry* 143:378–383.

Carnes, P. (1997). *The Betrayal Bond.* Wickenburg, AZ: Gentle Path.

Ceniceros, S., and Brown, G. R. (1998). Acupuncture: a review of its history, theories and indications. *Southern Medical Journal* 91:1121–1125.

Chard, K. M., Weaver, T. L., and Resick, P. A. (1997). Adapting cognitive processing therapy for child sexual abuse survivors. *Cognitive and Behavioral Practice* 4:31–52.

Charney, D. S., Deutch, A. Y., Krystal, J. H., et al. (1993). Psychobiologic mechanisms of posttraumatic stress disorder. *Archives of General Psychiatry* 50:294–305.

Chaves, J. F. (1993). Hypnosis in pain management. In *Handbook of Clinical Hypnosis*, ed. J. W. Rhue, S. J. Lynn, and I. Kirsch, pp. 511–532. Washington, DC: American Psychological Association.

Chengappa, K. N. R., Ebeling, T., Kang, J. S., et al. (1999). Clozapine reduces severe self-mutilation and aggression in psychotic patients with borderline personality disorder. *Journal of Clinical Psychiatry* 60:477–484.

Chu, J. A. (1998). *Rebuilding Shattered Lives: The Responsible Treatment of Complex and Post-Traumatic Dissociative Disorders.* New York: John Wiley.

Chu, J. A., and Dill, D. L. (1990). Dissociative symptoms in relation to childhood physical and sexual abuse. *American Journal of Psychiatry* 147:887–892.

Clemmens, M. C. (1997). *Getting Beyond Sobriety.* San Francisco: Jossey-Bass.

Cohen, B. M., Giller, E., W.[sic], L., eds. (1991). *Multiple Personality Disorder from the Inside Out.* Baltimore: Sidran.

Cohen, J. A., and Mannarino, A. P. (1998). Factors that mediate treatment outcome of sexually abused pre school children: six and 12-month followup. *Journal of the American Academy of Child and Adolescent Psychiatry* 31:44–51.

Cohen, K. S. (1997). *The Way of Qigong: The Art and Science of Chinese Energy Healing.* New York: Ballantine.

Cole, P., and Putnam, F. W. (1992). Effect of incest on self and social functioning: a developmental psychopathology perspective. *Journal of Consulting and Clinical Psychology* 60:174–184.

Collinge, W. (1998). *Subtle Energy.* New York: Warner.

Conn, L., and Lion, J. (1983). Self-mutilation: a review. *Psychiatric Medicine* 1:21–33.

Connors, R. (1996a). The functions of self-injury for trauma survivors. *American Journal of Orthopsychiatry* 66:197–206.

———. (1996b). Levels of clinical response. *American Journal of Orthopsychiatry* 66:207–216.

———. (1998). Openings: the use of the self in healing work. *Voices: The Art and Science of Psychotherapy* 34(3):32–38.

Conterio, K., and Lader, W. (1998). *Bodily Harm.* New York: Hyperion.

Coons, P. M., and Milstein, V. (1990). Self-mutilation associated with dissociative disorders. *Dissociation* 3:81–87.

Cornell, W., and Olio, K. (1991). Integrating affect in treatment with adult survivors of physical and sexual abuse. *American Journal of Orthopsychiatry* 61(1):59–69.

Courtois, C. (1988). *Healing the Incest Wound: Adult Survivors in Therapy.* New York: W. W. Norton.

Cowdry, R. W., and Gardner, D. L. (1988). Pharmacotherapy of borderline personality disorder. *Archives of General Psychiatry* 45:111–119.

Cusack, K., and Spates, C. R. (1999). The cognitive dismantling of eye movement desensitization and re-processing (EMDR) treatment of posttraumatic stress disorder (PTSD). *Journal of Anxiety Disorders* 13:87–99.

Davidson, J. R. T., and van der Kolk, B. A. (1996). The psychopharmacological treatment of posttraumatic stress disorder. In *Traumatic Stress: The Effects of Overwhelming Experience on Mind, Body and Society,* ed. B. A. van der Kolk, A. C. McFarlane, and L.Weisaeth, pp. 510–524. New York: Guilford.

Davies, J. M., and Frawley, M. G. (1994). *Treating the Adult Survivor of Childhood Sexual Abuse: A Psychoanalytic Perspective.* New York: Basic Books.

Deiter, P. J., and Pearlman, L. A. (1998). Responding to self-injurious behavior. In *Emergencies in Mental Health Practice: Evaluation and Management*, ed. P. M. Kleepsies, pp. 235–257. New York: Guilford.

de Silva, P., and Marks, M. (1999). The role of traumatic experiences in the genesis of obsessive-compulsive disorders. *Behavior Research and Therapy* 37:941.

de Young, M. (1982). Self-injurious behavior in incest victims: a research note. *Child Welfare* 61:577–584.

de Zulueta, F. (1993). *From Pain to Violence: The Traumatic Roots of Destructiveness.* Northvale, NJ: Jason Aronson.

DiClemente, R. J., Ponton, L. E., and Hartley, D. (1991). Prevalence and correlates of cutting behavior: risk for SIV transmission. *Journal of the American Academy of Child and Adolescent Psychiatry* 30:735–739.

Dolan, Y. (1991). *Resolving Sexual Abuse.* New York: W. W. Norton.

Dominiak, G. (1992). Psychopharmacology of the abused. In *Sexual Trauma and Psychopathology*, ed. S. Shapiro and G. Dominiak, pp. 81–112. New York: Lexington.

Dossey, L. (1993). *Healing Words: The Power of Prayer and the Practice of Medicine.* San Francisco: HarperCollins.

Dugan, T. F., and Coles, R., eds. (1989). *The Child in Our Times: Studies in the Development of Resiliency.* New York: Brunner/Mazel.

Dutton, D. G. (1995). *The Batterer: A Psychological Profile.* New York: Basic Books.

Dutton, D. G., and Painter, S. (1981). Traumatic bonding: the development of emotional attachments in battered women and other relationships of intermittent abuse. *Journal of Victimology* 6:139–155.

Ehrenberg, D. B. (1992). *The Intimate Edge: Extending the Reach of Psychoanalytic Interaction.* New York: W.W. Norton.

Eimer, B. N., and Freeman, A. M. (1998). *Pain Management Psychotherapy: A Practical Guide.* New York: Wiley.

Elkind, S. N. (1992). *Resolving Impasses in Therapeutic Relationships.* New York: Guilford.

Farber, S. (1998) The body speaks, the body weeps: Eating disorders, self-mutilation and body modifications. *The Renfrew Perspective* 4(2):8–9.

Favazza, A. R. (1996). *Bodies Under Siege: Self-mutilation and Body Modification in Culture and Psychiatry,* 2nd ed. Baltimore: Johns Hopkins University Press.

Favazza, A. R., and Conterio, K. (1988). Female habitual self-mutilators. *Acta Psychiatry Scandinavica* 78:1–7.

Favazza, A. R., and Rosenthal, R. J. (1993). Diagnostic issues in self-mutilation. *Hospital and Community Psychiatry* 44(2):134–140.

Favazza, A. R., and Simeon, D. (1995). Self-mutilation. In *Impulsivity and Aggression,* ed. E. Hollander and D. Stein, pp. 185–200. New York: Wiley.

Feldenkrais, M. (1993). *Body Awareness as Healing Therapy.* Berkeley: Frog.

Figley, C. (1995). *Compassion Fatigue.* New York: Brunner/Mazel.

Figueroa, M. (1988). A dynamic taxonomy of self-destructive behavior. *Psychotherapy* 25:280–287.

Finney, L. (1992). *Reach for the Rainbow: Advanced Healing for Survivors of Sexual Abuse.* New York: Perigee.

Ford, J. D. (1999). Disorders of extreme stress following warzone military trauma: Associated features of posttraumatic stress disorder or comorbid but distinct syndromes? *Journal of Consulting and Clinical Psychology* 67:3–12.

Ford, J. D., Fisher, P., and Larson, L. (1997). Object relations as predictors of treatment outcome with chronic PTSD. *Journal of Consulting and Clinical Psychology* 64:547–559.

Ford, J. D., and Kidd, P. (1998). Early childhood trauma and disorders of extreme stress as predictors of treatment outcome with chronic posttraumatic stress disorder. *Journal of Traumatic Stress* 11:743–761.

Fraiberg, S. (1959). *The Magic Years.* New York: Scribner's.

Freedman, S. A., Brandes, D., Peri, T., and Shalev, A. (1999). Predictors of chronic posttraumatic stress disorder: a prospective study. *British Journal of Psychiatry* 174:353–359.

Freud, S. (1947). The ego and the id. *Standard Edition* 19: 3–66.

Freyd, J. (1996). *Betrayal Trauma.* Cambridge: Harvard University Press.

Gallo, F. P. (1999). *Energy Psychology: Explorations at the Interface of Energy, Cognition, Behavior and Health.* Boca Raton, FL: CRC.

Garbarino, J. (1999a). *Lost Boys: Why Our Sons Turn Violent and How We Can Save Them.* New York: Free Press.

———. (1999b). Small wars: the cultural politics of childhood. *Readings: A Journal of Reviews and Commentary in Mental Health* 14(1):14–17.

Gardner, D., and Cowdry R. (1985). Alprazolam-induced dyscontrol in borderline personality disorder. *American Journal of Psychiatry* 143:19–22.

Gelinas, D. (1983). The persisting negative effects of incest. *Psychiatry* 46:312–332.

Gerber, R. (1996). *Vibrational Medicine.* Sante Fe: Bear.

Goldbart, S., and Wallin, D. (1996). *Mapping the Terrain of the Heart: Passion, Tenderness and the Capacity to Love.* Northvale, NJ: Jason Aronson.

Gorski, T. T., and Miller, M. (1986). *Staying Sober: A Guide for Relapse Prevention.* Independence, MO: Independence Press.

Green, A. H. (1978). Self-destructive behavior in battered children. *American Journal of Psychiatry* 141:520–525.

Greenspan, G. S., and Samuel, S.E. (1989). Self-cutting after rape. *American Journal of Psychiatry* 146:789–790.

Grove, D. (1989). *Resolving Feelings of Anger, Guilt and Shame: The Seminar for Mental Health Professional.* Edwardsville, IL: David Grove Seminars.

Grunebaum, H. U., and Klerman, G. L. (1967). Wrist slashing. *American Journal of Psychiatry* 124:527–534.

Gunderson, J., and Sabo, A. (1993). The phenomenological and conceptual interface between borderline personality disorder and PTSD. *American Journal of Psychiatry* 150:19–27.

Hamilton, N. (1992). *Self and Others: Object Relations Theory in Practice.* Northvale, NJ: Jason Aronson.

Hartman, C. R., and Burgess, A. W. (1993). Information processing of trauma. *Child Abuse and Neglect* 17:47–58.

Hawton, K. (1990). Self-cutting: Can it be prevented? In *Dilemmas and Difficulties in the Management of Psychiatric Patients,* ed. K. Hawton and P. Cowan, pp. 91–103. Oxford: Oxford University Press.

Hawton, K., Houston, K., and Shepperd, R. (1999). Suicide in young people. *British Journal of Psychiatry* 175:271–276.

Herman, J. L. (1992). *Trauma and Recovery.* New York: Basic Books.

Herman, J. L., and van der Kolk, B. A. (1987). Traumatic origins of borderline personality disorder. In *Psychological Trauma,* ed. B. A. van der Kolk, pp. 111–126. Washington, DC: American Psychiatric Press.

Hill, M. (1990). On creating a theory of feminist therapy. *Women and Therapy* 9:53–65.

Holiman, M. (1997). *From Violence Toward Love: One Therapist's Journey.* New York: W. W. Norton.

Holmes, J. (1998). *John Bowlby and Attachment Theory.* New York: Routledge.

Hunt, V. V. (1996). *Infinite Mind: Science of the Human Vibrations of Consciousness,* 2nd ed. Malibu, CA: Malibu Publishing.

Hyman, J. W. (1999). *Women Living with Self-Injury.* Philadelphia: Temple University Press.

Ingerman, S. (1991). *Soul Retrieval: Mending the Fragmented Self.* San Francisco: Harper.

James, M. (1981). *Breaking Free: Self-Reparenting for a New Life.* Reading, MA: Addison-Wesley.

Johnson, J. G., Cohen, P., Brown, J., et al. (1999). Childhood maltreatment increases risk for personality disorders during early adulthood. *Archives of General Psychiatry* 56:600–606.

Jones, J. C., and Barlow, D. H. (1990). The etiology of posttraumatic stress disorder. *Clinical Psychology Review* 10:299–328.

Jordan, J. V. (1991a). The meaning of mutuality. In *Women's Growth in Connection,* ed. J. V. Jordan, A. G. Kaplan, J. B. Miller, et al., pp. 81–96. New York: Guilford.

———. (1991b). Do you believe that the concepts of self and autonomy are useful in understanding women? In *Some Misconceptions and Reconceptions of a Relational Approach,* ed. J. B. Miller, J. V. Jordan, A. G. Kaplan, et al., pp. 4–5. *Work in Progress,* no. 49. Wellesley, MA: Stone Center Working Paper Series.

Jordan, J. V., Kaplan, A. G., Miller, J. B., et al. (1991). *Women's Growth in Connection.* New York: Guilford.

Kaminsky, P., and Katz, R. (1996). *Flower Essence Repertory.* Nevada City, CA: Flower Essence Society.

Kaplan, L. (1978). *Oneness and Separateness: From Infant to Individual.* New York: Simon & Schuster.

Kaufman, G. (1985). *Shame: The Power of Caring,* 2nd ed. Cambridge, MA: Schenkman.

Kelly, E. W. (1997). Relationship-centered counseling: a humanistic model of integration. *Journal of Counseling and Development* 75:337–345.

Kepner, J. I. (1995). *Healing Tasks: Psychotherapy with Adult Survivors of Childhood Abuse.* San Francisco: Jossey-Bass.

Kernberg, O. (1985). *Borderline Conditions and Pathological Narcissism.* Northvale, NJ: Jason Aronson.

Khan, L. I. H. (1994). Sand play: meaning, method and metaphor. *Dissertations Abstracts International Section A: Humanities and Social Sciences* 55:4-A.

Kidder, R. (1995). *How Good People Make Tough Choices.* New York: William Morrow.

Kluft, R. (1985). *Childhood Antecedents of Multiple Personality.* Washington, DC: American Psychiatric Press.

Krieger, D. (1993). *Accepting Your Power to Heal.* Sante Fe, NM: Bear.

Lam, J. N., and Grossman, F. K. (1997). Resiliency and adult adaptation in women with and without self-reported histories of child sexual abuse. *Journal of Traumatic Stress* 10:175–196.

Lebegue, B. (1992). Sudden self-harm while taking fluoxetine. *American Journal of Psychiatry* 149:1113.

LeDoux, J. E. (1996). *The Emotional Brain.* New York: Simon & Schuster.

Leibenluft, E., Gardner, D., and Cowdry R. (1987). The inner experience of the borderline self-mutilator. *Journal of Personality Disorders* 1:317–324.

Levenkron, S. (1997). *Cutting: Understanding and Overcoming Self Mutilation.* New York: W. W. Norton.

Levy T. M., and Orlans, M. (1998). *Attachment, Trauma and Healing: Understanding and Treating Attachment Disorder in Children and Families.* Washington, D.C.: Child Welfare League of America Press.

Lew, M. (1990). *Victims No Longer: Men Recovering from Incest and Other Sexual Child Abuse.* New York: HarperCollins.

Linehan, M. M. (1993). *Cognitive-Behavioral Treatment of Borderline Personality Disorder.* New York: Guilford.

Little, J., and Taghavi, E. (1991). Disinhibition after lorazepam augmentation of antipsychotic medication. *American Journal of Psychiatry* 148:1099.

Love, P., and Robinson, J. (1994). *Hot Monogamy: Essential Steps to More Passionate, Intimate Lovemaking.* New York: Plume/Penguin.

Mahler, M. (1975). *The Psychological Birth of the Human Infant.* New York: Basic Books.

Malon, D. W., and Berardi, D. (1987) Hypnosis with self-cutters. *American Journal of Psychotherapy* 16(4):531–541.

Markowitz, P. J., Calabrese, J. R., Schulz, S. C., and Meltzer, H. Y. (1991). Fluoxetine in the treatment of borderline and schizotypal personality disorders. *American Journal of Psychiatry* 148:1064–1067.

Marmar, C. R., Weiss, D. S., Schlenger, W. E., et al. (1994). Peritraumatic dissociation and posttraumatic stress in male Vietnam theater veterans. *American Journal of Psychiatry* 151:902–907.

Maroda, K. (1998). *The Power of Countertransference.* Northvale, NJ: Jason Aronson.

Matsakis, A. (1994). *Post-Traumatic Stress Disorder: A Complete Treatment Guide.* Oakland, CA: New Harbinger.

Mazelis, R. (1990). What is SIV about? Self-inflicted violence. *The Cutting Edge* 1(1):1.

——. SIV and multiple personality disorder. *The Cutting Edge* 2(1):1–3.

——. SIV: struggling with shame. *The Cutting Edge* 3(2):1–3.

———. SIV: the issue is survival. *The Cutting Edge* 4(2):1–3.

———. SIV: programs, rituals and disbelief. *The Cutting Edge* 8(1):1–3.

———. (1998). SIV: biology and medicine. *The Cutting Edge* 9(2):1–4.

———. (1999). SIV: victim, perpetrator or neither? *The Cutting Edge* 10(1):1–3.

McArthur, R. (1998). Learning to love. *Venture Inward,* January/February, pp. 32–36.

McCann, L., and Pearlman, L. A. (1992). Constructivist self-development theory: a theoretical model of psychological adaptation to severe trauma. In *Out of Darkness: Exploring Satanism and Ritual Abuse,* ed. D. K. Sakheim and S. E. Devine, pp. 185–206. Lexington, MA: Lexington.

McClory, R. (1986). Mutilation: the new wave in female self-abuse. *Reader: Chicago Free Weekly* September 5, pp. 1, 30, 32, 37, 38.

McCraty, R., Barrios-Choplin, B., Rozman, D., et al. (1998). The impact of a new emotional self-management program on stress, emotions, heart rate variability, DHEA and cortisol. *Integrative Physiological and Behavioral Science* 33:151–170.

McFarlane, A. C. (1988). Recent life events and psychiatric disorder in children: the interaction with preceding adversity. *Journal of Clinical Psychiatry* 29:677–690.

———. (1999). Risk factors for the acute biological and psychological response to trauma. In *Risk Factors for Posttraumatic Stress Disorder,* ed. R. Yehuda, pp. 163–190. Washington, DC: American Psychiatric Press.

McGee, M. D. (1997). Cessation of self-mutilation in a patient with borderline personality disorder treated with naltrexone. *Journal of Clinical Psychiatry* 58:32–33.

McLane, J. (1996). The voice on the skin: self-mutilation

and Merleau-Ponty's theory of language. *Hypatia* 11:107–118.

Menninger, K. (1935). A psychoanalytic study of the significance of self-mutilation. *Psychoanalytic Quarterly* 4:408–466.

Miller, A. (1990). *Banished Knowledge: Facing Childhood Injuries,* trans. L. Vennewitz. New York: Anchor/Doubleday.

Miller, D. (1994). *Women Who Hurt Themselves.* New York: Basic Books.

Mitchell, R. R., and Friedman, H. S. (1994). *Sand Play: Past, Present and Future.* London: Routledge.

Morgan, H., Burns-Cox, C., Pocock, H., and Pottle, S. (1975). Deliberate self-harm: clinical and socio-economic characteristics of 368 patients. *British Journal of Psychiatry* 127:564–574.

Morrison, A. P., Bowe, S., Larkin, W., and Nothard, S. (1999). The psychological impact of psychiatric admission: some preliminary findings. *Journal of Nervous and Mental Disorders* 187:250–253.

Moss, M., Frank, E., and Anderson, B. (1990). The effects of marital status and partner support on rape trauma. *American Journal of Orthopsychiatry* 60:379–391.

Napier, N. (1993). *Getting Through the Day: Strategies for Adults Hurt as Children.* New York: W. W. Norton.

Neswald, D. W. (1991). Common programs observed in survivors of satanic ritual abuse. *The California Therapist,* September/October, pp. 47 50.

Nicholls, S. S., Deiter, P. J., and Pearlman, L. A. (1999). *Self-harming behaviors and reasons for self-harm.* Unpublished research.

Ochberg, F. (1996). The counting method for ameliorating traumatic memories. *Journal of Traumatic Stress* 9:873–880.

Ogata, S. N., Silk, K. R., Goodrick, S., et al. (1989). Childhood and sexual abuse in adult patients with borderline personality disorder. *American Journal of Psychiatry* 147:1008–1013.

Olson, P. (1990). The sexual abuse of boys: a study of the long-term psychological effects. In *The Sexually Abused Male, Vol. I: Prevalence, Impact and Treatment,* ed. M. Hunter, pp. 137–152. Lexington, MA: Lexington Books.

O'Sullivan, R. L., Christenson, G. A., and Stein, D. J. (1999). Pharmacotherapy of trichotillomania. In *Trichotillomania,* ed. D. J. Stein, G. A. Christenson, and E. Hollander, pp. 93–123. Washington, DC: American Psychiatric Press.

Palmer, S. E., Brown, R. A., Rae-Grant, N. I., and Loughlin, M. J. (1999). Responding to children's disclosure of familial abuse: what survivors tell us. *Child Welfare* 78:259–282.

Pattison, E., and Kahan, J. (1983). The deliberate self-harm syndrome. *American Journal of Psychiatry* 140:867–872.

Pearlman L.A., and Saakvitne, K. W. (1995). *Trauma and the Therapist: Countertransference and Vicarious Traumatization in Psychotherapy with Incest Survivors.* New York: W. W. Norton.

Pearsall, P. (1999). *The Heart's Code.* New York: Broadway Books/Random House.

Pelcovitz, D., van der Kolk, B. A., Roth, S., et al. (1997). Development of a criteria set and a structured interview for disorders of extreme stress. *Journal of Traumatic Stress* 10:3–16.

Pennebaker, J. W. (1997). *Opening Up: The Healing Power of Expressing Emotions.* New York: Guilford.

Pert, C. B. (1999). *Molecules of Emotion: The Science Behind*

Mind-Body Medicine. New York: Touchstone/Simon & Schuster.

Peterson, M. R. (1992). *At Personal Risk: Boundary Violations in Professional-Client Relationships.* New York: W. W. Norton.

Pistole, M. C. (1999). Caregiving in attachment relationships: a perspective for counselors. *Journal of Counseling and Development* 77:437–446.

Pitman, R. K. (1990). Self-mutilation in combat-related PTSD. *American Journal of Psychiatry* 147:123–124.

Potier, M. (1993). Giving evidence: women's lives in Ashworth maximum security psychiatric hospital. *Feminism and Psychology* 3:335–347.

Primeau, F., and Fontaine, R. (1987). Obsessive disorder with self-mutilation: a subgroup responsive to psychotherapy. *Canadian Journal of Psychiatry* 32:699–701.

Putnam, F. (1985). Dissociation as a response to extreme trauma. In *Childhood Antecedents of Multiple Personality,* ed. R. Kluft, pp. 65–98. Washington, DC: American Psychiatric Press.

———. (1989). *Diagnosis and Treatment of Multiple Personality Disorder.* New York: Guilford Press.

Rieker, P., and Carmen, E. (1986). The victim-to-patient process: the disconfirmation and transformation of abuse. *American Journal of Orthopsychiatry* 56:360–370.

Rivera, M. (1996). *More Alike Than Different: Treating Severely Dissociative Trauma Survivors.* Toronto: University of Toronto Press.

Rogers, A. G. (1995). *A Shining Affliction: A Story of Harm and Healing in Psychotherapy.* New York: Penguin.

Romans, S. E., Martin, J. L., Anderson, J. C., et al. (1995). Sexual abuse in childhood and deliberate self-harm. *American Journal of Psychiatry* 152:1336–1342.

Root, M. P. P. (1989). Treatment failures: the role of sexual victimization in women's addictive behavior. *American Journal of Orthopsychiatry* 59:542–549.

Ross, C. A. (1989). *Multiple Personality Disorder: Diagnosis, Clinical Features and Treatment.* New York: Wiley.

———. (1997). The problem of attachment to the perpetrator. *Many Voices,* February, pp. 6–7.

Ross, R. R., and McKay H. B. (1979). *Self-mutilation.* Lexington, MA: Lexington Books.

Roth, A. S., Ostroff, R. B., and Hoffman, R. E. (1996). Naltrexone as a treatment for repetitive self-injurious behavior: an open-label trial. *Journal of Clinical Psychiatry* 57:233–237.

Roth, S., Newman, E., Pelcovitz, D., et al. (1997). Complex PTSD in victims exposed to sexual and physical abuse. *Journal of Traumatic Stress* 10:539–555.

Rothbaum, B. O., and Foa, E. B. (1996). Cognitive-behavioral therapy for posttraumatic stress disorder. In *Traumatic Stress: The Effects of Overwhelming Experience on Mind, Body and Society,* ed. B. A. van der Kolk, A. C. McFarlane, and L. Weisaeth, pp. 491–509. New York: Guilford.

Russek, L. G., and Schwartz, G. E. (1996). Narrative descriptions of parental love and caring predict health status in midlife: a 35-year follow-up of the Harvard Mastery of Stress study. *Alternative Therapies* 2:55–62.

Rutter, M. (1987). Psychosocial resilience and protective mechanisms. *American Journal of Orthopsychiatry* 57:316–331.

———. (1999). Resilience concepts and findings: implications for family therapy. *Journal of Family Therapy* 21:119–144.

Saakvitne, K. W., Gamble, S., Pearlman, L. A., and Lev, B. T. 2000. *Risking Connection.* Lutherville, MD: Sidran.

Saakvitne, K. W., and Pearlman, L. A. (1996). *Transforming the Pain: A Workbook on Vicarious Traumatization.* New York: W. W. Norton.

Sakheim, D. K., and Devine, S.E. (1992). Bound by the boundaries: therapy issues in work with individuals exposed to severe trauma. In *Out of Darkness: Exploring Satanism and Ritual Abuse*, ed. D. K. Sakheim and S. E. Devine, pp. 279–293. Lexington, MA: Lexington Books.

Saporta, J., and Case, J. (1993). The role of medications in treating adult survivors of childhood trauma. In *Treatment of Adult Survivors of Incest*, ed. P. L. Paddison, pp. 101–134. Washington, DC: American Psychiatric Press.

Satir, V. (1987). The therapist story. *Journal of Psychotherapy and the Family* 3(1):17–25.

Saunders, E., and Arnold, F. (1991). Borderline personality disorder and child abuse: revisions in clinical thinking and treatment approach. *Work in Progress*, no. 51. Wellesley, MA: Stone Center Working Paper Series.

Scharff, D. E. (1992). *Refinding the Object and Reclaiming the Self.* Northvale, NJ: Jason Aronson.

Schwartz, G. E., and Russek, L. G. (1996). Energy cardiology: a dynamical energy systems approach for integrating conventional and alternative medicine. *Advances: The Journal for Mind–Body Medicine* 12:4–24.

"The Shadows." (1997). Evaluating. *Many Voices*, December, pp. 8–10.

Shapiro, F. (1995). *Eye Movement Desensitization and Processing.* New York: Guilford.

———. (1999). Eye movement desensitization and processing (EMDR) and the anxiety disorders: clinical and research implications for an integrated psychotherapy treatment. *Journal of Anxiety Disorders* 13:35–67.

Sheldrake, R. (1988). *The Presence of the Past.* New York: Times Books.

Shneidman, E. S. (1985). *Definition of Suicide.* New York: Wiley.

Shur, R. (1994). *Countertransference Enactment.* Northvale, NJ: Jason Aronson.

Signorile, M. (1995). *Outing Yourself.* New York: Fireside/Simon & Schuster.

Simmons, K. P., Sack, T., and Miller, G. (1996). Sexual abuse and chemical dependency: implications for women in recovery. *Women and Therapy* 19:17–30.

Simpson, C. A., and Porter, G. L. (1981). Self-mutilation in children and adolescents. *Bulletin of the Menninger Clinic* 45:428–438.

Smucker, M. R., Dancu, C., Foa, E. B., and Niederer, J. L. (1995). Imagery rescripting: a new treatment for survivors of childhood sexual abuse suffering from posttraumatic stress. *Journal of Cognitive Psychotherapy* 9:3–17.

Soloff, P., George, A., Nathan, S., et al. (1986). Progress in pharmacotherapy of borderline disorders. *Archives of General Psychiatry* 43:691–697.

Sonne, S., Rubey, R., Brady, K., et al. (1996). Naltrexone treatment of self-injurious thoughts and behaviors. *Journal of Nervous and Mental Disease* 184:192–194.

Spitz, R. (1965). *The First Year of Life: A Psychoanalytic Study of Normal and Deviant Development of Object Relations.* New York: International Universities Press.

Stanley, M. A., and Cohen, L. J. (1999). Trichotillomania and obsessive-compulsive disorder. In *Trichotillomania,* ed. D. J. Stein, G. A. Christenson, and E. Hollander, pp. 93–123. Washington, DC: American Psychiatric Press.

Stein, D. (1997). *Essential Reiki.* Freedom, CA: The Crossing Press.

Stein, D. J., and Christenson, G. A. (1999). Trichotillomania: descriptive characteristics and phenomenology. In *Trichotillomania*, ed. D. J. Stein, G. A. Christenson, and E. Hollander, pp. 93–123. Washington, DC: American Psychiatric Press.

Stern, D. (1985). *The Interpersonal World of the Infant.* New York: Basic Books.

Strean, H. S. (1999). Resolving some therapeutic impasses by disclosing countertransference. *Clinical Social Work Journal* 27:123–140.

Strong, M. (1998). *A Bright Red Scream: Self-Mutilation and the Language of Pain.* New York: Viking.

Surrey J. L. (1991). What do you mean by mutuality in therapy? In *Some Misconceptions and Rreconceptions of a Relational Approach,* ed. J. B. Miller, J. V. Jordan, A. G. Kaplan, et al. *Work in Progress,* No. 49. Wellesley, MA: Stone Center Working Paper Series.

Tanya. (1997). Untitled. *The Cutting Edge* 8(1):5.

Tauber, R.T. (1997). *Self-Fulfilling Prophecy: A Practical Guide for Its Use in Education.* Westport, CT: Praeger.

Terr, L. (1990). *Too Scared to Cry.* New York: Basic Books.

Trautmann, K., and Connors, R. (1994). *Understanding Self-injury: A Workbook for Adults.* Pittsburgh: Pittsburgh Action Against Rape.

Urquiza, A. J., and Crowley C. (1986). Sex differences in the survivors of child sexual abuse, paper presentation quoted by Courtois, C. (1988). *Healing the Incest Wound: Adult Survivors in Therapy.* New York: W. W. Norton.

Urquiza, A. J., and Keating, L.A. (1990). The prevalence of sexual victimization of males. In *The Sexually Abused Male,* vol. 1, ed. M. Hunter, pp. 89–104. Lexington, MA: Lexington Books.

Valentine, L., and Feinauer, L. (1993). Resilience factors associated with female survivors of childhood sexual abuse. *American Journal of Family Therapy* 21:216–224.

VandeCreek, L., and Knapp, S. (1993). *Tarasoff and Beyond: Legal and Clinical Considerations in the Treatment of Life-Endangering Patients.* Sarasota, FL: Professional Resource Press.

van der Kolk, B. A. (1989). The compulsion to repeat the trauma: re-enactment, revictimization and masochism. *Psychiatric Clinics of North America* 146:1530–1540.

———. (1996a). The complexity of adaptation to trauma: self-regulation, stimulus discrimination, and characterological development. In *Traumatic Stress: The Effects of Overwhelming Experience on Mind, Body and Society,* ed. B. A. van der Kolk, A. C. McFarlane, and L. Weisaeth, pp. 182–213. New York: Guilford.

———. (1996b). The body keeps score: approaches to the psychobiology of posttraumatic stress disorder. In *Traumatic Stress: The Effects of Overwhelming Experience on Mind, Body and Society,* ed. B. A. van der Kolk, A. C. McFarlane, and L. Weisaeth, pp. 214–241. New York: Guilford.

———. (1996c). Trauma and memory. In *Traumatic Stress: The Effects of Overwhelming Experience on Mind, Body and Society,* ed. B. A. van der Kolk, A. C. McFarlane, and L. Weisaeth, pp. 279–302. New York: Guilford.

———. (1998). *The impact of trauma on memory and development.* Conference presentation at Lakewood Hospital, Canonsburg, PA, February.

———, ed. (1987). *Psychological Trauma.* Washington, DC: American Psychiatric Press.

van der Kolk, B. A., and Kadish, W. (1987). Amnesia/dissociation/returned of the repressed. In *Psychological Trauma,* ed. B. A. van der Kolk, pp. 173–190. Washington, DC: American Psychiatric Press.

van der Kolk, B. A., McFarlane, A. C., and van der Hart, O. (1996a). A general approach to treatment of posttraumatic stress disorder. In *Traumatic Stress: The Effects of Overwhelming Experience on Mind, Body and Society*, ed. B. A. van der Kolk, A. C. McFarlane, and L. Weisaeth, pp. 417–440. New York: Guilford.

van der Kolk, B. A., McFarlane, A.C., and Weisaeth, L., eds. (1996b). *Traumatic Stress: The Effects of Overwhelming Experience on Mind, Body and Society.* New York: Guilford.

van der Kolk, B. A., Perry J. C., and Herman, J. L. (1991). Childhood origins of self-destructive behavior. *American Journal of Psychiatry* 148:1665–1671.

Waites, E. (1993). *Trauma and Survival: Post-traumatic and Dissociative Disorders in Women.* New York: W. W. Norton.

Walant, K. (1995). *Creating the Capacity for Attachment.* Northvale, NJ: Jason Aronson.

Walker, S. (1992). Ivan Pavlov, his dog and chiropractic. *Digest of Chiropractic Economics,* March/April, pp. 36–46.

Walsh, B., and Rosen, P. (1988). *Self-Mutilation: Theory Research and Practice.* New York: Guilford.

Watkins, J. G. (1995). Hypnotic abreactions in the recovery of traumatic memories. *International Society for the Study of Dissociation News* 13(6):1,6.

Watkins, J. G., and Watkins, H. H. (1981). Ego states therapies. In *Handbook of Innovative Psychotherapies*, ed. R. Corsini, pp. 252–270. New York: Wiley.

Weil, A. (1995). *Spontaneous Healing.* New York: Knopf.

Weiner, B. A., and Wettstein, R. M. (1993). *Legal Issues in Mental Health Care.* New York: Plenum.

Wells, J. H., Haines, J., Williams, C. L., and Brain, K. L. (1999). The self-mutilative nature of severe onychophagia: a comparison with self-cutting. *Canadian Journal of Psychiatry* 44:40–47.

West, C. (1999). *First Person Plural: My Life as a Multiple.* New York: Hyperion.

White, B. (1992). *Workshop presentation.* Second National Conference on Sexual Misconduct by Clergy, Psychotherapists and Health Professionals, Minneapolis, MN, October.

Wilber, K. (1985). *The Holographic Paradigm and Other Paradoxes: Exploring the Leading Edge of Science.* Boston: Shambala.

Wilson, J. P. (1995). *Toward integrative models for the future.* Keynote speech at Trauma, Loss and Dissociation: The Foundations of 21st Century Traumatology conference, Alexandria, VA, February.

Wilson, J. P., and Lindy, J. D. (1994a). Empathic strain and countertransference. In *Countertransference in the Treatment of PTSD*, ed. J. P. Wilson and J. D. Lindy, pp. 5–30. New York: Guilford.

Wilson, J. P., and Lindy, J. D., eds. (1994b). *Countertransference in the Treatment of PTSD.* New York: Guilford.

Winchel, R., and Stanley M. (1991). Self-injurious behavior: a review of the behavior and biology of self-mutilation. *American Journal of Psychiatry* 148:306–317.

Winnicott, D. (1965). *The Maturational Process and the Facilitating Environment.* New York: International Universities Press.

Wise, M. L. (1989). Adult self-injury as a survival response in victim-survivors of childhood abuse. *Journal of Chemical Dependency Treatment* 3:185–201.

Wisechild, L. (1988). *The Obsidian Mirror: An Adult Healing from Incest.* Seattle: Seal.

Wright, M. S. (1988). *Flower Essences: Reordering Our Understanding and Approach to Illness and Health.* Jefferston, VA: Perelandra.

Wylie, M. S. (1996). Going for the cure. *The Family Therapy Networker*, July/August: pp. 21–37.

Yehuda, R. (1999a). Biologic factors associated with susceptibility to posttraumatic stress disorder. *Canadian Journal of Psychiatry* 44:34–39.

Yehuda, R., ed. (1999b). *Risk Factors for Posttraumatic Stress Disorder.* Washington, DC: American Psychiatric Press.

Yehuda, R., and McFarlane, A. (1995). The conflict between current knowledge about post-traumatic stress disorder and its original conceptual basis. *American Journal of Psychiatry* 152:1705–1713.

Young, E. B. (1990). The role of incest issues in relapse. *Journal of Psychoactive Drugs* 22:249–258.

Young, W. (1992). Recognition and treatment of survivors reporting ritual abuse. In *Out of Darkness: Exploring Satanism and Ritual Abuse,* ed. D. K. Sakheim and S. E. Devine, pp. 249–278. Lexington, MA: Lexington Books.

Zanarini, M. C., Gunderson, J. G., Marino, M. F., et al. (1989). Childhood experience of borderline patients. *Comprehensive Psychiatry* 30:18–25.

Zlotnick, C., Shea, M. T., Pearlstein, T., et al. (1996). The relationship between dissociative symptoms, alexithymia, impulsivity sexual abuse, and self-mutilation. *Comprehensive Psychiatry* 37:12–16.

Zlotnick, C., Shea, M. T., Recupero, P., et al. (1997). Trauma, dissociation, impulsivity and self-mutilation among substance abuse patients. *American Journal of Orthopsychiatry* 67:650–654.

Zukav, G. (1990). *The Seat of the Soul.* New York: Fireside Books/Simon & Schuster.

Zweig-Frank, H., Paris, J., and Guzder, J. (1994a). Psychological risk factors for dissociation and self-mutilation in female patients with borderline personality disorder. *Canadian Journal of Psychiatry* 39:259–264.

———. (1994b) Psychological risk factors for dissociation and self-mutilation in male patients with BPD. *Canadian Journal of Psychiatry* 39:266–268.

Credits

Index

About The Author

Robin E. Connors, Ph.D., a clinician and consultant in private practice in Pittsburgh, Pennsylvania, is the co-author of *Understanding Self-Injury: A Workbook for Adults*. Her articles "Self-Injury in Trauma Survivors: Functions and Meanings" and "Self-Injury in Trauma Survivors: Levels of Clinical Response" appeared in the *American Journal of Orthopsychiatry* in 1996, and she has published in several dozen other professional publications. She has held various positions in community and hospital settings, including clinical supervisor at Pittsburgh Action Against Rape, consultant to Lakewood Psychiatric Hospital, teacher at Arsenal Family and Children's Center, and research assistant at Western Psychiatric Institute and Clinic. Dr. Connors has taught many training courses to therapists in diverse settings, practiced as a divorce mediator, edited a newsletter offering legal information to mental health professionals, and worked as a freelance writer. She currently specializes in work with women experiencing life transitions, trauma survivors, and couples.